In the current chaos that is children can be overwhelme̶ for their attention and claiming authority. In such a moment, those teachers are rare and valuable who are able to take a wider view of what is developing, to connect the various strands of the apparent moral anarchy around us, and see how these can be addressed in a manner that is consistent with a biblical way of thinking while also clear and comprehensible to the lay person. Sharon James has a long and impressive record of being precisely such a person. In this book she achieves a remarkable feat: she addresses the lies that our culture currently exalts as truth and does so in a way that crosses the generational divide and will be helpful both to young people and those who wish to understand them and help them think through the deepest challenges of our day.

Carl R. Trueman
Professor, Grove City College, Pennsylvania
Fellow, Ethics and Public Policy Center, DC

This is a remarkable book. Sharon James brings the skills of a trained historian to the task of explaining what has gone so horribly wrong in society today. Her analysis is consistently fascinating, insightful, and filled with biblical wisdom. The book concludes with a call for Christians to courageously proclaim the truths about God and His creation that will overcome the destructive lies so influential in modern thinking. Anyone seeking to understand why society seems to be falling apart, and what we can do about it, needs to read this book. Highly recommended!

Wayne Grudem
Distinguished Research Professor of Theology and Biblical Studies,
Phoenix Seminary, Arizona

The world of propositions is divided into truth and lies. The truth is, God created with purpose and design, God reveals the truth about Himself, His world, and our condition, God redeems fallen sinners by the work of His eternal Son, and God will bring all to a culmination of utterly just judgment. Lies seek to deconstruct every one of the absolutely true realities. The ostensible purpose of these lies also is a lie. Seeking to free humanity from supposed shackles of intrinsic principles of right and wrong, truth and falsehood, in order to establish an unshackled pursuit of immediate pleasure, the intellectual constructors of these lies have only brought deception, bondage, terror, shackles, and death. Sharon James has unpacked with clarity and force both the sphere of lies and its leading proponents and the sphere of truth and the revelation of its God of love, justice, and redemption. Clearly and forcefully and in pursuit of a purpose of persuasion, James has given us a succinct analysis of today's culture of death, how we got here, assurance that it will not have final victory, and clear guidance out of the bondage of these destructive lies.

Tom J. Nettles
Senior Professor of Historical Theology
The Southern Baptist Theological Seminary, Louisville, Kentucky

Although most people around us are not well versed in the history of modern thought, their thinking and practices are highly influenced by what Sharon James takes us though in the first section of this book. We see the academics, scientists and philosophers and artists who shaped contemporary culture to give birth to the naturalistic post-modern worldview, with no God, no truth and no real morality. James then goes on to show us truth of God the creator and God the Son as King and Saviour from our corrupt way of thinking and acting and the only pathway to truth and hope. This is a detailed but highly readable and valuable resource to help us engage with the people around us and contextualise the timeless truth of Jesus.

Graham Nicholls
Director, Affinity, Cambridge, UK

'The fool says in his heart, "There is no God"' (Ps. 14:1). Such foolishness, as we have on a global scale, has a devastating price to pay—a world in shambles. In her book *The Lies We Are Told, The Truth We Must Hold*, Sharon James shows us that it all started with the denial of the existence of God, absolute morality, and universal truth. Instead, the world conjured up its own notions of truth and justice. The only antidote is to return to a biblical worldview, which Sharon very deftly lays out in the second half of her book. I highly recommend this work!

John MacArthur
Pastor, Grace Community Church, Sun Valley, California
Chancellor, The Master's University and Seminary

Dedicated with love and gratitude to

Daniel, Lydia and Judson

*'One generation commends your works to another;
they tell of your mighty acts.'*
(Ps. 145:4)

'One word of truth outweighs the world.'
(Aleksandr Solzhenitsyn)

THE LIES WE ARE TOLD,

THE TRUTH WE MUST HOLD

Worldviews and Their Consequences

SHARON JAMES

CHRISTIAN
FOCUS

Scripture, unless otherwise marked, is taken from the *Holy Bible, New International Version*®, NIV® Copyright ©1973, 1978, 1984 by Biblica, Inc.® Used by permission. All rights reserved worldwide.

Scripture quotations marked 'ESV' are taken from *The Holy Bible, English Standard Version*, copyright © 2001 by Crossway Bibles, a publishing ministry of Good News Publishers. Used by permission. All rights reserved. ESV Text Edition: 2011.

Scripture quotations marked 'NKJV' are taken from the *New King James Version*. Copyright © 1982 by Thomas Nelson, Inc. Used by permission. All rights reserved.

Scripture quotations marked 'BSB' are taken from the *Berean Study Bible*. Copyright © 2021 Berean Study Bible. All rights reserved.

Scripture quotations from the *King James Version* are marked with 'KJV'.

Copyright © Sharon James 2022

paperback ISBN 978-1-5271-0796-0
ebook ISBN 978-1-5271-0865-3

10 9 8 7 6 5 4 3 2 1

Published in 2022
by
Christian Focus Publications, Ltd.
Geanies House, Fearn,
Ross-shire, IV20 1TW, Scotland.
www.christianfocus.com

Cover design by Pete Barnsley

Printed and bound by
Bell & Bain, Glasgow

CONTENTS

Acknowledgements

This book had its genesis when I led several groups of students at Emmanuel Church, Leamington Spa, through 'The Truth Project' and a series of studies on worldview. I'm grateful to all those who contributed to the discussions. I developed some of that material in a series of talks delivered at Word Alive 2014, entitled 'God's Good Design for Human Society'; my thanks to the organisers of that event. Some of the material in this book has also appeared in other articles, books, and talks; I have tried to acknowledge this where appropriate.

I work as part of a team at The Christian Institute. It's been a privilege to offer a variety of seminars to the staff, and I always value their discussions and ideas. Thanks to Dave Greatorex, Michael Taylor and Rachel Gillies for their input on this project. I'm grateful to a number of friends who have read and commented on parts of the book, including Colin Reeves and Julia Jones. Many friends and colleagues have encouraged me and pointed me to helpful resources; a special thank you to Willemien Gunnink and Ranald Macaulay for some timely suggestions. My thanks to the whole team at Christian Focus Publications; but especially to Rosanna Burton. Thanks also to Pete Barnsley and James Amour for their work on the cover and design; Anne Norrie for the editing; and Margaret Roberts, Kate MacKenzie and Maegan Roper for all their help. I am deeply grateful to Pastor

Conrad Mbewe for contributing the Foreword. The views expressed in this book are my own, as are any and all mistakes made.

This book is intended as a simple primer, a 'road map' of some of the complex worldview issues that challenge Bible-believing Christians today. I've leaned on the detailed work done by others (both Christian and non-Christian). At the end of each chapter, and at the end of the book, I point to resources which go into greater depth on each of these topics.

I have been in awe of my husband Bill's unfailing fidelity to truth over the four decades I have known him. I could not have written this book without him. Equally, I could not have completed this project without the encouragement and faithful prayer support of many family members and friends. I am thankful to God for you all.

Sharon James,
London, 2021

Tables and Illustrations

Chapter Summaries

PART ONE: THE LIES WE ARE TOLD

1: By the end of the nineteenth century, increased acceptance of evolutionary theory had contributed to a naturalistic worldview: 'There is no Creator God, and there won't be a judgement.' This had profound implications: human beings are no longer given unique dignity, there is no purpose in history, death is the end and there is no absolute morality or universal religious truth.

2: Trailblazers in the liberation of humanity from the fear of God included Ludwig Feuerbach, Charles Darwin and Karl Marx. Once God is denied, the next thing to be challenged is the notion that there is one absolute moral code which we all have to obey. This led straight to the horrors of the gulags and the inhumanities perpetrated during the Cultural Revolution. Bad ideas bear bitter fruit.

3: Friedrich Nietzsche, Sigmund Freud, Wilhelm Reich and Margaret Sanger saw themselves as saviours, liberating people from the repression of traditional morality. They dreamed of a future of unlimited personal freedom. But in a fallen sinful world, the dream of unbounded freedom unravels inexorably into nightmare. As moral norms are eroded, the powerful use their power to exploit the weak. Violence and evil are not only normalised, they are celebrated. Sexual liberation has resulted in historically unprecedented global rates of fatherlessness.

4: Without a transcendent authority, who, or what, is left to judge between competing claims to truth? Confidence that our problems would be solved by human reason and science collapsed into the radical doubt of postmodernism. The pioneers of critical theory wanted to bring about a society where all inequalities in outcome were removed. The 'hegemony' of established institutions had to be undermined. This could be attempted by using radical doubt (aka critical theory) to question all objective truth, including scientific truth (and much that had previously assumed as 'common sense'). Critical theory has taken root in all the major institutions of the West. At a popular level, we are all now expected to join the battle to achieve 'absolute' freedom and 'absolute' equality.

5: Critical theory began in the universities, but as graduates entered all the various professions, the result at a popular level has been the rise of 'identity politics'. Many view the West as inherently evil (racist, patriarchal, capitalist). Some activists want to destroy the very structures which have created freedom and prosperity: 'Smash the patriarchy' (aka the family), 'Smash capitalism' (aka wealth creation and private property), 'Smash the police' (aka law and order), 'Smash down the statutes' (aka our collective memory and history). The essential unity of the human race, and the essential dignity of human identity, are both undermined by the current insistence on pushing people into groups defined by their diverse characteristics.

6: How has the Christian church responded to the rise of a worldview that denies God and denies ultimate truth? Confusingly, some clergy seem to have cheered it on! Challenges to the authority of Scripture lie behind the rise of unbelief within the professing church. Some 'Christian' ministers paint evil as good, good as evil, and mock the idea of judgement and hell.

Part Two: The Truth We Must Hold

7: God is the Creator, and the ground of truth, justice and morality. Our creation in the image of God is the only firm foundation for the respect of human rights. The Bible affirms both the dignity of every individual person, and the essential unity of the human race. Because of the fall into sin, oppression and suffering are endemic to human existence. Every individual is morally responsible, but forgiveness is offered to all in Christ.

8: The biblical worldview is the foundation of human flourishing in society. God designed family and work. The married family should not be undermined. Property should be protected and work should be rewarded. We need to learn from the past and allow for innovation in the present. Civil authorities should be supported. All human institutions are answerable to God, which provides a bulwark against oppression. The division of the world into nation states offers protection from the threat of global tyranny.

9: Christ is King. The biblical worldview is the foundation of future hope. God has good purposes for this world. He will bring about complete justice, and restoration of the whole creation, when Christ returns.

10: Christians are not just to know the truth, but to live it. We are created to live for God's glory. Worship should be the pulse of our existence. When we love and fear God, we won't fear anyone or anything else. Loving God and loving our neighbour includes sharing the good news of salvation and working for our neighbour's good.

Further Resources: Be equipped to live out and tell out the truth!

Foreword

Unless you are talking to a child that has never been exposed to other people, you can be sure you are not writing on a blank slate. The world has its own views of life and all of them are stained with sin. As a result, they are opposed to the revealed truth of God to different degrees. These are the lies that are etched onto the tablets of human hearts, causing them to have little or no room for God and His truth. Sadly, some of these lies are within the four walls of the church. Like termites secretly eating away the inside of wooden pillars of a building until it comes crashing down, they are stealthily destroying the church from within. Sometimes it is the sheer numbers of those who are following such teachers and their teachings that causes us to turn a blind eye to the obvious departures from biblical truth. In some cases, churches have been emptied by the conspicuous unbelief in the pulpits.

While we are not expected to know all the untruths that the world is spewing out in every generation, it is helpful for any teacher to have some working understanding of the major philosophical ideas that have shaped his or her generation, including the individuals who have been the main proponents of those ideas. This is also true for those of us who are pastors. Apart from teaching the truth, this equips us to better oppose such false views. Or at the least, we should be able to quote some of the world's teachers when some divine light shines through their belief system, as the apostle Paul did when he wrote,

'One of the Cretans, a prophet of their own, said, "Cretans are always liars, evil beasts, lazy gluttons." This testimony is true. Therefore rebuke them sharply, that they may be sound in the faith, not devoting themselves to Jewish myths and the commands of people who turn away from the truth' (Titus 1:12–14). It also equips young adults to better understand their world.

There is no doubt that any thinking person listening to what is in the popular news and social media will soon be asking in frustration, 'What is life? Why is the world in such a mess? How can it get fixed? Is there any hope?' Often, these questions are due to the failure of all these false teachings to satisfy the deepest craving of the human soul. This is often the case in the hearts of young adults, after being bombarded with these popular ideas in the halls of learning. The absence of a solid answer is what leads these young hearts into a meaningless future and jettisons their capacity to contribute to a better world.

Sharon James has brought together in this book some of the main ideas that have shaped the world's thinking—especially the Western world. I am glad that she has included false prophets who are largely within the Christian enclave because their influence on our entire generation cannot be ignored. They have added to the mess. Like a good teacher, she has simplified these lies enough for an average reader to understand and appreciate. She has also shown that today's worldviews are basically built upon those of previous eras. Reading the first half of this book leaves you saying, 'No wonder our world is in such a mess! You cannot hold on to such teachings in God's created order and remain with a sane world!'

Sharon James does not end there. She goes on to show us the biblical worldview. She puts God where He ought to be—at the centre of the universe—and shows the implication of this for human beings and for the whole world and its future. The panoramic view is breath-taking! It is like standing on the sun and seeing all the planets in the solar system going around in beautiful symmetry. The confusion turns to picturesque order. Everything begins to make sense—personal, family, work, and national life. Instead of being left in a state of confusion and despair, this worldview leaves you with hope in the Lord Jesus. You feel as if you are building your house on solid granite while the world around you is sinking. You want to reach out and help. I am grateful for this book and pray that it will bless many readers!

Conrad Mbewe
Founding Chancellor, African Christian University, Zambia,
and Pastor of Kabwata Baptist Church, Lusaka
September 2021

Introduction

Le Disciple, a French novel published in 1889, described the life of a respected philosopher.[1] Each day he studied from 6 am to 10 pm, aside from meals, a daily walk, and visits from students. In the words of his caretaker, he 'wouldn't hurt a fly'. His peaceful routine was shattered when he was called to attend a criminal inquest. A former student had been so inspired by his teacher's philosophy of liberation that he had put it into practice, and was on trial for murder.

Ideas have consequences. Their outworking can be murderous.

The current presuppositions of Western culture affect us all. We are aware of environmental pollution, and protest if our children breathe in dangerous fumes. But we, and our children, daily absorb the 'air' of current assumptions. Lies have been told. Lies have been believed. They are incorporated into the worldview of our culture. Like poison gas they cannot be seen, but they have deadly effects on individuals, societies, and whole civilisations.

The first set of ideas flows from 'Enlightenment' thinking and the 'scientific revolution': natural causes explain everything.[2] We don't need to look to God for explanations. We won't have to give account

---

1   Bourget, P, *Le Disciple*, 1889.

2   There were committed Christians in both movements.

to God. This worldview, (modernism), rejects reliance on external authorities such as God or the Bible, and looks to human reason alone.

But trying to derive certain knowledge by basing it on individual reason is a doomed project. When seven billion plus individuals all look to their own reason, who is to judge between their competing views and claims?

So modernism collapsed into postmodernism. We are now in the world of 'my truth' and 'your truth'. Without absolute truth, there is only power. Some have more power than others. It's increasingly argued that those who enjoy privilege (because of factors such as race and sex) hold onto their position by pushing down those below them in the rank. The privileged are the oppressors. If they deny their privilege, they are (it is assumed) only confirming it. So, despite the collective insistence 'there is no absolute truth', some advocates of Social Justice[3] do insist that they know what is right and wrong; just and unjust. Increasingly it's believed that Christians are on the wrong side of the argument and the wrong side of history. Religious belief, especially biblical morality, is blamed for propping up a repressive and patriarchal system that enshrined inequality. Those who speak out for biblical Christianity face accusations such as 'bigot', 'transphobe', or 'fundamentalist'. Many Christians are scared into silence. Others, wanting to avoid confrontation, go along with current trends, and keep quiet about the ways in which biblical truth is denied. Some celebrate the whole package, and rewrite biblical morality to suit the current times.

I am going to argue in this book that each of these options (silence, acquiescence, celebration) buys into lies and ignores the truth. They shut down the only real answer for human suffering. It is right to be angry about injustice and suffering. But we need to understand the real causes if we are going to arrive at real solutions. We don't need to

---

3   When Social Justice is capitalised, it denotes an ideology that includes concepts such as 'systemic' injustice. The biblical worldview is the foundation for true justice (chapter 7). See chapters 4 and 5 for a critique of the concept of 'systemic' injustice.

be ashamed of Christ; we don't need to be intimidated by the claims of those who are militantly opposed to the Bible.

The only solid basis for defending human dignity and achieving justice is a biblical worldview.

In **Part 1** we look at the lies we have been told. We also examine the evidence. How has it worked out when these bad ideas have been applied? In **Part 2** we turn to the truth which leads to real liberation and justice. When we understand that Jesus Christ is Lord of all of life, we can be even *more* passionate in our desire to see righteousness prevail in this world.

I aim to equip you with a road map to navigate the minefield of current claims. This book offers a basic primer, which draws on some of the best of some of the longer books that have been published recently. It also provides short selections from the various thinkers we are going to look at, to enable you to see what they say in their own words. That's why there are lots of quotations along the way. There are pointers to further reading at the end of each chapter, as well as at the end of the book.

In order to understand our inherent human significance, to know genuine freedom, and to work for real justice, we need to know the truth.

Then you will know the truth and the truth will set you free. (John 8:32)

Part 1

The

LIES

We Are Told

'The fool says in his heart: "There is no God."'
(Ps. 14:1)

1 'There Is No God and No Absolute Morality'

Christians today are expected to keep their faith to themselves. Claims about God's truth and about absolute morality, we're told, belong only to the realm of *personal experience.*

In 2011 a study of attitudes among young adults in America was published which found:

> Six out of ten (60 percent) of the emerging adults we interviewed expressed a highly individualistic approach to morality. They said that morality is a personal choice, entirely a matter of individual decision. Moral rights and wrongs are essentially matters of individual opinion, in their view ... In this world of moral individualism, then, anyone can hold their own convictions about morality, but they also *must keep those views private.* Giving voice to one's own moral views is itself nearly immoral ...[1]

The idea of moral judgement has morphed into the derogatory term 'judgementalism', and morality is associated with a negative 'moralism'.[2] Christians may be told: 'Believe what you want, worship

---

1   Smith, C et al, *Lost in Transition: The Dark Side of Emerging Adulthood,* (OUP US, 2011), pp. 21, 24, emphasis mine.

2   Furedi, F, 'The Diseasing of Judgment', *First Things,* January 2021, https://www.firstthings.com/article/2021/01/the-diseasing-of-judgment (accessed 30 December, 2020).

as you wish, and run your home as you please, but don't bring your faith into the public square!'

The 'public square' relates to what goes on outside our own religious practice at home and at church. It concerns interactions with our neighbours and community (work, education, business, voluntary associations, public services), what goes on in our nation (media, academia, politics), and globally (international bodies and corporations). 'Public truth' is thought to be based on physical and material things that can be scientifically proven. Anything non-material, it is assumed, floats in the realm of the unprovable and personal.

Our culture is infused with a *naturalistic* worldview (this world is all there is). It stands against the *theistic* worldview (this world is created by God). Our culture, then, is deeply opposed to biblical Christianity.

We can easily feel intimidated. But we should remember that two thousand years ago the apostle Paul lived in a culture which was even more hostile than ours to the truth claims of Christ. Yet Paul was confident that there is a truth that every human being knows:

> The wrath of God is being revealed from heaven against all the godlessness and wickedness of men who *suppress the truth* by their wickedness, since what may be known about God is *plain to them,* because God has made it *plain to them.* For since the creation of the world God's invisible qualities – his eternal power and divine nature – have been clearly seen, being understood from what is made, so that men are without excuse. (Rom. 1:18-20, emphasis mine)

We have all perceived God's invisible attributes. God has plainly revealed Himself to all, and the truth has been 'clearly seen' (v. 20). Despite the clarity of this revelation, people 'suppress the truth' (v. 18). 'They exchanged the truth of God for a lie' (v. 25).

A World Without Windows

The devil is the father of lies (John 8:44), he has never stopped telling lies, and his biggest lie is to deny the existence of the Creator. The glory of creation, from the vast scale of the universe to the complexity of every cell, proclaims that there is a Creator God. But we are more likely to fall for the lie if we accept the (false) assumption that 'real truth' only has to do with physical and material things that can be scientifically proven (you can't examine God in a laboratory).

The naturalistic worldview suggests that people used to believe in God in a pre-scientific age, but now that 'science' can explain everything, we can dispense with that old superstition.

The British Humanist Society has a video for school children in which comedian Stephen Fry tells them that science is the 'testing of theories against evidence' and that it's 'reality', as opposed to religion and the supernatural (by implication 'unreality').[3]

> So we are to shut the windows, pull the blinds down, and exclude any thought that there might be anything 'out there', beyond the things we can see and touch and taste and hear and feel. We are left in a prison (albeit a comfortable prison) from which there is no escape. No exit to the world outside. No access to transcendence, eternal values, mystery, or God.[4]

This is often assumed to be a 'scientific' worldview: objectively true, and based on firm evidence. It's really a philosophical worldview, a pseudo-religion, which offers an alternative explanation for evil and an alternative offer of 'salvation'. The Bible teaches that suffering and injustice came into the world as a result of the 'Fall' (that is, disobedience to God), and that the *ultimate* solution lies in the

---

3 How do we know what's true and false? British Humanist Society https://www.youtube.com/watch?v=Yk5IWzTfWeM (accessed 11 January, 2021). See chapter 7 for comment.

4 Berger, P, et al eds, *Against the World, For the World: The Hartford Appeal and the Future of American Religion*, (Seabury, 1976). Sociologist Peter Berger coined the phrase 'world without windows' to describe a worldview which rejects the supernatural, and believes that all there is, is matter. He also described it as the 'prison of modernity'.

redemption secured by Christ. The Bible also teaches that the world is God's handiwork, and that it is our duty to comprehend and develop the resources of the world for the blessing of humanity. Sociologist Rodney Stark has argued convincingly that Christian theology was 'essential for the rise of science'.[5] Christianity and science should never be pitted against each other. But the naturalistic worldview claims that ignorance, inequality, superstition and religion (not sin!) cause human suffering. It can *only* be solved by means of science and the exercise of human reason (including the elimination of religion).[6]

Here are some of the most common lies about humans and about society, believed by many, promoted in our education system, and often assumed in public life. They all flow from a worldview that rejects God.

NO CREATOR GOD: WE JUST EVOLVED

The first lie is that we exist as the result of a process of random chance and the evolutionary process. Human beings are shaped only by chemical, physical and economic forces, and we are not essentially any different to other living beings. **Jacob Bronowski (1908-1974)**, presenter of a famous BBC series called *The Ascent of Man,* affirmed that:

> Man is a part of nature, in the same sense that a stone is, or a cactus, or a camel.[7]

---

5   Stark, R, *For the Glory of God: How Monotheism Led to Reformation, Science, Witch-Hunts and the End of Slavery,* (Princeton University Press, 2003), section 2 'God's Handiwork: The Religious Origins of Science', pp. 121-199, p. 123.

6   The stated objective of the British Humanist Society until July 2011 was 'the moral and social development of the community free from theistic or dogmatic beliefs or doctrines'; since then they have had 'rebranding' to appear more tolerant, but they are currently campaigning to end all faith schools in Britain. The Christian Institute, *Curriculum and Assessment (Wales) Bill: Compulsory Atheism Lessons,* 2021, p. 11.

7   Bronowski, J, *The Ascent of Man,* 1965/2011.

All reality is made up only of matter. Our mind, thoughts and beliefs are just chemical actions of the brain. We do not have an eternal soul. There is no supernatural realm. This belief is the basis of humanism, which 'begins from man alone, and makes man the measure of all things'.[8] **Carl Sagan (1934-1996)**, named as 'Humanist of the Year' in 1981, asserted:

The cosmos is all there ever is, there ever was, or ever will be.[9]

If it is true that our thoughts and beliefs are just chemical actions of the brain, why should we give them credence? Charles Darwin realised the implications of his own theory:

The horrid doubt always arises whether the convictions of man's mind, which has developed from the mind of the lower animals, are of any value or at all trustworthy. Would anyone trust the conviction of a monkey's mind, if there are any convictions in such a mind?[10]

The utilitarian ethicist **Peter Singer (b. 1946)** argues that the logical deduction of evolution through random mutation and natural selection is that there is nothing special about humanity, and no absolute reason to protect human life above animal life.

Racists violate the principle of equality by giving greater weight to the interests of members of their own race ... Sexists violate the principle of equality by favoring the interests of their own sex.

8   Schaeffer, F, Koop, E C, *Whatever Happened to the Human Race?* (Marshall Morgan and Scott, 1980), p. 97.

9   Sagan, C, *Cosmos: A Personal Journey,* (Random House, 1980), p.4. This is reiterated in the 3 Humanist Manifestos of 1933, 1973 and 2003: https://americanhumanist.org/what-is-humanism/manifesto1/, https://american humanist.org/what-is-humanism/manifesto2/, https://americanhumanist. org/what-is-humanism/manifesto3/, (accessed 4 January 2021).

10   'Darwin's "Horrid Doubt": The Mind', *Evolution News and Science Today,* Discovery Institute, September 11, 2014, https://evolutionnews. org/2014/09/darwinshorrid/ (accessed 18 June, 2020).

Similarly speciesists allow the interests of their own species to override the greater interests of members of other species.[11]

The idea that humans are special, he argues, arose from Christianity and the belief that humans alone have a soul that will never die. The Christian teaching was that to kill was to consign a person to their eternal destiny, and that to take innocent human life was to sin against God the Creator.[12] Singer rejects Christianity, and places all of sentient life on a continuum. Actions causing pain to, or destruction of, beings with intelligent awareness (like whales), are wrong. Similar actions upon beings with seemingly no intelligent awareness (like human embryos) are not wrong. Animals and humans should be treated with consistent criteria of compassion: you may need to kill in order to relieve pain. The killing of disabled babies, for instance, is justified in view of their likely suffering.

Nor is there an absolute obligation to protect human life above the environment itself.

Increasingly, some in the 'deep green' radical environmentalist movement argue that the earth itself is the greatest good, and that it is threatened by human life. Finnish activist **Pentti Linkola (1932-2020)**, for example, believed that humans are like a tumour on the earth, consuming more than our fair share of nature's resources. The vast majority of humans should be killed. The remainder should be controlled by an authoritarian environmentalist state, with people forcibly sterilized and private cars confiscated.[13]

No Creator God: No Judgement

The second lie arises from the first. If there is no Creator, we're not answerable to a Creator and there won't be a judgement. The atheist philosopher **Friedrich Nietzsche (1844-1900)** insisted that there is no

---

11   Singer, P, *Writings on an Ethical Life,* (Fourth Estate, 2002), p. 35.

12   Ibid., p. 129.

13   Linkola, P, *Human Flood,* 1989, translated by Heinonen H and Moynihan M,   http://www.penttilinkola.com/pentti_linkola/ecofascism_writings/humanflood/ (accessed 26 March 2020).

transcendent morality, so we are not constrained by an external moral code. Human will alone determines what *we* want to do. He believed it's harmful to be restricted by religions or social conventions.[14]

American sociologist **Philip Rieff (1922-2016)**, author of *The Triumph of the Therapeutic* (1966), maintained that the distinguishing mark of modernity was the assumption that we are not accountable to anyone other than ourselves. If we won't have to give account to God, then who has the right to tell us what to do? The idea gained ground that the exercise of *all* authority is toxic. Today it is often assumed to be demeaning, even psychologically damaging, to submit to authority.

If there's no God, we can create our own identity, choose our own destiny, and construct our own morality. We only have this one life on earth, so we should fulfil ourselves while we can. Our highest goal is often viewed as self-actualization.[15]

If we are simply driven by natural biological instincts, it's often assumed that behaviour is inevitably determined by sexual desires (we look at the impact of Freud's thinking in chapter 3). One of the most pervasive lies believed today is that guilt is necessarily a harmful emotion. Christian morality is thought to be evil, as it arouses so many guilt feelings. This is all the logical outworking of putting ourselves at the centre of our universe, rather than acknowledging and worshipping our Creator.

Within the cultural framework of extreme individualism, everyone must do what is right in their own eyes. Refusal to affirm whatever moral choice someone makes is taken to mean that we do not value or respect them as human beings. It may even be viewed as hating them. With increasing criticism of the very idea of authority, and the advance of the idea that moral judgements are indicative of being closed-minded, people became reluctant to express views

---

14 More on Nietzsche in chapter 3.

15 A simple definition of self-actualization is: 'the complete realization of one's potential, and the full development of one's abilities and appreciation for life', https://www.simplypsychology.org/self-actualization.html (accessed 3 March, 2021).

about morality in public. By 2021, it was common to hear the slogan 'criticism is violence' on university campuses.[16]

'TRUE TRUTH'?

If we go along with the lie that truth is only to do with what we see, touch or feel, (physical reality), then anything outside of the material realm is seen as a matter of individual preference or opinion.[17] God, morality and faith get pushed back into a personal realm that cannot be demonstrated to be true. Values are for each person to decide for themselves. Religion cannot be proved.

This worldview insists that discussion of God and morality should be confined to individual experience, separate from day-to-day realities of education, business, law, medicine, technology, and social work. Well-meaning Christians may pray, read the Bible, and go to church on Sundays, but live the rest of the time as if God didn't exist. This 'naturalistic' worldview controls much of education, the media, and public life.

Naturalistic Worldview
1 No Creator God, we just evolved
2 No Creator God, no judgement
3 'True Truth' has to do with physical reality

What are some of the implications of this worldview?

NO UNIQUE DIGNITY FOR HUMAN LIFE

The theory of evolution and the resulting naturalistic worldview sees humans as a product of chance in an impersonal universe. If human beings *are* just a chance product of a long, unfolding process of natural development, one implication is that there is *no* intrinsic value or

---

16 Furedi, F, 'The Diseasing of Judgment', *First Things,* January 2021, https://www.firstthings.com/article/2021/01/the-diseasing-of-judgment (accessed 30 December, 2020).

17 For example, gender ideology suggests that subjective experience can override physical reality.

dignity to every human life. You begin to judge the value of life by criteria such as usefulness, enjoyment, autonomy, or awareness. It is no surprise that the Second Humanist Manifesto (1973) insisted that all should have the right to both abortion and euthanasia, and that suicide should be legalised.[18]

Over many decades, the natural historian **Sir David Attenborough (b. 1926)** has thrilled audiences worldwide with his wildlife documentaries. Arguably, no one has done more to bring the glories of creation right into people's homes. Attenborough fails to give glory to the Creator for the wonders of the universe. He regards us as mere products of evolution, so that the human race is like a plague on the Earth which needs to be managed and controlled.[19] When you deny the Creator, you deny the unique dignity of human beings made in His image.

Environmentalist Pentti Linkola, mentioned above, was also dismissive of human dignity:

> ... humanity, by squirting and birthing all these teeming, filth-producing multitudes from out of itself, in the process also suffocates and defames its own culture ...[20]

With that view of humanity, we are not surprised to know that he asked:

> Who misses all those who died in the Second World War? Who misses the twenty million executed by Stalin? Who misses Hitler's six million Jews?[21]

---

18 Humanist Manifesto II, 1973, Articles 6 and 7, https://americanhumanist. org/what-is-humanism/manifesto2/ (accessed 13 January, 2021).

19 Attenborough, D, 'Humans are Plague on Earth', *The Daily Telegraph,* 22 January, 2013, https://www.telegraph.co.uk/news/earth/earthnews /9815862/Humans-are-plague-on-Earth-Attenborough.html (accessed 7 October, 2020).

20 Linkola, P, *Human Flood,* 1989, translated by Heinonen H and Moynihan M, http://www.penttilinkola.com/pentti_linkola/ecofascism_writings/ humanflood/ (accessed 26 March 2020).

21 Ibid.

He and other 'deep green' environmentalists have argued that human society could even have *an obligation* to use abortion, infanticide, euthanasia and eugenic policies to regulate world population.

That should shock us. But it's the logical outworking of a materialistic view of the universe. The Christian writer **Francis Schaeffer (1912-1984)** observed:

> If man is not made in the image of God, nothing then stands in the way of inhumanity.[22]

If we are just products of chance and matter, then there is no purpose in history and nothing after death. This robs life of meaning and purpose beyond survival. British evolutionary biologist, and author of *The God Delusion*, **Richard Dawkins (b. 1941)** writes:

> Natural selection, the blind, unconscious, automatic process which Darwin discovered, and which we now know is the explanation for the existence and apparently purposeful form of life, has no purpose in mind ... It has no vision, no foresight, no sight at all. If it can be said to play the role of watchmaker in nature, it is the blind watchmaker.[23]

Professor **William Provine (1942-2015)** was a leading atheist and historian of science. He was brutally honest about the implications of atheism:

> Let me summarize my views on what modern evolutionary biology tells us loud and clear — and these are basically Darwin's views. There are no gods, no purposes, and no goal-directed forces of any kind. There is no life after death. When I die, I am absolutely certain that I am going to be dead. That's the end of me.[24]

---

22 Schaeffer, F, Koop, E C, *Whatever Happened to the Human Race?* (Marshall Morgan and Scott, 1980), p. 15.

23 Quoted in Blanchard, J, *Does God Believe in Atheists?* (Evangelical Press, 2000), p. 120.

24 Provine, W B, debate with Johnson, P E, at Stanford University, April 30, 1994, http://www.arn.org/docs/orpages/or161/161main.htm (accessed 18 June, 2020).

No Absolute Morality

If there is no Creator, we are not answerable to a Creator, there are no absolute moral standards, and we make our own rules. To feel guilt is unhealthy, even pathological. The Christian teaching about God's moral law and the need for repentance is viewed as psychological and emotional abuse, an assault on individual freedom.

Evolutionary biologist **Julian Huxley (1887-1975)** became the first Director General of UNESCO[25] in 1946, and first President of the British Humanist Association in 1963. He opposed the idea of absolute moral truth, because:

> ... the provision of dogma, whose absolute truth is buttressed by authority or guaranteed by revelation ... is likely to break down in the face of the accumulation of new facts and new knowledge.[26]

Canadian psychiatrist **Brock Chisholm (1896-1971)**, first Director General of the World Health Organization, wanted people to be liberated from old-fashioned morality. Children needed to be brought up without rigid ideas of what was right and wrong. People had to break away from the:

> ... poisonous certainties fed us by our parents, our Sunday and day school teachers, our politicians, our priests, our newspapers and others with a vested interest in controlling us.[27]

Professor Frank Furedi points out that during the 1940s and 1950s, many began to use the terms *authority* and *authoritarian* interchangeably. Then, in the 1950s the word *obedience* began, increasingly, to be used alongside the term *unquestioned*. Implication? Obedience was something for unthinking people![28]

---

25 The United Nations Educational, Scientific and Cultural Organization.

26 Quoted by Furedi, F, 'The Diseasing of Judgment', *First Things*, January 2021, https://www.firstthings.com/article/2021/01/the-diseasing-of-judgment (accessed 30 December, 2020).

27 Ibid.

28 Ibid.

The notion of so-called 'poisonous pedagogy' argues that the exercise of *all* authority is toxic. Many young people are never trained to respect authority. In 1993, British sociologist Richard Hoggart observed that when elderly people in the deprived area of Leeds where he had grown up spoke of youth delinquency, they qualified any statement with: *'but it's only my opinion of course.'* In a world where God and absolute moral standards are denied, we all have to be non-judgemental. We should not be surprised that in the same housing estate, Hoggart found that there was little confidence in the role of parents to guide their children, and that tragically, children were growing up in what was, effectively, a 'violent, jungle world'.[29]

William Provine, mentioned above, was a man of integrity. As an evolutionary theorist he aimed to live an ethical life, but he was candid about having no firm basis for that:

> There is no ultimate foundation for ethics, no ultimate meaning in life, and no free will for humans, either ... Finally, there is no reason whatsoever that ethics can't be robust, even if there is *no ultimate foundation for ethics.* If you're an atheist and know you're going to die, what really counts is friendship ... [30]

Christian apologist James Sire asks:

> If we are only material beings, a product of unintentional, uncaring sources, why do we think we can know anything at all? And why do we think we should be good?[31]

CULTURAL RELATIVISM

Western civilisation was founded on the biblical worldview that draws a clear distinction between good and evil. That is why Winston

---

29   Quoted in Himmelfarb, G, *The Demoralization of Society,* (IEA, 1995), p. 241.

30   'William Provine, RIP: Noble in His Honesty', *Evolution News and Science Today,* 3 September, 2015, Discovery Institute, https://evolutionnews.org/2015/09/william_provine/ (accessed 18 June, 2020), emphasis mine.

31   Sire, J, *The Universe Next Door,* (first published 1973, 4th edition, IVP Academic, 2004), p. 240.

Churchill was able to see with absolute clarity that Nazism was a moral evil which had to be opposed without compromise; equally he realised the moral evil of Communist totalitarianism.[32] But eight decades after the Second World War, it's deeply unfashionable to imply that Western democracy is superior to any other political system because *moral relativism* has led to *cultural relativism.*

George Blake was a British spy working for Soviet Russia between 1953 and 1960. He was fully aware of the oppression in Russia, the show trials and gulags. And yet, despite that, he deliberately worked to destroy the network of agents who were trying to bring freedom and democracy to Eastern Europe. Many of the agents he betrayed were killed, some of them after being tortured.[33] Blake was ultimately arrested and found guilty of treason. He died on 26 December 2020. Obituaries paid tribute to his 'courage'. Andrew Roberts, Churchill's biographer, roundly condemned the *'moral equivalence'* of such obituaries:

> A profoundly evil man died on Boxing Day, though one would hardly have known it from the entirely *judgement-free tone of his obituaries* ... Countries that enjoy representative institutions, the rule of law, free and fair elections, freedom of speech, freedom of association and of the press are indeed *morally superior* to those countries that hate and fear such things, and try remorselessly to undermine them. People like George Blake, who dedicated their lives to trying to replace democracy with Communist tyranny, thus ought to be identified when they die with the crimes against humanity that they perpetrated, instead of being presented as the moral equivalent of our own espionage agents in the West.[34]

---

32   Roberts, A, *Churchill: Walking with Destiny,* (Penguin Books, 2019), passim, especially p. 967.

33   Roberts, A, 'The Death of George Blake Reveals How Little We Now Respect Western Values', *The Daily Telegraph,* 28 December, 2020, https:// www.telegraph.co.uk/news/2020/12/28/death-george-blake-reveals-little-now-respect-western-values/ (accessed 4 January, 2021).

34   Ibid.

NO UNIVERSAL RELIGIOUS TRUTH

The moral equivalence, rightly condemned by Andrew Roberts, is just one symptom of the current assumption that it's arrogant to claim to know what is universally true. We hear of 'your truth' and 'my truth', and you've probably heard the mantra:

Well, that may be true for you, but it's not true for me!

We are expected to keep moral beliefs and faith in a personal 'spiritual' compartment, and many of the supposedly most brilliant intellects of the age promote a worldview that denies God and dismisses absolute morality. But a consistent application of naturalism leads to despair. As humanist philosopher **Bertrand Russell (1872-1970)** wrote:

Mankind ... is like a group of shipwrecked sailors on a raft in a vast sea at night. There is darkness all around. One by one they fall off the raft into the waters and disappear. When the last man has fallen off, the sea will roll on, and the holes made in the water by their bodies will be covered over. Nature cares not for man.[35]

This worldview gives no firm basis for human dignity or value. To believe that everything is really only matter or energy offers no foundation for meaning, morality, love or hope.

It is no accident that the word 'demoralization' has a double meaning. Originally, 'demoralize' meant to corrupt or to undermine morals. That assumed that there are such things as absolute morals to undermine. But now, 'demoralize' means to discourage – to undermine morale. The connection is obvious. When you lose any sense of objective morality, you will be demoralized in both senses of the word.

Before 1960, suicide had been rare among American young people. By 1980, nearly 400,000 adolescents were attempting suicide each year, and by 1987, suicide had become the second largest cause of death

---

35   Attributed to Bertrand Russell, quoted in Smart, S, ed, *The Spectator's Guide to Worldviews,* (Blue Bottle, 2007), p. 119.

among teens, after car accidents.[36] In 1994, **Kurt Cobain (b.1967)**, lead singer of Nirvana, committed suicide. His album 'Nevermind' had sold ten million copies, and his worldview can be summed up in his lyric:

> Silence, Here I am, Here I am, Silent.
> Death is what I am, Go to hell, Go to jail ...
> Die.[37]

Cobain's suicide was followed by at least 68 copycat suicides. Vishal Mangaldwadi writes:

> Cobain's music appealed to contemporary America because it was a full-throttled disharmony of rage, anguish, hatred, despair, meaninglessness, and obscenity. His song titles included, 'I hate myself, I want to die' and 'Rape me.'[38]

Back in the seventh century B.C., the prophet Jeremiah grieved over the self-destructive stupidity of rejecting God and His truth:

> My people have committed two sins: They have forsaken me, the spring of living water, and have dug their own cisterns, broken cisterns that cannot hold water. (Jer. 2:13)

During the twentieth century, the brave new world of freedom from the 'constraints' of religion increasingly lurched towards pessimistic nihilism. A naturalistic worldview offers no ultimate purpose to life, and no firm grounds for hope.

FURTHER READING

Furedi, F, 'The Diseasing of Judgment', *First Things,* January 2021, https://www.firstthings.com/article/2021/01/the-diseasing-of-judgment (accessed 30 December, 2020)

---

36 Mangalwadi, V, *The Book That Made Your World: How the Bible Created the Soul of Western Civilization,* (Nelson, 2011), p. 4.

37 Cobain, K, 'Endless, Nameless', (*Nevermind,* 1991).

38 Mangalwadi, V, *The Book That Made Your World,* p. 9.

Pearcey, N, *Total Truth: Liberating Christianity from its Cultural Captivity,* (Crossway, 2004)

Summary: By the end of the nineteenth century, increased acceptance of evolutionary theory had contributed to a naturalistic worldview: 'There is no Creator God, and there won't be a judgement'. This had profound implications: human beings are no longer given unique dignity, there is no purpose in history, death is the end and there is no absolute morality or universal religious truth.

2 'No God': From Atheism to Death Camps

'There is no God, there is no judgement.' In this chapter we look at three of the trailblazers in this 'liberation': Ludwig Feuerbach, Charles Darwin and Karl Marx. And we ask, how did their ideas work out in practice?

Ludwig Feuerbach (1804-1872): God Is Just a Comfort Blanket

At the beginning of the nineteenth century the Christian worldview was the majority assumption in the West (including Europe and North America). It was a 'given' that there is 'transcendent' (spiritual or eternal) reality, as well as the material realm. A bridge from the old world to the new was provided by German anthropologist and philosopher Ludwig Feuerbach.

In 1841 he published *The Essence of Christianity*. On a surface level it seemed spiritual, but underneath the pious phrases the message was plain. The *idea* of God is a comfort blanket to help people through the hardships of life. Humans created God because they wanted Him. God is a human projection. The concept of Christ's resurrection arose from the *desire* to believe in life after death. Here are some extracts from *The Essence of Christianity:*

Consciousness of God is self-consciousness, knowledge of God is self-knowledge ... *God is the manifested inward nature,* the expressed self of a man ... the historical progress of religion consists in this: that what by an earlier religion was regarded as objective, is now recognised as subjective; that is, *what was formerly contemplated and worshipped as God is now perceived to be something human.*[1]

The divine being is nothing else than the human being ... contemplated and revered as another, a distinct being. All the attributes of the divine nature are, therefore, attributes of the human nature.[2]

Providence is the conviction of man of the infinite value of his existence ... Faith in Providence is faith in one's own worth, the faith of man in himself ... *God's love for me [is] nothing else than my self-love deified.*[3]

God is the Love that satisfies our wishes, our emotional wants ... [4]

God is the affirmation of human feeling; prayer [is] the certainty that the power of the heart is greater than the power of Nature ... [5]

The resurrection of Christ is therefore the satisfied desire of man for an immediate certainty of his personal existence after death ... [6]

The fundamental dogmas of Christianity are realised wishes of the heart—the essence of Christianity is the essence of human feeling.[7]

---

1   Feuerbach, L, *The Essence of Christianity,* translated Evans, M, (aka Eliot, George), (London, 1890), https://www.gutenberg.org/files/47025/47025-h/47025-h.htm#ch27 (accessed 26 June 2020), p. 13, emphasis mine.

2   Ibid., p. 14, emphasis mine.

3   Ibid., p. 105, emphasis mine.

4   Ibid., p. 121.

5   Ibid., p. 123.

6   Ibid., p. 135.

7   Ibid., p. 140.

We have reduced the supermundane, supernatural, and superhuman nature of God to the elements of human nature as its fundamental elements ... *The beginning, middle and end of religion is MAN.*[8]

This represented a revolution in thinking: God is no longer in the centre, human beings are. A door opened to a world where we no longer assume that there is a transcendent, spiritual, eternal reality. We don't have to answer to God 'out there', only to 'God within'. Each person becomes their own Messiah. The 'death of God' seemed to present the opportunity for unlimited human freedom and fulfilment. Self-reliance became the creed of the idealists and transcendentalists, such as Ralph Waldo Emerson, Henry David Thoreau and Walt Whitman.

Charles Darwin (1809-1882): Made Atheism Intellectually Possible

Few today have heard of Feuerbach, but few have not heard of Darwin. *On the Origin of Species,* published in 1859, is widely acknowledged to be a book that changed the world.

Charles Darwin was born in 1809. His father was a leading doctor in Shrewsbury, England. His mother was a daughter of the famous potter, Josiah Wedgwood. Charles initially went to Edinburgh University to study medicine, but he didn't get on with medical studies and moved down to Cambridge University. His father hoped that he might go on to become a clergyman, thinking that if Charles could settle down in a quiet country rectory he would be able to spend time on his great passion, natural science.

After his studies at Cambridge, Charles was offered a place on an exploratory voyage to the Pacific. The Captain of HMS Beagle wanted someone with scientific interests who could collect, observe, and note anything worth recording in the field of natural history. The five-year expedition (1831-1836) proved perfect for Darwin's interest in the natural world. On return to England, he declined to enter the church.

---

8   Ibid., p. 184, emphasis mine.

An annual allowance from his father secured his independence, and the freedom to pursue his scientific interests.

During the first part of his life Darwin professed Christianity in a conventional way, but over time he lost faith altogether. At first he was reluctant to admit his unbelief too publicly. During the mid-nineteenth century, open atheism was scandalous. There was also a personal reason. In 1839 Charles married his cousin Emma, a daughter of the famous and wealthy Wedgwood family. Emma believed in God and fretted about the eternal destiny of her husband. Charles loved her, and did not want to upset her. But the final demise of his religious faith came when their ten-year-old daughter Annie died in 1851.

With a substantial allowance from his father, plus a generous dowry from Emma's father, Charles could live on private means. He spent all his time on detailed investigations in natural science and geology. By 1837 he had conceived his theory of natural selection, but he still hesitated about putting his controversial arguments before the public. However, the intellectual climate was shifting by the mid-1850s. Thomas Huxley, Herbert Spencer, and others formed a secularist, non-clerical 'alternative' to the traditional clerical Oxbridge elite. This network would make it easier for Darwin's theories to gain ground.[9]

In the event, Darwin was pushed into publication when a scientific colleague called Alfred Russel Wallace (1823-1913) sent him an essay which described the same idea of natural selection. Wallace and Darwin both presented papers at the Linnean Society in 1858,[10] and *On The Origin of Species* was published the next year. Twelve years later, *The Descent of Man* (1871) developed Darwin's idea of human evolution. The implication that man is simply an advanced animal was explored in *The Expression of Emotions in Man and Animals* (1872).

---

9   Desmond, D, Moore, J, Browne, J, *Charles Darwin,* (Oxford University Press, 2007), p. 56.

10   The Linnean Society of London, founded 1788, is the world's oldest active biological society, named after the Swedish naturalist Carl Linnaeus (1707-1778) whose collections have been in its keeping since 1829.

Darwin died in 1882. The foundation of modern secular humanism, that life can be explained without God, is 'grounded in the life and work of Darwin'.[11]

HISTORY RESTARTED

The impact of Darwin's ideas extended far beyond the field of biology. To view mankind as part of a continuum with nature rather than the product of special creation was an 'intellectual revolution' which:

> ... has caused man to reinterpret his past, rethink his present, and revise his anticipations for the future. Darwin is seen as giving the world a comprehension of itself so unlike the view held in the past that, in a sense, he *restarted history*.[12]

Atheist philosopher Daniel C. Dennett writes about the fantasy of a *'universal acid'*, so corrosive that it cannot be held in any container. There are people who would like to see Darwin's idea contained within the field of biology, but:

> ... it eats through just about every traditional concept, and leaves in its wake a revolutionized world-view, with most of the old landmarks still recognizable, but transformed in fundamental ways.[13]

Today, 'Social Darwinism' prevails in many university departments. This, broadly, affirms that:
- Social structures are engineered and controlled by impersonal forces rather than by God.
- Society is moving upward (from the primordial slime until now).
- Human beings are a higher sort of animal.

---

11 Carter, J D, *Western Humanism: A Christian Perspective: A Guide for Understanding Moral Decline in Western Culture,* (Point of Grace, 2005), p. 150.

12 Breese, D, *Seven Men who Rule the World from their Grave,* (Moody Press, 1992) p. 18, emphasis mine.

13 Dennett, D C, *Darwin's Dangerous Idea: Evolution and the Meanings of Life,* (Simon and Schuster, 1995), p. 63.

- The mind (our thoughts and beliefs) are just chemical actions of the brain.[14]

Michael Denton, a leader in the 'intelligent design' movement, writes:

> The influence of evolutionary theory on fields far away from biology is one of the more spectacular examples in history of how a *highly speculative idea* for which there is really no *hard scientific evidence* can come to fashion the thinking of a whole society and *dominate the outlook of an age* ... One might have expected that a theory of such cardinal importance, a theory that literally changed the world, would have been something more than metaphysics, something more than a myth.[15]

The Culture of Death

Christianity introduced an ethic which regarded every human life as sacred, because we are made in the image of God. John Ling points out that Western human medicine combined the best of Greek medicine, as summed up in the Hippocratic Oath, and the Judeo-Christian ethic of life as laid out in Scripture. 'For well over two thousand years, these two grand pillars have underpinned medical ethics and medical practice.'[16] These two millennia represented the 'Golden Age of Medicine', when medical care rested on the solid foundation of respect for life as given by God. But that solid foundation has been undermined, and we have seen a tragic drift towards a culture of death. The British Medical Association proposed in 1997 to revise the Hippocratic Oath to allow for the killing of unborn human life.

The theory of evolution sees humans as the product of chance in an impersonal universe. Once a society rejects the belief that all human life has been created by God with unique dignity, the door opens to a utilitarian system of ethics. The value of a life can be assessed by criteria such as usefulness, enjoyment, or awareness. It's an easy progression

---

14 Breese, *Seven Men who Rule the World from their Grave,* pp. 137-8.

15 Denton, M, *Evolution: A Theory in Crisis,* (Adler & Adler, 1986), p. 358, emphasis mine.

16 Ling, J, *Bioethical Issues,* (Day One, 2014), p. 23.

to arguing that the 'less fit' should be eliminated. Today, advances in reproductive technology mean that pregnant women are routinely scanned, and if their babies give any sign of 'abnormality' there may be pressure to abort the child.

THE EVIL IDEA OF RACIAL SUPREMACY

Evolutionary ideas lay directly behind the flawed 'science' of eugenics, which in turn fed into the evil idea of racial supremacy.

> Biological racism – the Social Darwinian belief that mankind is organized hierarchically by race, with the whites at the top – was considered scientific fact ... in the late nineteenth century.[17]

That is, considered scientific fact by many who bought into Darwin's evolutionary theory. By contrast, as we will see in Part Two, the biblical truth is that all humans are of one race.

The 'science' of eugenics emerged in Britain in the mid-nineteenth century, as an offshoot of Darwinism. Darwin's half-cousin Francis Galton (1822-1911) coined the word 'eugenics', meaning the improvement of the human species through genetic engineering. Galton wrote *Hereditary Genius* in 1869. This claimed:

> Consequently, as it is easy ... to obtain by careful selection a permanent breed of dogs or horses gifted with peculiar powers of running, or of doing anything else, so it would be quite practicable to produce a highly-gifted race of men by judicious marriages during several consecutive generations.[18]

Galton founded the Eugenics Society in London in 1908, to investigate human heredity and carry out social-action programmes. His ideas were scientifically flawed. He claimed, for example, that mental handicap could be eliminated if affected people were segregated or

---

17 Roberts, A, *Churchill: Walking with Destiny,* (Penguin Books, 2019), p. 976.

18 Galton, F, *Hereditary Genius,* 1869, Introduction, http://galton.org/ books/hereditary-genius/ (accessed 17 July, 2020).

sterilized.[19] Despite that, by the first part of the twentieth century, many in the West advocated state adoption of eugenic policies.[20] In America, for example, many prominent figures promoted eugenics. They hoped to improve the country's health by increasing births and immigration amongst the 'fit', and decreasing births and immigration amongst the 'unfit'.[21] During the first decades of the twentieth century, more than thirty states in America adopted policies which meant individuals could be forcibly sterilised if they were disabled, ill, or belonged to socially disadvantaged groups. Most US states abandoned the practice after World War II, amidst revulsion at the Nazi programme of eugenics.

Karl Marx (1818-1883): Overthrow the Old Society

> The workers have nothing to lose but their chains. They have a world to gain. Workers of the world unite![22]

These electrifying words concluded the Communist Manifesto, written in 1848 by Karl Marx and Friedrich Engels. Marx was born

---

19 Ling, J, *Bioethical Issues,* (Day One, 2014), p. 135.

20 See John Maynard Keynes' lecture in Berlin in 1926, 'The End of laissez-Faire', https://fee.org/articles/when-keynes-lectured-mises-on-eugenics-migration-and-population-control/ (accessed 25 February 2021). The British politician and founder of the welfare state, William Beveridge believed that those men with 'general defects' should be denied not only the vote, but 'civil freedom and fatherhood': https://www.theguardian.com/commentisfree/2012/feb/17/eugenics-skeleton-rattles-loudest-closet-left?INTCMP=SRCH (accessed 25 February, 2021).

21 Shockingly, many Christians endorsed these ideas and policies – a sobering warning against compromising biblical principles under pressure from what the 'science' says. Durst, D L, 'Evangelical Engagements with Eugenics, 1900–1940', *Ethics and Medicine: An International Journal of Bioethics,* Vol. 18.2, 2009, https://pubmed.ncbi.nlm.nih.gov/14700040/ (accessed 30 June, 2020).

22 Marx, K, *The Communist Manifesto,* https://www.marxists.org/archive/marx/works/download/pdf/Manifesto.pdf (accessed 2 July 2020), p. 34.

to a Jewish family in 1818, in a small Prussian city. He studied law at Bonn, and then philosophy at Berlin. Having adopted revolutionary ideals, Marx became a journalist, first in Cologne, then in Paris and Brussels. 1848 was the year of revolutions in Europe. Marx, as a known instigator of revolution, was forced to move with his family to the relatively tolerant safe haven of London, where he remained until his death in 1883.

What would revolution look like? Total overthrow of society. Marx was critical of those who: 'see in poverty nothing but poverty, without seeing in it the *revolutionary, subversive side, which will overthrow the old society*.'[23] Engels explained:

> ... this struggle ... has now reached a stage where the exploited and oppressed class (the proletariat) can no longer emancipate itself from the class which exploits and oppresses it (the bourgeoisie), without at the same time forever freeing *the whole of society* from exploitation, oppression, class struggles.[24]

This would only be achieved by violent revolution: a fight against private property, the married family, national borders, and all the religious and legal norms which propped the old capitalist structure up.

> The proletariat, the lowest stratum of our present society, cannot stir, cannot raise itself up, without the whole superincumbent strata of official society being sprung into the air ... The Communists disdain to conceal their views and aims. They openly declare that their ends can be attained only by the *forcible overthrow of*

---

23 Marx, K, *The Poverty of Philosophy,* https://www.marxists.org/archive/marx/works/1847/poverty-philosophy/ch02.htm#a1, (accessed 2 November, 2020), emphasis mine.

24 After Marx died in March 1883, Engels wrote a preface to a new German edition of the Manifesto. Engels, F, Preface to 1883 German Edition, *Manifesto of the Communist Party,* 1848, p. 6. https://www.marxists.org/archive/marx/works/download/pdf/Manifesto.pdf (accessed 2 July 2020), p. 20, emphasis mine.

all existing social conditions. Let the ruling classes tremble at a Communistic revolution.[25]

ABOLISH PRIVATE PROPERTY!

In the *Communist Manifesto* (1848), Marx wrote: 'the theory of the Communists may be summed up in the single sentence: Abolition of private property.' He believed 'that man's material needs and wants were the primary driving forces that formed human nature.'[26] He claimed that societies had passed through a communal and primitive stage, where all was held in common; the slave stage; the feudal society and then the era in which he lived: bourgeois or capitalist society. The goal of history was the overthrow of capitalism and the establishment of communism. Marx believed that intellectual activists such as himself, and the workers in society, should join in revolutionary activity to topple the capitalist establishment.

A cartoon drawn in America in 1911 summed up the Marxist view of society: a social pyramid with exploited workers at the base.[27] Rulers are at the top: 'We rule you', then the clergy: 'We fool you', then the armed forces: 'We shoot at you' and the bourgeoisie: 'We eat for you'. Trampled down by all those groups are the proletariat: 'We work for all – We feed all'.

The assumption is that the State (representing the rulers) oppresses the workers; religious leaders keep workers subservient by promoting a 'false consciousness', and law enforcement agencies are primarily concerned with protecting the property of the rich. The bourgeoisie are those who own the means of production in society; and as a class are perceived as the enemy who must be eliminated. These various layers of oppression must all be overthrown. The key demands of the *Communist Manifesto* included:

---

25 Marx, K, Engels, F, *Manifesto of the Communist Party,* 1848, https://www. marxists.org/archive/marx/works/download/pdf/Manifesto.pdf (accessed 2 July 2020), p. 20, emphasis mine.

26 Marx, K, *The Communist Manifesto*, p. 32.

27 Pyramid of Capitalist System, Nedeljkovich, Brashick and Kuharich, (Cleveland: The International Publishing Co., 1911).

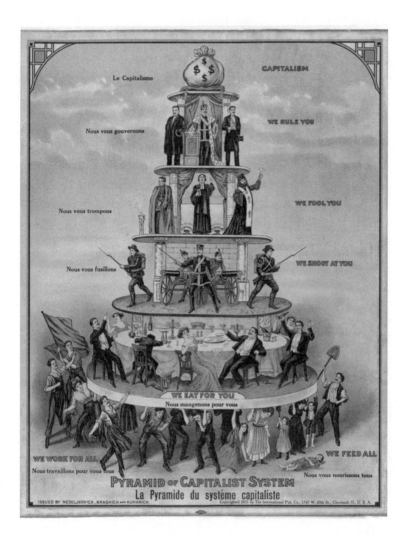

Pyramid of Capitalist System, 1911

- Abolition of privately owned property and land.
- Heavy taxation.
- Abolition of inheritance rights.
- The State to own banks, means of communication, transport, factories and all instruments of production.
- The State to control labour, by means of industrial armies; all citizens to work; 'contradictions' between town and countryside to be eliminated.

The lower middle class, small manufacturers, shopkeepers, artisans and peasants would have to join the revolutionary proletariats. If they tried to protect the small stake they had carved out in the established system (their own homes, shops, small businesses or farms), it would identify them with the bourgeoisie, that is:

> ... not revolutionary, but conservative. Nay more, they are reactionary, for they try to roll back the wheel of history ... The 'dangerous class', [lumpenproletariat] the social scum, that passively rotting mass thrown off by the lowest layers of the old society, may, here and there, be swept into the movement by a proletarian revolution; its conditions of life, however, prepare it far more for the part of a bribed tool of reactionary intrigue.[28]

These poor people, then, would be regarded as *the enemy* along with the middle classes. To achieve 'justice' the 'enemy' had to be eliminated. Hatred of the bourgeoisie justified any act of terror. When a bomb was thrown into a Russian cafe filled with two hundred people, those responsible boasted that they had wanted 'to see how the foul bourgeois will squirm in death agony'.[29]

---

28 Marx, K, Engels, F, *Manifesto of the Communist Party,* p. 20.

29 Morson, G S, 'Suicide of the Liberals', *First Things,* October 2020, https://www.firstthings.com/article/2020/10/suicide-of-the-liberals (accessed 13 January, 2021)

ABOLISH THE FAMILY!

The married family was a target, because the 'bourgeois family' was inseparable from private property. A family owning their own home could not be tolerated. It symbolised their shameful bourgeois privilege. The desire of parents to work for, and leave an inheritance for, their children is one of the main incentives to acquire property.

> *Abolition [Aufhebung] of the family!* Even the most radical flare up at this infamous proposal of the Communists. On what foundation is the present family, the bourgeois family, based? On capital, on private gain. In its completely developed form, this family exists only among the bourgeoisie.[30]

Marx and Engels were open about their aims. They didn't want to achieve a level of prosperity in society where all families could aspire to their own homes. The only way to eliminate noxious inequality was to rid society of the family:

> The Communist revolution is the most radical rupture with traditional property relations; no wonder that its development involved the most radical rupture with traditional ideas.[31]
>
> What will be the influence of communist society on the family? It will transform the relations between the sexes into a purely private matter which concerns only the persons involved and into which society has no occasion to intervene. It can do this since it does away with private property and educates children on a communal basis, and in this way *removes the two bases of traditional marriage – the dependence rooted in private property, of the women on the man, and of the children on the parents.*[32]

ABOLISH THE RULE OF LAW!

On 21 November 1917, Lenin abrogated 'the courts, the bar and the legal profession, and left the people without the only protection

---

30   Marx, K, Engels, F, *Manifesto of the Communist Party,* p. 25, emphasis mine.

31   Ibid., p. 26.

32   Ibid., p. 52, emphasis mine.

they had ever had from arbitrary intimidation and arrest'.[33] The state could now control the population unconstrained by the rule of law. **György Lukács (1885-1971)** a writer and philosopher, worked for the communist party in Hungary after the First World War. He maintained that the whole bourgeois legal system would have to be dismantled:

> the ideological foundation of legality ... is a view of the world that has to be overcome if the Communist Party wishes to create a healthy foundation for both its legal and illegal tactics ... the question of legality or illegality reduces iself ... for the Communist Party to a mere system of tactics ... in this wholly unprincipled solution lies the only possible practical and principled rejection of the bourgeois legal system.[34]

In answer to a question, Lukács insisted that 'Communist ethics makes it the highest duty to accept the necessity to act wickedly.'[35] The Marxist priority was the destruction of capitalism, *whatever* the cost.

ABOLISH RELIGION AND MORALITY!

Like Feuerbach, Marx taught that religion is an illusion, created by human beings as a comfort blanket to warm and cheer through the uncertainties of life. He believed religion to be a dangerous diversion, preventing people from seeing the need to overthrow capitalism.

> Religion is the sigh of the oppressed creature ... It is the opium of the people[36]

---

33 Scruton, R, *Fools, Frauds and Firebrands: Thinkers of the New Left,* (Bloomsbury Continuum, 2015), p. 30.

34 Lukács, G, *History and Class Consciousness: Studies in Marxist Dialectics,* 1968, translated, Livingstone, R, (Merlin Press, 1971), pp. 263-4, https://monoskop.org/images/3/3b/Lukacs_Georg_History_and_Class_Consciousness_Studies_in_Marxist_Dialectics.pdf (accessed 21 December, 2020).

35 Scruton, R, *Fools, Frauds and Firebrands,* p. 119.

36 In fact, Marx lifted this punchy saying from Heinrich Heine, Johnson, P, *Intellectuals,* (Weidenfeld and Nicolson, 1988), p. 56.

Communism abolishes eternal truths, *it abolishes all religion, and all morality.*[37]

Religion was regarded as a reactionary force to be done away with.[38] It was to be extirpated by force. Believers were viewed as traitors to the revolution. Children were to be liberated from the tyranny of religion. A propaganda campaign in Soviet Russia depicted the church as a place of danger. A typical poster depicted a little girl fighting to escape the evil grasp of an elderly woman, who is pulling the child away from school and into church.[39]

Not only was religion attacked, there was also an assault on the concepts of absolute morality and personal responsibility. The philosophy of *personal responsibility* (that we are individually accountable for our actions) was still dominant in the nineteenth century. In 1859, Samuel Smiles published what would become an international best seller entitled *Self-Help: with Illustrations of Character and Conduct.* The central message was that 'character is power, more than knowledge is power'. Perseverance, energy, integrity and diligence could empower the humblest person to be useful and productive.[40] This certainty about individual moral responsibility was the joint heritage of Christianity and the classical world.

By the beginning of the twentieth century, it was increasingly assumed that individuals should be regarded as *victims of their circumstances.* Marx promoted the idea that the behaviour of human beings was driven, not so much by what appeared to be their own free will, as by powerful underlying economic forces and class structures.

As structural forces took front place, personal conscience and individual free will were undermined. Once the spotlight was on

---

37   Marx, K, *Communist Manifesto,* p. 31.

38   Marx, K, Engels, F, *Manifesto of the Communist Party,* p. 52.

39   See p. 58. Soviet anti-religious propaganda posters, poster 11, https://russiatrek.org/blog/art/soviet-anti-religious-propaganda-posters/ (accessed 13 January 2021); the slogan on the poster reads 'Religion is Poison: Protect Children!' and the building on the right is a school.

40   Smiles, S, *Self-Help,* http://files.libertyfund.org/files/297/Smiles_0379.pdf (accessed 14 July, 2020)

Soviet Poster: 'Religion is Poison: Protect Children!'

structures, individual freedoms could be sacrificed for the good of the many. *The 'good' was what was good for the proletariat.* 'Evil' was what harmed the proletariat. *Killing and stealing could be regarded as 'good' if it benefited the proletariat:*

> For Marxism there is no reason (literally no reason: our universe, the movement posits, is the kind of universe where there cannot conceivably be any reason) for not killing or torturing or exploiting a human person if his liquidation or torture or slave labor will advance the historical process.[41]

Universal Christian morality was regarded as a false consciousness, which only delayed revolution.

ABOLISH NATIONAL BORDERS!

The existence of sovereign states was regarded as a barrier to the triumph of the proletariat. Independent states seek to protect their own interests, and they use the rule of law to secure property rights. Communists wanted workers of all nations to rise in violent revolution against all governments.

> The nationalities of the peoples associating themselves in accordance with the principle of community will be compelled to mingle with each other as a result of this association and thereby to dissolve themselves, just as the various estate and class distinctions must disappear through the abolition of their basis, private property.[42]

---

41 Professor Wilfred Cantwell Smith, quoted by Denis Prager, 'The Left's Moral Compass Isn't Broken', *The Daily Signal,* 17 September, 2020, https://www.dailysignal.com/2020/09/17/the-lefts-moral-compass-isnt-broken/ (accessed 7 October, 2020).

42 Marx, K, Engels, F, *Manifesto of the Communist Party,* p. 52.

CONCERN FOR 'THE PEOPLE' – CONTEMPT FOR REAL PEOPLE

Marx's interest in 'the proletariat' was purely theoretical. Passionate about 'The People', he didn't care about individual people. They were dispensable in light of his grand vision of the future. They:

> ... were simply the eggs from which a glorious omelette would one day be made. And he would be instrumental in making it.[43]

Most of Marx's time was spent in the British Library, he didn't bother to visit mills, factories, mines or other industrial workplaces.[44] He was hostile to socialists of working class origin, and 'any leaders who had secured a large following of working men by preaching practical solutions to actual problems of work and wages rather than doctrinaire revolution.'[45] He had his fixed theories, and then distorted evidence to back them up.[46]

Profligate in spending money, terrible at managing it, and incapable of earning very much of it – Marx's mother apparently said bitterly that she wished her son would spend less time writing about capital, and more time trying to earn some. He lived beyond his means, and the main victims were his wife and children. Two of his daughters ended up committing suicide. Marx's income never fell below £200 a year (three times that of an average skilled workman), but he refused to live in a 'proletarian' way. He insisted on living on around £500 a year which meant constant debt, many begging letters to family and friends, and regular visits to the pawn shop. Friedrich Engels (who was the son of a wealthy manufacturer) subsidised Marx throughout his life.[47]

Marx exploited the one 'worker' he had first-hand contact with. Helen Demuth, known to the family as 'Lenchen', entered service at the age of just eight in his wife's family. When Marx married Jenny in

---

43 Dalrymple, T, *Our Culture: What's Left of It: The Mandarins and the Masses,* (Ivan R Dee, 2005), p. 88.

44 Johnson, P, *Intellectuals,* p. 60.

45 Ibid., p. 61.

46 Ibid., pp. 66-9.

47 Ibid., pp. 73-7.

1845, Jenny's mother 'gave her' Helen, (by then aged twenty-two), as a servant/housekeeper. Helen worked for the Marx family until her death in 1890, receiving only board and lodging, never a wage. Worse still, when she gave birth to Marx's son in 1851, Marx refused to have the child under his own roof. Helen was forced to foster him out to a poor family.[48]

When Marx died, only eleven people attended his funeral in Highgate Cemetery. He had fallen out with most of his colleagues.

From Dream to Nightmare

After Marx's death, his ideas were forced onto nations such as Russia, China and Cambodia with terrifying effect.

'MEN HAVE FORGOTTEN GOD'

Vladimir Ilyich Ulyanov, better known as **Lenin (1870-1924)**, tried to enforce Marx's dogmatic atheism in Russia. He believed 'there can be nothing more abominable than religion'.[49] People who would not reject belief in God were sent to mental institutions, prisons, or concentration camps where millions died. Lenin was responsible for over four million deaths. **Joseph Stalin (1878-1953)** continued the suppression of religion, as well as the liquidation of any enemies of the revolution. That included the educated; and also the 'kulaks', a term applied to all reasonably well-to-do peasants. Stalin was responsible for more than forty-two million deaths.

The great Russian writer **Aleksandr Solzhenitsyn (1918-2008)** documented the evils of this tyranny in *The Gulag Archipelago*,[50]

---

48 Ibid., pp. 79-81.

49 Blanchard, J, *Does God Believe in Atheists?* (Evangelical Press, 2000), p. 67.

50 In Russian, the term GULAG is an acronym for Main Directorate of Camps. And an archipelago is a string of islands. Solzhenitsyn was evoking the picture of a string of prison camps reaching right across the vast expanse of the Soviet Union. Solzhenitsyn, A, *The Gulag Archipelago,* (Abridged edition, Penguin, 2018). Jordan Peterson regards *The Gulag Archipelago* as possibly the most important book of the twentieth century. He believes that it should be read by every high school student.

written between 1958 and 1968, and first published in 1973. Solzhenitsyn was a graduate in Physics, Mathematics and Literature. He served in World War II, attaining the rank of captain. At the end of the war, some of his letters commenting negatively on army conditions were intercepted. He was arrested and sentenced to eight years in forced labour camps, followed by internal exile.

Solzhenitsyn offered an eye-witness description of the way that society was corrupted and destroyed by nihilism and totalitarianism, the inevitable outworking of Marxist ideology. In 1983 he observed:

> ... if I were asked today to formulate as concisely as possible the main cause of the ruinous revolution that swallowed up some 60 million of our people, I could not put it more accurately than to repeat: *'Men have forgotten God; that's why all this has happened.'*[51]

Marxist ideology places no moral constraints on those in power. All those regarded by the ideology as 'reactionary' could be arrested, sent to labour camps and worked to death. Families were separated. There was no recourse to 'justice'. Anyone judged to be an 'enemy of the revolution' was, effectively, dehumanised, but that category was infinitely expandable. One suspect conversation or joke might condemn you.

Children were encouraged to inform on their parents. One of the 'heroes' of the Soviet Union was Pavlik Morozov, who allegedly informed on his father to the Party in 1932. His father was sent to a work camp and then executed. Pavlik was, in turn, murdered (under disputed circumstances). Four members of the family were accused of his death, rounded up and shot. A statue was erected in Pavlik's honour. Tens of thousands of schoolchildren were taken to visit this shrine to a child who had put Party before family. The message: 'that's what we would expect you to do!'[52]

---

51 Solzhenitsyn, A, 'Templeton Award Speech', 1983, https://www. templetonprize.org/laureate-sub/solzhenitsyn-acceptance-speech/ (accessed 2 July, 2020), emphasis mine.

52 'Squalid truth of Stalin's little martyr killed for informing on his father', *History News Network,* 13 March 2005, https://web.archive.org/

The idea of 'group guilt' was hardwired into Marxist thinking. In 1956 Nikita Khrushchev, the leader of the USSR who took over from Stalin, admitted that Stalin had repressed or killed:

> not only ... actual enemies, but also ... individuals who had not committed any crimes against the party or the Soviet government.[53]

Seventy-five year old Tatiana was interviewed in Moscow in 2017. Her mother had been sentenced to eight years in a gulag because of her 'association' with someone deemed to be an enemy of the state. Tatiana and her twin brother were born in the gulag. Her father and infant brother both died there, victims of harsh conditions and lack of food. Eventually Tatiana, aged six, was released with her mother.[54]

THE GREAT TERROR

In 1949, **Mao Tse-Tung (1893-1976)** established the People's Republic of China in order to implement Marx's revolutionary ideas. He, too, tried to abolish religious practice. In total, his regime was responsible for the deaths of over seventy million people.[55]

The 'great terror' commenced in 1966, when young people all over the country were incited to accuse, attack, and ultimately torture and kill their teachers. Every vestige of culture from the past had to be purged: books were burned, statues were toppled. One Communist leader admitted that during the 'Cultural Revolution' the country became a vast torture chamber.[56]

Mao died in 1976. But that wasn't the end of communist totalitarianism in China. There has been a greater measure of

---

web/20050314010149/http://hnn.us/readcomment.php?id=27304 (accessed 15 July 2020).

53 Bartholomew, J, 'Life in a Gulag', *The Spectator*, 20 May, 2017, https://www.spectator.co.uk/article/life-in-a-gulag (accessed 4 September, 2020).

54 https://www.spectator.co.uk/article/life-in-a-gulag (accessed 4 September, 2020).

55 Chang, J, Halliday, J, *Mao: The Unknown Story*, (Vintage Books, 2006), p. 651.

56 Ibid., p. 546.

economic freedom in recent years, but, at the time of writing, Uighur people in Xinjiang province have been systematically rounded up, their passports confiscated, parents separated from children, people forced into labour camps, and shocking atrocities committed.[57]

A SPLENDID VICTORY!

Pol Pot (1925-1998) aimed to establish an atheistic Communist regime in Cambodia. He brutally enforced Marx's vision of eliminating the bourgeoisie. Between 1975 and 1977 a quarter of the population perished. Mao congratulated Pol Pot for having abolished the inequalities of the class system by transforming Cambodia into one vast slave-labour-state:

> You have scored a splendid victory. Just a single blow and no more classes![58]

By 1980 about twenty-eight nations, representing more than 1.5 billion people (more than one-third of the world's population), were governed by Marxist regimes.[59] All were characterised by loss of individual freedom, widespread poverty and suppression of religious practice.

When I was a student at the end of the 1970s, it was common for students to wear sweatshirts emblazoned with images of their hero, the revolutionary leader **Che Guevara (1928-1967)**. This was a man who ruthlessly eliminated countless individuals in his quest for 'group justice'. Che Guevara gave a speech in 1964, after he and Castro had taken power in Cuba:

---

57 https://www.washingtonpost.com/opinions/global-opinions/new-evidence-of-chinas-concentration-camps-shows-its-hardening-resolve-to-wipe-out-the-uighurs/2020/09/03/aeeb71b4-ebb2-11ea-99a1-71343d03bc29_story.ht (accessed 30 September 2020).

58 Chang, J, Halliday, J, *Mao,* p. 650.

59 Blanchard, J, *Does God Believe in Atheists?* p. 69.

We continue to speak of the small farmer, the poor, small farmer, and we never say that the farmer, no matter how poor and small he is, manifestly generates capitalism... *he must be eliminated.*[60]

THE NIGHT THE WALL CAME DOWN

On the evening of 9 November 1989, guards at the checkpoints on the wall between communist East Berlin and free West Berlin gave up trying to hold back the crowds. Thousands rushed from east to west, where they were greeted with cheers, champagne, flowers, and cash handouts. Over the following days, 'wall-peckers' gathered to dismantle the ultimate symbol of oppression and tyranny. Borders had to be fortified to force people to *stay in* communist regimes. People were not lining up to emigrate into the 'socialist utopias'. They were desperate to get out.

EXECUTIONS ON CHRISTMAS DAY

Today, some still remember the horrors uncovered during the 1990s, once Nicolae and Elena Ceaușescu had been toppled from power in Romania. The Marxist ideal of eliminating the contradiction between town and country, and erasing the traditional ways of life of the past, had been brutally enforced. Villages had been demolished. High-rise apartments were built in the middle of fields. Christianity was forbidden. Family and community life were viciously attacked. The result? People lacked food, heat, and light, while the Ceaușescus lived in obscene luxury. By the 1980s, the population could only be kept under by the brutal *Securitate.*[61] Thousands of dissenters were imprisoned, tortured and killed. An estimated one in four of the population were informers for the secret police. Popular fury eventually erupted after 42 years of communist rule and 21 years of the Ceaușescus' dictatorship. Nicolae and Elena were executed on Christmas day 1989.

---

60 Collier, P, Horowitz, D, *Destructive Generation: Second Thoughts about the Sixties,* (Encounter Books, 1989), p. 270, emphasis mine.

61 Internal Security Force in Romania, 1948-1989.

The total death toll of the murderous tyranny of Marxist governments in the twentieth century far exceeded the horrors of Nazi Germany, but the crimes of the Marxist regimes are relatively unknown. Maybe the reason for this ignorance is that, as the poet TS Eliot observed, 'Humankind cannot bear very much reality'.[62]

VIEWS FROM WITHIN AND WITHOUT – PEOPLE AS 'HUMAN MATERIAL'

Czeslaw Milosz (1911-2004) was born in Lithuania. Following the Second World War, he worked for the People's Republic of Poland. Milosz became disillusioned with the authoritarianism and totalitarianism of the communist regime and went into exile, first in Paris, then in America. In *The Captive Mind*, (1953), he described 'enslavement through consciousness': the way in which the communist regime sought to change the thought patterns of citizens. 'In the people's democracies, a battle is being waged for mastery over the human spirit.'[63] All were to be convinced that 'good and evil are definable solely in terms of service or harm to the interests of the Revolution.'[64] Humans didn't exist as individuals, they were regarded as '*human material*'.[65]

Milosz vividly described the human and social cost of this 'new faith':

> In the countries of the New Faith, the cities lose their former aspect. The liquidation of small private enterprises gives the streets a stiff and institutional look. The chronic lack of consumer goods renders the crowds uniformly gray and uniformly indigent [poor]. When consumer products do appear, they are of a single second-rate quality. Fear paralyses individuality and makes people adjust

---

62 Eliot, T S, 'Burnt Norton', I.

63 Miłosz, C, *The Captive Mind,* translated by Zielonko, J, (Penguin, 1953), p. 191.

64 Ibid., p. 75.

65 Ibid., p.108, emphasis mine.

themselves as much as possible to the average type in their gestures, clothing and facial expressions.[66]

But even as the authorities stamp out private enterprise, human nature ensures that it springs up again:

Hardly is one clandestine workshop or store liquidated in one neighbourhood or city than another springs up elsewhere. Restaurants hide behind a sliding wall of a private house; shoemakers and tailors work at home for their friends. In fact, everything that comes under the heading of speculation sprouts up again and again. And no wonder! State and municipal stores consistently lack even the barest essentials. In the summer, one can buy winter clothes; in the winter, summer wear – but usually of the wrong size and of poor quality. The purchase of spool of thread or a needle is a major problem, for the one state store in the town may not carry them for a year. Clothes that are given to be mended may be held by the local crafts' cooperative for six months. The inns ('Points of Collective Nourishment') are so crowded that people lose the desire to drink with their friends. They know they will have to sit down at a table with strangers and wait, sometimes as long as an hour, before the waiter appears. All this creates a field for private services. A worker's wife goes to a nearby town, buys needles and thread, brings them back and sells them: the germ of capitalism. The worker himself of a free afternoon mends a broken bathroom pipe for a friend who has waited months for the state to send him a repair man. In return, he gets a little money, enough to buy himself a shirt: a rebirth of capitalism. He hasn't time to wait in line on the day the state store receives a new shipment of goods, so he buys the shirt from a friend. She has cleverly managed to buy three, let us say, through her friendship with the salesgirl and now she resells them at a small profit. She is speculating. What she earns as a cleaning woman in a state factory is not enough to support her three children, since her husband was arrested by the security police. If these manifestations of human enterprise

66   Ibid., p. 66.

were not wiped out, it is easy to guess what they would lead to. A worker would set up a plumbing repairs shop. His neighbour, who secretly sells alcohol to people who want to drink in relative privacy would open a cafe. The cleaning woman would become a merchant, peddling her goods. They would gradually expand their businesses, and the lower middle class would reappear. Introduce freedom of the press and of assembly, and publications catering to this clientele would spring up like mushrooms after the rain. And there would be the petty bourgeoisie as a political force.[67]

Most painful of all are the descriptions of the fate that befell the Baltic states under communism – three small nations where innumerable peasant farmers had cultivated small farms, and sold butter and eggs to surrounding countries. They were, of course, regarded as 'bourgeois', and deported en masse to labour camps in Siberia. Milosz described a letter written in 1949 by a mother and her two daughters:

> Their letter was a terse account of their work on a kolkhoz [state-owned collective farm]. The last letters of every line were slightly stressed, and reading vertically one made out the words 'Eternal Slave'. If such a letter happened to fall into my hands, then how many other, similarly disguised expressions of despair must have found their way to people who could not make any use of them. And, calculating the possibilities, how many such letters remained unwritten; how many of those who might have written them died of hunger and overwork, repeating those hopeless words 'Eternal Slave'?[68]

Balint Vazsonyi (1936-2003) made his musical debut in Budapest, Hungary aged just twelve. He went on to become an internationally acclaimed concert pianist. He was in a unique position to comment on the outworking of socialism, as he lived through the 1944 German National Socialist (Nazi) occupation of Hungary, and then, after the Second World War, the 1948-9 Soviet invasion, occupation, and

---

67   Ibid., pp. 192-3.

68   Ibid., p. 232, emphasis mine.

imposition of communism. As a teenager he was reported to have made negative comments about the regime, and was summoned to answer to the police. He witnessed children informing on their parents, people being sentenced to death for belonging to the wrong 'group', and a corrosion of civil society as ideology overrode the rule of law.

In 1956 it seemed as if Hungary might break free from Soviet occupation. But then the uprising was brutally crushed. Around 200,000 Hungarians, Vazsonyi among them, attempted to walk to freedom, risking death if they were detected by border guards. Having safely crossed the Austrian border, Vazsonyi was met by volunteer American students who had come over to Europe to form a 'human chain' to protect escapees from inadvertently re-entering Hungarian territory. He ultimately settled in America, and became a music professor. In *America's Thirty Years War* (1998), he argued that America was throwing away its heritage of freedom, which rested on the rule of law, individual rights, security of property, and the acceptance that all citizens equally could identify as American. Arguing from history and experience, he showed that the ideology of group identity and 'Social Justice'[69] leads straight to totalitarianism. Group rights are incompatible with individual rights:

> ... the Rule of Law and the Search for Social Justice cannot exist side-by-side because social justice requires that those who possess more of anything have it taken away from them. The Rule of Law will not permit that. It exists to guarantee conditions in which more people can have *more* liberty, *more* rights, *more* possessions. Prophets of social justice – communists – whether by that or any other name – focus on who should have *less*. Because they have nothing to give, they can only take away. First, they take away opportunity. Next, they take away possessions. In the end they have to take away life itself.[70]

---

69 See Introduction, footnote 3, Social Justice as an ideology; also critique in chapter 5 and the biblical vision of true justice in chapters 7 and 8.

70 Vazsonyi, B, *America's Thirty Year War: Who is Winning?* (Regnery Publishing, 1998), p. 59. Articles available on Vazsonyi's website: http://

Because Vazsonyi had witnessed socialism in two manifestations, he rejected the idea that it would bring about real justice. He is one of many who lived through the nightmare of State-enforced socialism in Eastern Europe and Russia in the twentieth century, who have described the appalling consequences.

British-born **Peter Hitchens (b. 1951)** voluntarily took up the cause of revolutionary socialism when he was young.[71] He changed his mind after living and travelling in Marxist and ex-Marxist countries. He saw for himself the devastation wrought by this ideology. In 2018 he looked back on the years he spent in Moscow before the end of the Soviet regime:

> 22 years ago, I came to live in a dark and secretive building where my neighbours were KGB[72] men and the aristocrats of the old Kremlin elite. Here, in this mysterious and often dangerous place, I saw what lies just beneath our frail and fleeting civilisation — bones, blood, death, injustice, despair, horror, loss, corruption and fear. I grasped for the first time how wonderfully safe and lucky I had been all my life in the unique miracle of freedom and law that is — or was — England.[73]

Hitchens described a visit back to Russia:

> For thousands of miles in every direction, undeniable and no longer denied [is] the rusting, leaking, sagging evidence that this revolution had failed and that international socialism was a discredited, bankrupt idea.[74]

---

www.balintvazsonyi.org/ (accessed 17 July, 2020).

71 Hitchens was a revolutionary socialist from 1968-1975. Hitchens, P, *Short Breaks in Mordor: Dawns and Departures of a Scribbler's Life,* (privately published, 2018).

72 Acronym for the Committee for State Security; the secret police force in the Soviet Union from 1954 to 1991.

73 Hitchens, P, *Short Breaks in Mordor: Dawns and Departures of a Scribbler's Life,* journey 3.

74 Ibid.

What had started as a dream of egalitarian utopia had ended as a hideous nightmare.

DELIBERATELY BLIND, WILFULLY DEAF

At the beginning of the twenty-first century we have witnessed vast movements of people desperately seeking to leave their own countries in order to settle in the United Kingdom, countries in Europe, or the USA. The intellectual elite in the West accuses America of being the 'matrix of oppression', despite the fact that hundreds of thousands would do anything to have the opportunity to settle there.

In July 2020 an assistant professor at Princeton University wrote about the inspiration she derived from the Combahee River Collective Statement.[75] This had been written in 1974 by a group of feminists in Boston. A key demand was the abolition of capitalism:

> We realize that the liberation of all oppressed peoples necessitates the destruction of the political-economic systems of capitalism and imperialism as well as patriarchy.[76]

When this statement was released, hundreds of thousands of people were still being exploited as slave labour in the gulags which stretched across the Union of Soviet Socialist Republics. Countless school teachers (and other 'transmitters of culture') were still being ruthlessly tortured to death during the 'cultural revolution' in Maoist China. In that context to call for the dismantling of capitalism was displaying wilful ignorance.

Today there is still *less* excuse to celebrate the overthrow of free markets. When capitalism is thrown out, every marker of human flourishing decreases. The great socialist experiment in Venezuela has unfolded as an unimaginable catastrophe. What was once Latin America's most prosperous state has been reduced to penury. Thriving private enterprises have been replaced with desperate bartering. By

---

75   We come back to this Statement in chapter 5.

76   The Combahee River Collective Statement, https://americanstudies. yale.edu/sites/default/files/files/Keyword%20Coalition_Readings.pdf emphasis mine (accessed 18 November, 2020).

2018 more than 2.3 million Venezuelans had attempted to escape.[77] And yet, the academic elite ignore historical and present reality. In June 2020 the Princeton academic mentioned above suggested that conditions are so appalling for minority Americans, that the question should be asked: *'how bad could communism or socialism really be?'*[78]

To which one could reply: Why not find out what actually happened in Russia, China and Cambodia?[79] Why not interview the people fleeing Venezuela?[80]

David Horowitz and Peter Collier were progressive activists during the 1970s, who, along with many others, when confronted with the devastation wrought by Marxism, responded: 'But that wasn't true socialism! We have yet to experience the real thing!' They later publicly rejected that false illusion, and gave a powerful testimony of the destructive ideology that had enthralled them.[81]

DISCREDITED BUT NOT DESTROYED

In the first instance, Marxism was imposed on nations after violent revolution. It has been discredited as a political philosophy. But the impact of Marx's ideas extends far beyond those nations directly governed according to his economic and political ideals. Marxist

---

77 Mitchell, J, 'Maduro's Madness: How Venezuela's Great Socialist Experiment has brought a Country to its Knees', *The Spectator,* 25 August, 2018, https://www.spectator.co.uk/article/maduro-s-madness (accessed 30 July, 2020).

78 Taylor, K Y, 'Until Black Women Are Free, None of Us Will Be Free', *The New Yorker,* July 20, 2020, https://www.newyorker.com/news/our-columnists/until-black-women-are-free-none-of-us-will-be-free?utm_source=pocket-newtab-global-en-GB (accessed 30 July, 2020).

79 For example: Solzhenitsyn, A, *The Gulag Archipelago,* (Abridged edition, Penguin, 2018); Chang, J, Halliday, J, *Mao*; Cormack, D, *Killing Fields, Living Fields,* 1997, (rep. Christian Focus, 2014).

80 Mitchell, J, 'Maduro's Madness: How Venezuela's Great Socialist Experiment has brought a Country to its Knees', *The Spectator,* 25 August, 2018, https://www.spectator.co.uk/article/maduro-s-madness (accessed 30 July, 2020).

81 Horowitz, D, Collier, P, *Destructive Generation: Second Thoughts about the Sixties,* 1989, second edition, (Encounter Books, 2006), p. 4.

principles have been adopted by many with influence in academia, the media, law and government. Wherever people view the interactions of persons of different racial groups, genders, or sexual behaviours in terms of oppression and class warfare, they echo Marx's demand that the oppressed class rise up in revolution.[82]

Further Reading

Breese, D, *Seven Men Who Rule the World from the Grave,* available in digital format (Moody, 1990), https://www.logos.com/product /7705/seven-men-who-rule-the-world-from-the-grave

Chang, J, Halliday, J, *Mao: The Unknown Story,* (Vintage Books, 2006)

Cormack, D, *Killing Fields Living Fields: An Unfinished Portrait of the Cambodian Church,* 2001, (rep. Christian Focus, 2014)

Johnson, P, *Intellectuals: A fascinating examination of whether Intellectuals are Morally Fit to Give Advice to Humanity,* (Weidenfeld & Nicolson, 1989/2013)

Solzhenitsyn, A, *The Gulag Archipelago,* (Vintage Classic, Abridged edition, 2018)

Summary: Trailblazers in the liberation of humanity from the fear of God included Ludwig Feuerbach, Charles Darwin and Karl Marx. Once God is denied, the next thing to be challenged is the notion that there is one absolute moral code which we all have to obey. This led straight to the horrors of the gulags and the inhumanities perpetrated during the Cultural Revolution. Bad ideas bear bitter fruit!

---

82 We will see in chapter 5 how Marxist principles have been applied to the arena of social and cultural conflicts.

3 'No Absolute Morality': From Relativism to Fatherlessness

'We can live free from any fear of God!' We've seen the contributions of Feuerbach, Darwin and Marx to this thinking. The people we look at in this chapter built on this foundation. If there's no God and no judgement, we don't have to conform to an absolute moral code. Our desires can be set free.

Friedrich Nietzsche, Sigmund Freud, Wilhelm Reich and Margaret Sanger pioneered an assault on Christian morality. In their own day their ideas seemed extreme. But their legacy is the 'new morality' prevailing in Western culture: a *reversal* of moral codes:

- Sexual freedom used to be regarded as sinful: it's now seen as healthy.
- Modesty, chastity and sexual restraint used to be considered virtues: they're now viewed as pathological.
- The 'natural' family of a married father and mother was accepted as the fundamental building block of society: it's now often thought to be a seedbed of abuse and an outdated relic of heteronormativity.

Friedrich Nietzsche (1844-1900): No Transcendent Morality

Nietzsche was born in 1844, near Leipzig, Germany (then Prussia). His father, a Lutheran minister, died when he was four, and he was brought up by his mother, grandmother, sister, and two aunts. As a young man, Nietzsche specialised in classical philology (the study of language in written historical sources). Aged just twenty-four, he was appointed as a professor at the University of Basel. He later turned to philosophy; having been deeply influenced by the thought of the German philosopher **Arthur Schopenhauer (1788-1860)**, the author of *On the Sufferings of the World*, (1851). Schopenhauer believed that the universe is the product of blind force. His atheistic pessimism led him to conclude that it's better to be dead (and free from suffering) than alive. Nietzsche eventually rejected much of Schopenhauer's thinking, but retained his stress on the supremacy of the human will.

Nietzsche suffered constant ill-health. By the age of forty-five he was failing physically and mentally, possibly due to syphilis. He had always despised compassion and disparaged women, but his own illness forced him to rely on care from female relatives. Tragically, he died aged fifty-six, having lost touch with reality.

GOD IS DEAD

Never characterised by humility, Nietzsche regarded himself as a historic saviour figure. He had the grand vision of cleansing Western civilisation of any idea of the transcendent. He rejected any idea of God or an externally defined morality. In one of his writings, a madman celebrates the death of God:

> God is dead. God remains dead. And we have killed him.[1]

Nietzsche rejected attempts to believe in a universal morality without a supernatural God:

---

1   Nietzsche, F, *The Joyful Wisdom* (The Gay Science), translated by Common, T, (Macmillan, 1924), https://archive.org/details/completenietasch10nietuoft/page/168/mode/2up (accessed 6 January, 2021), Section 125, p. 168.

Nietzsche looked down on those 'English flatheads', those 'little moralistic females à la Eliot',[2] who thought it possible to have morality without religion. 'They are rid of the Christian God and now believe all the more firmly that they must cling to Christian morality'; they become 'moral fanatics' to compensate for their religious emancipation. For the moment, 'morality is not yet a problem.' But it would become a problem once they discovered that without Christianity there is no morality. *When one gives up the Christian faith, one pulls the right to Christian morality out from under one's feet.*[3]

Nietzsche set out to prove that morality is a human construct, created in response to particular social contexts and events. Reason and conscience should be subject to the human will alone. Here are a few of his messianic claims:

> What defines me, what sets me apart from all the rest of mankind, is that I have *unmasked* Christian morality.[4]

> ... the *unmasking* of Christian morality is an event without equal ... He who exposes it is a ... destiny – he breaks the history of mankind into two parts ... Everything hitherto called 'truth' is recognized as the most harmful, malicious, subterranean form of the lie; the holy pretext of 'improving' mankind as the cunning to *suck out* life itself and make it anaemic. Morality as *vampirism* ... He who unmasks morality has therewith unmasked the valuelessness of all values which are or have been believed in ... [5]

---

2   English novelist Mary Ann Evans, aka George Eliot, author of *Middlemarch* and other novels.

3   Himmelfarb, G, *The De-moralization of Society: From Victorian Virtues to Modern Values,* (Institute of Economic Affairs, 1995), p. 188, quoting Nietzsche, *Twilight of the Idols,* emphasis mine.

4   Nietzsche, F, *Why I am so Wise,* first published 1889, translated by R. J. Hollingdale, (Penguin Books, Great Ideas, 2004), p. 66, emphasis his.

5   Ibid., p. 68, emphasis his.

In his book *On the Genealogy of Morals* (1887), Nietzsche set out to trace the origins of morality. Rather than being God-given and permanent, morality emerged (he said) in response to historic situations. He claimed that in ancient Rome most of the Christians were slaves. They resented their masters, and began to 'valorise' the qualities they had no choice but to exhibit (weakness, submission, compliance). Christians comforted themselves by elevating these pitiful qualities, and saying that God valued them. So began the notion that these feeble characteristics were 'worthy'! This 'new moral code' stood in contrast to pagan thinking which praised power. The final revenge of the slaves was to persuade their masters to embrace this new system of thought. Their real motivation wasn't love and compassion, it was hatred and resentment.[6]

No hard evidence was offered for any of this. But Nietzsche concluded that it was unnecessary to remain constrained by this pseudo-morality. In *The Anti-Christ* (1888), he asked:

> What is more harmful than any vice? [it is] Active sympathy for the ill-constituted and weak – Christianity.[7]

MORALITY REVERSED: IMPURITY IS PURITY

In *Beyond Good and Evil* Nietzsche claimed that only within the slave mentality did 'pity, the kind and helping hand, the warm heart, patience, industriousness, humility, friendliness come into honour.'[8] He reversed everything usually assumed about morality. His rewriting of history made heroes into villains and vice versa.[9] He defined chastity as immorality, and purity as impurity:

---

6   Law, S, *The Great Philosophers: The Lives and Ideas of History's Greatest Thinkers,* (Quercus Publications, 2007), pp. 137-8.

7   Nietzsche, F, *The Anti-Christ,* translated by Hollingdale, R J, (Penguin Classics, 1990), p. 128. Note that the German title might more accurately be understood as The Anti-Christian.

8   Nietzsche, F, *Beyond Good and Evil,* translated by Hollingdale, R J, (Penguin Classics, 1990), p. 197.

9   Trueman, C, *The Rise and Triumph of the Modern Self,* (Crossway, 2020), Epilogue to Part 2, p. 197.

The preaching of chastity is a public incitement to anti-nature. Every expression of contempt for the sexual life, every befouling of it through the concept 'impure', is *the* crime against life – is the intrinsic sin against the holy spirit of life.[10]

These ideas would be promoted by the advocates of 'free love'. Around the beginning of the twentieth century this group was limited to members of the intellectual elite (such as the 'Bloomsbury' circle in London).[11] Later, the same ideas would be propagated through the whole of Western society.

We can see a direct outworking of Darwin's account of the survival of the fittest in *Beyond Good and Evil:*

A good and healthy aristocracy ... accepts with good conscience the sacrifice of innumerable men who for its sake have to be suppressed and reduced to imperfect men, to slaves and instruments. Its fundamental faith must be that *society should not exist for the sake of society* but only as a foundation and scaffolding upon which a *select species of being* is able to raise itself to its higher rank and in general to a higher existence.[12]

Logically, the 'death of God' would end the idea that every human being should be respected because they are created in the image of God. Nietzsche condemned the 'lie' of equal dignity for all humans:

The *fib of the equality of souls* undermined the aristocratic outlook in the most insidious way ... Christianity is the revolt of all grovelling creatures against that which has stature: the gospel of the 'lowly' makes for lowliness ...[13]

---

10 Nietzsche, F, *Why I am so Wise,* p. 57, emphasis his.

11 Himmelfarb, G, 'From Clapham to Bloomsbury', 1985, https://www.commentarymagazine.com/articles/gertrude-himmelfarb/from-clapham-to-bloomsbury-a-genealogy-of-morals/ (accessed 6 January, 2021).

12 Nietzsche, F, *Beyond Good and Evil,* p. 193, emphasis mine.

13 Nietzsche, F, *Works,* Vol. VIII, p. 273. Kröner, Leipzig, https://www.marxists.org/archive/lukacs/works/destruction-reason/ch03.htm#n80 (accessed 29 July 2020), emphasis mine.

VIRTUES OR VALUES?

Before Nietzsche, whether or not people lived according to Christian virtues, there was a widespread acceptance that such virtues were objectively good. He set out to destroy that assumption.

His legacy can be seen in that for many decades, education systems in many countries have incorporated 'values clarification'. Each child is expected to work out for themselves what is right and wrong. 'Values clarification' is not a neutral teaching tool. It challenges confidence in absolute morality and promotes moral relativism. In a classroom context it drives a wedge between a child and their parent's view of right and wrong, and between that child and religious belief.[14] Its widespread adoption represents the fulfilment of Nietzsche's dream: humanity's deliverance from traditional morality.[15] He proudly self-identified as anti-Christian, and he saw his prophetic role as the liberation of humanity from Christianity.

THE ROUTE TO NIHILISM

Nietzsche was bleakly consistent. If you 'kill' God, you also kill confidence that anything is real. Get rid of the transcendent, and you lose certainty about the imminent. This is the route to nihilism. In *Twilight of the Idols* Nietzsche mocked the idea of a 'true world' of objective reality:

> The true world we have abolished: what was left? the apparent world, perhaps? But no! Along with the true world we have also abolished the apparent one![16]

Nietzsche is remembered as the father of existentialism (which fed directly into postmodernism). His loathing of Christian morality was

---

14 Williams, E S, *Lessons in Depravity: Sexual Education and the Sexual Revolution,* (Belmont House, 2003), pp. 14-16.

15 Himmelfarb, G, *The De-moralization of Society,* (IEA, 1995), pp. 10-13.

16 Quoted by Lukács, G, *The Destruction of Reason,* https://www.marxists. org/archive/lukacs/works/destruction-reason/ch03.htm#n108 , Section 6, (accessed 6 January, 2021).

absorbed by Sigmund Freud, Wilhelm Reich, and Margaret Sanger, three of the architects of the sexual revolution.

Sigmund Freud (1856-1939): To Be Human Is to Be Sexual

Today any restriction on sexual expression is likely to be regarded as an attack on a person's individual identity. The idea that sexuality is a core element of personal identity is Freud's legacy, because he believed that to be human is to be sexual.[17] Central to that claim was his insistence that from early *infancy humans are capable of sexual expression and enjoyment. The current assumption that sexual fulfilment is a 'human right' can be traced back to Freud.*

Born in 1858 in Moravia (now the Czech Republic), Freud earned a medical degree from the University of Vienna when he was twenty-five. With another doctor, Josef Breuer, Freud examined the case of a patient known as Anna O. who suffered from a nervous cough, paralysis and other symptoms. While being treated, she remembered a number of traumatic experiences. Breuer and Freud concluded that there was no organic cause for Anna O.'s difficulties, but the emotional release of talking about past experiences ('the talking cure') mitigated her symptoms. Freud argued that patients exhibiting hysteria had suppressed traumatic experiences into their unconscious mind ('repression'). The 'psychoanalytic cure' included moving traumatic memories from the unconscious to the conscious mind. Neurosis could then be resolved.[18] His ideas received worldwide publicity after the First World War, when the cruel treatment given to those who had suffered so-called 'shell-shock' was exposed. Psychoanalysis seemed to offer a civilised alternative.[19]

---

17 Trueman, C, *The Rise and Triumph of the Modern Self,* chapter 6.

18 Carter, J D, *Western Humanism,* p. 159.

19 Johnson, P, *A History of the Modern World from 1917 to the 1980s,* (Weidenfeld and Nicolson, 1983), pp. 5-6. Freud is remembered for founding the discipline of psychoanalysis, and creating a revolutionary approach to understanding human personality.

Freud also developed a theory in which sexual and aggressive impulses battle for dominance over the defences people form against them. His theories, based mainly on his own analysis of himself, were criticised for lack of rigorous clinical evidence, and were controversial during his own lifetime and beyond.

RELIGION: A HUMAN CONSTRUCT

Freud regarded religion as a human construct grounded in ignorance, fear, fantasy and guilt. The idea of a protective God is based on the infant's need for a father-figure, and human fear of natural forces. The afterlife is a comforting fantasy to help people cope with death. Religion may have been useful as a means of restraining behaviour in the past, but in enlightened times, it should be replaced with science and reason.

SEX: DEPERSONALISED

Freud believed that everyone, from the earliest age, has sexual desires. On the most slender 'evidence', (observation of thumb-sucking and breast-feeding), Freud taught that infants experience erotic sensations from the beginning of life, and that boys experience sexual desire for their mothers (the so-called 'Oedipus complex'). Freud wrongly read adult desire backwards into the life of the child, and destroyed the notion of childish innocence.[20] If anyone disagreed with him, Freud could suggest that they were deluded and needed treatment (his 'trump card' of psychoanalysis).

Although Freud insisted that sexual desires needed to be curbed in order to keep stability in society, his thinking fed into the idea that personal guilt feelings were an illusion to be dispelled, and conscience a force to be subdued. In turn this contributed to the idea that Christian morality represses sexual desire in a dangerous way.

Freud regarded humans as highly developed animals, and understood sexual desire in solely physical terms. He allowed no place

---

20   Roger Scruton, 'An Unhappy Birthday to Sigmund the Fraud', *The Spectator*, 29 April 2006, https://www.spectator.co.uk/article/an-unhappy-birthday-to-sigmund-the-fraud (accessed 31 December, 2020).

for mystery, and no place of innocence. This depersonalised sexual activity, opening the way to the ubiquity of pornography and the cheapening of casual sexual encounters.[21] He criticised schools and conventional religion for inhibiting the sexual development of young people.

Freud's ambition has now been achieved. Many schools promote permissive sex education and undermine or ignore biblical Christianity. And the concept of sexual abuse has been twisted. Any sexual activity with children should be regarded as child abuse (which would rule out the explicit sharing of sexual information, such as that included in much sex education). The innocence of children should be protected without exception. But many now think it's abusive not to allow underage youngsters to express themselves sexually.

FAMILY: THE SOURCE OF OPPRESSION

Freud regarded the family as a breeding place for neuroses and other disorders:

> Freud ... believed that when humanity could throw off its illusions, it would also destroy neurosis, the thing which made it unhappy. But his diagnosis of what made it unhappy was *family life*. He taught us that in order to become sane, we must undermine and question what for most of us is the bedrock of our social and emotional security – our trust in, and love for, our parents. By teaching that neurosis can only be eliminated by overt hatred of our parents, he re-drew the inner map of millions of Europeans and Americans, making what had been a safe place into a battle ground.[22]

And so in some countries we now see the state interfering with the privacy of family life in order to ensure that children are not deprived

---

21 Ibid.

22 Wilson, A N, *God's Funeral,* (John Murray, 1999), p. 252, emphasis mine.

of their 'right' to sexual activity, or expression of their 'orientation' or 'gender identity'.[23]

Much of Freud's thinking has been discredited. But the idea that the family causes trauma had become orthodoxy in academia by the 1970s. It was passed on to those professionals (such as doctors, social workers, teachers, politicians and journalists) who trained at universities. In countries impacted by Western culture, public policy began to de-privilege the married family.

Wilhelm Reich (1897-1957): Father of the Sexual Revolution

By the end of the nineteenth century, a number of intellectuals had launched an attack on conventional morality.[24] During the early twentieth century, others continued the campaign.[25] But if we were to pick out the 'father' of the sexual revolution, it would be Wilhelm Reich, an Austrian doctor of medicine and a psychoanalyst, and author of *The Sexual Revolution* (1936).

SEXUAL LIBERATION FOR CHILDREN

Reich engaged in sexual activity himself as a child, and would later inflict sexual abuse on his young patients in the name of 'research'.[26]

---

23   Kuby, G, *The Global Sexual Revolution: Destruction of Freedom in the Name of Freedom,* (Lifesite 2015), translated by James Patrick Kirchner, first published in Germany in 2012. See chapters 12 and 13.

24   They included Robert Owen (1771-1858), the father of English socialism; Francis Place (1771-1854) a political radical and advocate of birth control; Richard Carlisle (1790-1843) who promoted the idea that sex was primarily about pleasure, and therefore a 'right' to be enjoyed by all, and George Drysdale (1825-1904) who argued that sexual satisfaction was a basic human need like food. Williams, E S, *Lessons in Depravity,* pp. 51-54.

25   Including Edward Carpenter (1844-1929), Havelock Ellis (1859-1939) and H G Wells (1866-1946).

26   Bayes, M, 'Breaking the Silence: Secrets of the Reichian Cult', http://www.rogermwilcox.com/Reich/Reich%20310.pdf (accessed 20 November, 2020). Sexual researcher Alfred Kinsey also abused children in the name of research. Reisman, J, 'Kinsey, Crimes and Consequences', http://www.

He believed that sexual suppression in childhood resulted in life-long unhappiness, and that to be fulfilled as a human being you need regular sexual satisfaction. Permissive sex education would liberate children from oppressive moral codes.[27]

In *The Mass Psychology of Fascism* (1933) Reich argued that fascism arose because people had suffered sexual repression. In 1936 he published *Sexuality in the Culture War*, later retitled *The Sexual Revolution*.[28] Suffering and cruelty in society, he argued, were due to Christian morality which wrongly deprived women and children of their sexual rights. '*Negation of life*' (i.e. sexual restraint) rested on the suppression of the sexuality of children, and society's insistence on pre-marital virginity and marital fidelity. It resulted in crime and war.

A free society would arise when all could enjoy sexual 'rights'. Reich wanted '*self regulation*' to replace Christian morality (everyone should choose their own morality and fulfil their own desires). He called this '*sexual hygiene*', or '*natural morality*', and argued that infants and children would be freed from inhibitions if they were used to seeing adults naked and making love. His cruel experiments on small children involved trying to remove their 'blockages' to sexual fulfilment.[29] His sexual revolution aimed to overthrow the traditional family. He wanted to replace compulsory (Christian) morality with compulsory sex education to liberate people from an early age from false notions of modesty and unhealthy sexual inhibitions. Here are some extracts from the Introduction to *The Sexual Revolution:*

---

drjudithreisman.com/archives/2014/01/kinsey_crimes_c.html (accessed 20 November, 2020).

27 Williams, E S, *Lessons in Depravity,* (Belmont House Publishing, 2003), pp. 98-101.

28 Reich, W, *The Sexual Revolution,* 1936, https://www.wilhelmreichtrust. org/sexual_revolution.pdf (accessed 14 July 2020).

29 Bayes, M, 'Breaking the Silence: Secrets of the Reichian Cult', http://www. rogermwilcox.com/Reich/Reich%20310.pdf (accessed 20 November, 2020).

Here and there one encounters hesitation, silence, even hostility, but sexual hygiene for the masses is making strong progress.[30]

... the mental-hygiene movement and the affirmation of the natural biological sexuality of children and adolescents are steadily progressing. They can no longer be stopped. The negation of life is being confronted by the affirmation of life.[31]

... suppression of the love life of children and adolescents is the central mechanism for producing enslaved subordinates and economic serfs ... [Being on the side of progress] is quite unmistakably a question of whether one fully affirms, supports, and safeguards the free life expressions of newborn infants, of small children, adolescents, and adult men and women, or whether one suppresses and destroys these expressions ...[32]

The inner forces which prevent this [freedom] are called sexual moralism and religious mysticism.[33]

The core of happiness in life is sexual happiness.[34]

Thus, capitalism and sexual suppression go together as do revolutionary 'morality' and sexual gratification.[35]

The new morality consists precisely in making moral regulation superfluous and in establishing the self-regulation of social life.[36]

Reich viewed himself in messianic terms, believing that his 'gospel' of sexual liberation would bring happiness to all. The way to get this good news out to the masses was by means of early compulsory sex education, so that children were accustomed to nudity and images

---

30 Reich, W, *The Sexual Revolution,* p. xiv.

31 Ibid., p. viii.

32 Ibid., p. xvi.

33 Ibid., p. xxv.

34 Ibid., p. xxvi.

35 Ibid., p. xxvii.

36 Ibid., p. xxvii.

of sexual activity. They should have opportunities for sexual play, and youngsters should have access to contraception when needed. Opposition from traditionalists, religious fundamentalists or social conservatives would have to be silenced. There could be no happy coexistence between the old and new morality:

> In its simplest formulation: today's social struggles are being waged between those forces interested in the safeguarding and affirming of life [i.e. sexual freedom], and those whose interests lie in its destruction and negation [i.e. traditional morality].[37]

INCITEMENT TO INCEST

What would this look like translated into public policy? Fast forward to 2009. The German government's Ministry for Family Affairs published booklets encouraging parents to sexually massage their children as young as 1 to 3 years of age:

> Fathers do not devote enough attention to the clitoris and vagina of their daughters. Their caresses too seldom pertain to these regions, while this is the only way the girls can develop a sense of pride in their sex.[38]

These booklets were later, rightly withdrawn. But this was, albeit briefly, a *State inciting parents to commit incest*. Parents who sexually abuse their children should be locked up, not encouraged.

---

37 Ibid., p. xvi.

38 'Germany and EU to Legalize Pedophilia and with it, Child Pornography as well!' *EU Times,* June 20th, 2009, https://www.eutimes.net/2009/06/germany-and-eu-to-legalize-pedophilia-and-with-it-child-pornography-as-well/ (accessed 23 July, 2020). See also Sielert, U, *Lisa and Jan*. Professor Sielert is a key leader in the movement for 'CSE' or Comprehensive Sexuality Education. Children must be 'positively' (i.e. sexually) 'caressed ahead of time by their parents. If they don't know what lust is, there will also be no sex play'. Quoted Kuby, G, *The Global Sexual Revolution, LifeSite*, 2015, p. 208, note 13. http://www.christendom-awake.org/pages/book-promotions/global-sexual-revolution/978-1-62138-154-9_int-2.pdf (accessed 23 July, 2020).

Reich's thinking has contributed to the industrial scale of child sexual abuse today, fuelled by online pornography. In common with other architects of the sexual revolution, Reich's personal life was troubled. Despite his hostility to marriage he married three times (and divorced three times as well). He spent years making and selling 'orgone accumulators', machines supposed to collect 'life energy'. He also constructed 'cloud buster machines' purporting to harness 'life energy' to manipulate weather. He was convicted of fraud and died in prison in the USA in 1957.

In May 1968, 11 years after Reich's death, France was paralysed by student riots. The President fled the country, and many feared revolution or civil war. Reich-inspired graffiti (see chapter 4) appeared on the walls of the Sorbonne.[39] At the same time, student demonstrators in Berlin, Germany, were hurling copies of Reich's *The Mass Psychology of Fascism* at the police. Reich's legacy was not only the sexual revolution of the 1960s, but the student unrest which erupted at the same time.[40]

Margaret Sanger (1879-1966): Sex As Salvation

Margaret Sanger, pioneer of contraceptive provision and founder of Planned Parenthood, also viewed sexual freedom as salvation. Like Reich, she believed that it was not enough to look for economic liberation for the masses – they needed sexual liberation.

CIVILISATION VIA CONTRACEPTION

Sanger believed that as long as pregnancy resulted in 'ever-growing broods', women would never enjoy sex. The misery of the world could be solved with contraception. She saw her own role in promoting freedom in messianic terms. In her grandly-titled book, *The Pivot*

---

39 http://www.bopsecrets.org/CF/graffiti.htm (accessed 12 October, 2020); this took place on the Sorbonne campus of the University of Paris, now Sorbonne University.

40 More on this in chapter 4.

of Civilisation,[41] she argued that the 'magic bullet' to tip humanity towards a better future was not Marxist revolution but contraception (and the sexual freedom that this would facilitate).

> The eloquence of those who led the underpaid and half-starved workers could no longer, for me, at least, ring with conviction. *Something more than the purely economic interpretation [i.e. Marxist revolution] was involved.* The bitter struggle for bread, for a home and material comfort, was but one phase of the problem. There was another phase, perhaps even more fundamental, that had been absolutely neglected by the adherents of the new dogmas. *That other phase was the driving power of instinct, a power uncontrolled and unnoticed.* The great fundamental instinct of sex was expressing itself in these *ever-growing broods,* in the prosperity of the slum midwife and her colleague the slum undertaker. In spite of all my sympathy with the dream of liberated Labor, I was driven to ask whether this urging power of sex, this deep instinct, was not at least partially responsible, along with industrial injustice, for the widespread misery of the world.[42]

Sexual energy had to be released, and separated from having children. Then women and men would equally be free to fulfil that 'driving power of instinct'. Sex had to be liberated from the restraint of lifelong faithful monogamy (Christian morality). Sanger's philosophy can be summed up as follows:

- What is the cause of human misery? Christian Morality
- What will solve human suffering? Sexual Liberation

The advocates of 'free love' wanted to spread this new gospel. Children and young people were still being brainwashed by parents, churches and schools into thinking that they had to keep sex for marriage. That had to be challenged by means of sex education. Sanger's organisation,

---

41   Sanger, M, *The Pivot of Civilisation,* published 1922, reprinted (Pergamon Press, 1950), https://www.gutenberg.org/files/1689/1689-h/1689-h.htm (accessed 2 July 2020).

42   Ibid., chapter 1, emphasis mine.

Planned Parenthood, from its inception, was not just about providing contraception. Increasingly, it also promoted sex education, with a view to informing children and young people of their 'sexual rights'. Sex education materials promoted by Planned Parenthood encouraged pre-marital sexual activity.[43] Children were (and are) helped to 'choose their own values'. Where children have imbibed traditional attitudes from their parents, role-playing is used as a way of transforming their thinking.[44]

SANGER'S DEMAND: 'STOP THE BREEDING OF IDIOTS'

The Pivot of Civilisation promoted the new pseudo-science of eugenics. Sanger wrote in 1925:

> The government of the US deliberately encourages and even makes necessary by its laws the breeding – with a breakneck rapidity – of idiots, defectives, diseased, feeble-minded, and criminal classes. Billions of dollars are expended by our state and federal governments and by private charities and philanthropies for the care, the maintenance, and the perpetuation of these classes. Year by year their numbers are mounting. Year by year more money is expended ... to maintain an increasing race of morons which threatens the very foundations of our civilization.[45]

Similar ideas lay at the heart of the Nazi 'race purification' programme. Sanger was enthusiastic about the euthanasia, sterilisation, abortion and infanticide programmes of Hitler's Reich.[46] She used Planned Parenthood to promote her racist vision of a superior society.[47] In 2020 Planned Parenthood removed Sanger's name from their

---

43 Wilson, A N, *God's Funeral,* pp. 110-11.

44 Grant, G, *Grand Illusions, The Legacy of Planned Parenthood,* (Adoit Press,1988), pp. 112-16.

45 Grant, G, *Killer Angel: A Biography of Planned Parenthood's Founder, Margaret Sanger,* (Ars Vitae, 1995), pp. 79-80.

46 Grant, G, *Grand Illusions,* p. 61.

47 Ibid., p. 96.

Lower Manhattan clinic, because of her connections to the eugenics movement.[48]

Sanger devoted her life to the abolition of Christian morality and the promotion of sexual liberation. Her own life was a mess: failed marriages, neglected children, numerous affairs, attempts to cover up her complicity with the Nazi regime, and desperate attempts to find meaning via occult activities.[49]

Sexual Liberation: Triumph or Tragedy?

'MY DUTY TO MYSELF'

Friedrich Nietzsche, Sigmund Freud, Wilhelm Reich and Margaret Sanger were each driven by a mission to deliver humanity from the constraints of Christian morality. 'You shall not commit adultery', they believed, was a direct attack on freedom. Humanity would only flourish once God's commandments had been relegated to history. Their goal was sexual revolution: a smashing down of all barriers to sexual liberation. They, and other champions of sexual freedom, have been stunningly successful. Their thinking took hold amongst the elites in the West, and was propagated in literature, theatre, and the media.

The Doll's House (1879), a play by the Norwegian playwright **Henrik Ibsen (1828-1906)**, depicted the plight of Nora, a wife trapped in a conventional marriage to Torvald Helmer. She ultimately realises that to be true to herself will necessitate leaving her family:

> Helmer: Can you neglect your most sacred duties?
>
> Nora: What do you call my most sacred duties?
>
> Helmer: Do I have to tell you? Your duties to your husband, and your children.

---

48 https://www.washingtonpost.com/history/2020/07/21/margaret-sanger-planned-parenthood-eugenics/ (accessed 23 July, 2020).

49 Grant, G, *Killer Angel,* chapter 10.

Nora: I have another duty which is equally sacred.

Helmer: ... What on earth could that be?

Nora: *My duty to myself* ... I don't want to see the children.... As I am now I can be nothing to them.

Dr Theodore Dalrymple (b. 1949) comments:

... with these chilling words, she severs all connection with her three children, forever. Her duty to herself leaves no room for a moment's thought for them. They are as dust in the balance. When, as I have, you have met hundreds, perhaps thousands, of people abandoned in their childhood by one or both of their parents, on essentially the same grounds ('I need my own space'), and you have seen the lasting despair and damage that such abandonment causes, you cannot read or see 'A Doll's House' without anger and revulsion. Now we see what Ibsen meant when he said that women's rights were of no fundamental interest to him. He was out to promote something much more important: universal egotism.[50]

By the second half of the twentieth century, the 'nuclear family' or, even more disparagingly the 'bourgeois' family, was despised by intellectuals. Universities taught psychologists, social workers, health workers and educationalists to regard it as the source of psychiatric dysfunction, the likely location of abuse, the place where children were victims of either over-controlling or over-indulgent parenting, and where women were kept in economic dependence on their over-bearing husbands. Radical feminists believed that the married family was at the root of 'patriarchy', or supposed 'man-rule'. Feminist sociologist **Carol Smart (b. 1948)** published *The Ties that Bind* in 1984, which claimed that 'the "family" is an ideological and economic site of oppression.'[51] It was regarded as incompatible with personal

---

50   Dalrymple, T, 'Ibsen and his discontents', *City Journal*, Summer 2005, http://www.city-journal.org/html/15_3_urbanities-isben.html (accessed 11 September, 2020).

51   Smart, C, *The Ties That Bind: Law, Marriage and the Reproduction of Patriarchal Relations*, (Routledge,1984, rep. 2012), p. 10.

fulfilment and freedom. In the new age of individualism it was thought wrong for a person to be bound by familial obligation or duty.

Peter A. D. Collier (1939-2019), threw himself into radical activism during the 1960s and 1970s. Later, having witnessed its catastrophic effects, he renounced 'progressivism'. Here he recalls the hatred of the traditional family:

> Two of my Movement comrades decided to get married. After a ceremony filled with gibberish about liberation and the Third World, there was a reception, featuring a large wedding cake frosted with the slogan 'Smash Monogamy!' ... Needless to say their marriage didn't last long, leaving in its rubble a pair of pathetic children, whom I still occasionally see walking around Berkeley looking like the survivors of an airplane disaster.[52]

Psychiatrist **David G Cooper (1931-1986)**, was another of those 1960s radicals who demanded the abolition of the traditional family, sexual freedom, legalisation of drugs, and communal child rearing. His book *The Death of the Family* was published by Penguin in 1971. He painted the nuclear family as the enemy of sexual and social independence. Before he had finished writing it, he had a mental and physical breakdown, no doubt exacerbated by his regular abuse of drugs. In the Dedication to this book, he testified:

> During the end of the writing of this book against the family, I went through a profound spiritual and bodily crisis ... The people who sat with me and tended to me with immense kindliness and concern during the worst of this crisis were my brother Peter and sister-in-law Carol and their small daughters. Just as a true family should.[53]

At that point he should have binned his book. But he went ahead and published a demand for the deconstruction of the very institution to which he had turned in his hour of need.

---

52 Horowitz, D, Collier, P, *Destructive Generation - Second Thoughts about the Sixties,* (Encounter Books,1989, second edition, 2006), p. 314.

53 Cooper, D, *The Death of the Family,* (Penguin, 1974), p. 157.

The anti-family ideology promoted by Cooper and others like him was soon embedded in popular culture. *Kramer vs Kramer,* an iconic legal drama starring Dustin Hoffman and Meryl Streep, was released in 1979. The opening scene portrayed a young mum, played by Meryl Streep, going into her little son's bedroom, kissing him goodnight, and then walking out for good – to find herself. This was a dramatic portrayal of the brutal reality of the pursuit of total individual freedom and self-fulfilment. Radical feminists told women to fulfil themselves, not to sacrifice themselves for others.

In countries impacted by Western culture, sexual freedom is now enshrined in law, public policy and education.[54] Sexual fulfilment and reproductive liberty are defined as fundamental human rights. In 1994 the 'Cairo Programme of Action' stated:

> Reproductive health is a state of complete physical, mental and social well-being and not merely the absence of disease or infirmity … Reproductive health therefore implies that people are able to have a satisfying and safe sex life and that they have the capability to reproduce and the freedom to decide if, when and how often to do so.[55]

Sexual morality is no longer placed in the context of community or family: it is all about individual fulfilment.

In the Spring of 2020 as fear of Covid-19 gripped whole populations, one journalist argued that this posed a great opportunity to finally abolish the family:

> … the private family qua mode of social reproduction still, frankly, sucks. It genders, nationalizes and races us. It norms us

---

54   James, S, 'Evangelical Response to the Reconfiguration of Family in England, 1960-2010', unpublished doctoral thesis, University of Wales, 2011; Morgan P, *The War Between the State and the Family: How Government Divides and Impoverishes, Institute of Economic Affairs,* 2007 https://iea. org.uk/wp-content/uploads/2016/07/upldbook406pdf.pdf (accessed 6 January, 2021).

55   'The Cairo Programme', 1994, http://www.iisd.ca/Cairo/program/ p07002.html (accessed 29 August 2011).

for productive work. It makes us believe we are 'individuals.' It minimizes costs for capital while maximizing human beings' life-making labor (across billions of tiny boxes, each kitted out – absurdly – with its own kitchen, micro-crèche and laundry) ... We deserve better than the family. And the time of corona is an excellent time to practice abolishing it.[56]

FREEDOM WITHOUT BOUNDARIES

The spectacular triumph of the sexual revolution may be seen if you consider America's third-oldest institution of higher education. Yale University was founded in 1701 with the purpose of training gospel ministers for the Congregational church. Three hundred years later, in 2001, Yale launched the Larry Kramer Initiative for Lesbian and Gay Studies. Three years after that, in 2004, Larry Kramer (1936-2020) gave a speech to New York's gay community in which he was searingly honest about his life during the AIDS outbreak:

> I have recently gone through my diaries of the worst of the plague years. I saw day after day a notification of another friend's death. I listed all the ones I'd slept with. There were a couple hundred. Was it my sperm that killed them ...? Have you ever wondered how many men you have killed? *I know I murdered some of them* ... The sweet young boy who didn't know anything and was in awe of me. I was the first man who xxxx him. I think I murdered him. The old boyfriend who didn't want to go to bed with me and I made him... .[57]

---

56 Lewis, S, 'The coronavirus crisis shows it's time to abolish the family', *Open Democracy*, 24 March 2020, https://www.opendemocracy.net/en/oureconomy/coronavirus-crisis-shows-its-time-to-abolish-family/ (accessed 9 September, 2020). See also, Lewis, S, *Full Surrogacy Now: Feminism Against Family,* (Verso, 2019).

57 Brown, M L, *A Queer Thing Happened to America, and What a Long, Strange Trip It's Been,* (Equal Time Books, 2011), p. 136, emphasis mine.

This was freedom without boundaries! Reich had claimed that conventional sexual boundaries represented the 'death principle'. The mother of that 'sweet young boy' would see things differently.

Reich had also claimed that children should be free to enjoy sexual gratification. The 'Gay Rights Platform' was drawn up in Chicago in 1972. It demanded the repeal of all state laws governing the age of consent.[58] While there are still age of consent laws on the statute books, they are rarely enforced. Sex education programmes promoted by international bodies such as the World Health Organization teach children about their 'sexual rights' and set out to free them from the constriction of the traditional norms of their parents.[59] All of this represents a veritable paedophile's charter.

But these sex education programmes also reflect the new orthodoxy that there is 'no normal' when it comes to sexual activity.[60] Sociologist Anthony Giddens speaks of 'the decline of perversion'. At one time it was assumed that man-woman marriage was the natural context for sexual union. Other forms of sexual activity were seen as the exception, and often condemned. That thinking was radically undermined by the publication of the Kinsey Reports, *Sexual behaviour in the human male* (1948) and *Sexual behaviour in the human female* (1953). **Alfred Kinsey (1894-1956)** had an agenda: he believed that people would only be free and fulfilled once the repressive restraints of Judaeo-Christian morality had been relegated to history. He wanted the repeal of any legislation which restricted sexual freedom. And he tried to show that 'science' proved that there is 'no normal' with regard to sexual behaviour.

Sexual behaviour in the human male sold 200,000 copies in two months. The 'take away' figure, believed by many, was that 10 per cent

---

58   Ibid., p. 30.

59   Kuby, G, *The Global Sexual Revolution,* (LifeSite, 2015), chapter 12, http://www.christendom-awake.org/pages/book-promotions/global-sexual-revolution/978-1-62138-154-9_int-2.pdf (accessed 23 July, 2020).

60   *Comprehensive Sex Education Materials,* https://www.comprehensive sexualityeducation.org/cse-materials-index/, (accessed 6 May, 2021).

of adult men in America had engaged in homosexual behaviour.[61] But what Kinsey passed off as 'a carefully planned population survey' were results from 'a male interviewee sample containing approximately 25 per cent prisoners or ex-prisoners, an abnormal percentage of sex offenders, and other sexually unconventional groups in numbers unrepresentative of society'.[62]

The most chilling chapters of Kinsey's two books concern 'Early Sexual Growth and Activity'. Kinsey laid out detailed 'evidence' that infants from a few months old 'enjoy' sexual stimulation.[63] But the descriptions he gave of the erotic arousal of infants and children can only be regarded as systematic and criminal abuse. When author and award-winning documentary maker Tim Tate investigated Kinsey's 'experiments' relating to 'early sexual activity', he found that much of Kinsey's 'evidence' had been supplied by predatory and habitual paedophiles.[64]

From Relativism to Fatherlessness

Freud, Reich and Sanger wanted to get rid of the constraints of the patriarchal family.

Today the number of children left fatherless by 'sexual liberation' is unprecedented in human history.[65] In 1964 only four small countries

---

61   Kinsey, A, *Sexual Behaviour in the Human Male,* (W B Saunders, 1948), p. 651; '10 per cent of the males are more or less exclusively homosexual for at least three years between the ages of 16 and 55.'

62   Muir, J Gordon, 'Let's Get Serious about Scientific Misconduct', *Scientist,* Jan 20, 1992, https://www.the-scientist.com/commentary/lets-get-serious-about-scientific-misconduct-60310, (accessed 6 May, 2021).

63   Kinsey, A, *Sexual Behaviour in the Human Male,* (W B Saunders, 1948), Chapter 5, pp. 157-92. There is a parallel chapter in *Sexual Behaviour in the Human Female,* 1953.

64   Tate, T, *Kinsey's Paedophiles,* Documentary, 1988, https://www.youtube.com/watch?v=UVC-1d5ib50 (accessed 6 May, 2021); see also Reisman, J, Kinsey, Sex and Fraud, 1990, http://www.drjudithreisman.com/archives/Kinsey_Sex_and_Fraud.pdf (accessed 6 May, 2021).

65   James, S, *God's Design for Women in an Age of Gender Confusion,* (Evangelical Press, 2019), chapter 4.

(Austria, Latvia, Iceland and Sweden) had more than 10 per cent of children born outside marriage. By 2016, more than 60 per cent of children were born outside marriage in twenty-five countries. A further twenty countries, including Belgium, Denmark, Norway, France and Sweden all had more than 50 per cent of children born outside marriage.[66]

The champions of sexual revolution promised a new dawn of human freedom and happiness. They were false prophets preaching a false gospel. Their assault on traditional morality and the married family has fuelled an epidemic of sexual violence. Children are innocent victims. In 2011, a federal study in the US showed that children living with their mother and boyfriend were about *eleven times* more likely to be abused than children living with their married biological parents.[67] Theodore Dalrymple, mentioned above, had a lifetime of experience working as a prison doctor and psychiatrist in a deprived area in Birmingham, England. He described the human cost of the sexual revolution:

> ... intellectuals in the twentieth century sought to free our sexual relations of all social, contractual, or moral obligations and meaning whatsoever, so that henceforth only raw sexual desire itself would count in our decision making ... If anyone wants to see what sexual relations are like, freed of contractual and social obligations, let him look at the chaos of the personal lives of members of the underclass ... Here are ... children who have children, in numbers unknown before the advent of chemical contraception and sex education; women abandoned by the father of their child a month before or a month after delivery; insensate jealousy, the reverse of the coin of general promiscuity, that results in the most hideous oppression and violence; serial step-

---

66 Chamie, J, 'Out-of-wedlock births rise worldwide', *Yale Global Online*, 16 March 2017, https://yaleglobal.yale.edu/content/out-wedlock-births-rise-worldwide (accessed 14 August 2018).

67 Wilcox, W B, 'Suffer the Little Children: Cohabitation and the Abuse of America's Children', *Public Discourse*, 22 April, 2011, http://www.thepublicdiscourse.com/2011/04/3181/ (accessed 14 September, 2018).

fatherhood that leads to sexual and physical abuse of children on a mass scale; and every kind of loosening of the distinction between the sexually permissible and impermissible.[68]

All too often, teenagers run away from situations of abuse. The Children's Society in Britain claims that 25 per cent of youngsters in step-families run away before the age of sixteen.[69] They may end up on the streets. They may dull the pain with alcohol or drugs or other substance abuse. They may turn to prostitution. But many policy-makers won't admit that family breakdown is a major driver for both poverty and homelessness.

DYSTOPIA NOT UTOPIA

It's not just sexual restraint that has been unloosed. When you ditch the idea of absolute morality, other social norms collapse and civility declines. Many modern commentators regard taboo-breaking and transgression of boundaries as commendable rather than blameworthy.[70]

The transgressiveness of the bohemian elite has been promoted by means of literature, entertainment, media comment, and academia, and has worked 'down' through society. The intellectuals who promote 'liberation' are cushioned from the worst damage, and some seem to have little awareness of what it's like to live in a deprived neighbourhood where the majority of the youth are free from moral restraints. It's the poor who really suffer. Living in an inner-city ghetto where law and order has broken down, and where stable family life has collapsed, leads to fear and despair.[71]

Many youngsters grow up with a worldview that mocks authority, despises the police, and denies moral absolutes. When they want to

---

68   Dalrymple, T, *Life at the Bottom,* (Ivan R Dee, 2001), pp. x-xi. Dalrymple's literary name is a pseudonym.

69   Children's Society, *Home Run,* 2001.

70   Dalrymple T, *Our Culture: What's Left of It: The Mandarins and the Masses,* (Ivan R Dee, 2005), p. x.

71   Ibid., pp. x-xi.

praise themselves, they describe themselves as 'non-judgemental'; in other words 'For them, the highest form of morality is amorality.'[72] No surprise then, that crime levels have rocketed:

> In 1921 ... there was 1 crime recorded for every 370 inhabitants of England and Wales; 80 years later it was 1 for every 10 inhabitants. There has been a twelvefold increase since 1941 and an even greater increase in crimes of violence.[73]

In 1949, novelist and journalist **George Orwell (1903-1950)** commented:

> For two hundred years we had sawed and sawed and sawed at the branch we were sitting on. And in the end, much more suddenly than anyone had foreseen, our efforts were rewarded, and down we came. But unfortunately there had been a little mistake. The thing at the bottom was not a bed of roses after all; it was a cess pit full of barbed wire.[74]

Freedom without boundaries ends up in dystopia not utopia.

FURTHER READING

Dalrymple T, *Our Culture: What's Left of It: The Mandarins and the Masses,* (Ivan R Dee, 2005)

Dalrymple, T, *Life at the Bottom: The Worldview that Makes the Underclass,* (Ivan R Dee, 2001)

Eberstadt, M, *Primal Screams: How the Sexual Revolution Created Identity Politics,* (Templeton Press, 2019)

Himmelfarb, G, *From Clapham to Bloomsbury: A Genealogy of Morals,* 1985, https://www.commentarymagazine.com/articles/gertrude-

---

72 Ibid., p. 14.

73 Ibid., p. 9.

74 Orwell, G, *Notes on the Way,* 1940, quoted in Mangalwadi, V, *The Book That Made Your World,* p. 3.

himmelfarb/from-clapham-to-bloomsbury-a-genealogy-of-morals/ (accessed 6 January, 2021)

Kuby, G, *The Global Sexual Revolution: Destruction of Freedom in the Name of Freedom,* (LifeSite, 2015)

Trueman, C, *The Rise and Triumph of the Modern Self,* (Crossway, 2020)

Summary: Friedrich Nietzsche, Sigmund Freud, Wilhelm Reich and Margaret Sanger saw themselves as saviours, liberating people from the repression of traditional morality. They dreamed of a future of unlimited personal freedom. But in a fallen sinful world, the dream of unbounded freedom unravels inexorably into nightmare. As moral norms are eroded, the powerful use their power to exploit the weak. Violence and evil are not only normalised, they are celebrated. Sexual liberation has resulted in historically unprecedented global rates of fatherlessness.

4 'No Universal Truth': The Death of Common Sense

A writer who says that there are no truths, or that all truth is 'merely relative,' is asking you not to believe him. So don't. (Roger Scruton)[1]

When one Christian post-grad student took a class in postmodernism, he was accused of being a fascist for affirming the existence of truth.[2] How have we arrived at the presumption that truth claims are fundamentalist, the exercise of authority is necessarily oppressive, and all inequality is evil?

THE COLLAPSE OF MODERNISM

Some of the leading Enlightenment thinkers denied the reality of universal sin. **Jean-Jacques Rousseau (1712-1778)** claimed that in our natural state we are basically good. If crimes were committed, then one could blame the family, or poverty, or social conditions.

Such philosophers placed confidence in human reason and virtue, and assumed that within a few decades, belief in God would be viewed

---

1   Scruton, R, *Modern Philosophy: A Survey,* (Sinclair-Stevenson, 1994), quoted in Kimball, R, https://newcriterion.com/issues/1994/6/saving-the-appearances-roger-scruton-on-philosophy (accessed 6 January, 2021).

2   Honeysett, M, *Meltdown: Making Sense of a Culture in Crisis,* (IVP, 2002), p. 203.

as one of the embarrassments of history. In reality, the murderous outworking of the French Revolution exposed the lie of innate human goodness. Many romanticise the French revolutionaries and their demand for 'Liberty, Equality, Fraternity'. They forget that the attempt to enforce equality necessitated the 'reign of terror'. In 1793, Bertrand Barère exclaimed in the Convention: *Let's make terror the order of the day!*[3] In 1794 Robespierre described terror as *an emanation of virtue.*[4] Between 1793 and 1794, 17,000 people in France were tried and executed; 23,000 were killed without trial or died in prison. Self-confident philosophers had denied human depravity. Now it was on full display.

Not only so – those who had predicted the 'death of God' were confounded by the widespread religious revivals of the later eighteenth and nineteenth centuries. But even as whole communities were transformed by those revivals, new challenges to Christianity arose, including Darwin's theory of evolution (see chapter 2).

The hope held out by modernism was that human problems could be solved by means of science, education, technology, industrialisation and social reform. The unfolding horrors of the twentieth century, beginning in the trenches of the First World War, exposed the emptiness of those promises. It became apparent that we can't derive certain knowledge by basing it on our own individual reason. Without an external transcendent authority (God) to judge the competing views of individuals, how do we negotiate between them? We are pushed to complete relativism.

As confidence faded in the bogus claims of modernism, you might hope there would be a turning back to God (the external authority who defines reality and truth). But that would mean submitting to God's moral demands. By nature, we rebel against those demands, and think that real freedom comes from doing what we want. Given the

---

3   http://www.vendeensetchouans.com/archives/2011/08/30/21907332.html (accessed 29 October, 2020).

4   https://sourcebooks.fordham.edu/mod/1794robespierre.asp (accessed 29 October, 2020).

choice between submission to God or freedom without boundaries, the false utopia of unlimited liberty proved irresistible.

Western civilisation was built on the biblical worldview: respect for the individual as created in God's image; the rule of law (rulers are accountable to God); and the creation patterns of family and work. Unprecedented numbers of people across the globe had been liberated from the grinding poverty of subsistence economies. Wealth creation had been made possible by the encouraging of innovation as well as the Christian work ethic.[5]

In a world made up of human *individuals,* respecting individual freedom won't ever achieve exact equality of *outcomes.* Freedom allows for natural variation in competence and motivation. And there will never be perfect justice in a fallen world. But in countries influenced by the Christian worldview, inequalities have been mitigated by the Christian virtues of generosity, compassion, and social responsibility.[6] Injustices have been challenged, and often addressed, by a variety of reform movements.

SUBVERT THE ESTABLISHMENT

Rather than continuing such campaigns for reform, radical activists of the twentieth century set out to subvert, and ultimately destroy, Western civilisation. They regarded it as irredeemably corrupted with *ideas* that sustained unequal *outcomes.*

Marx had believed that workers needed to be liberated from capitalism by means of violent revolution (which would also destroy the married family, the church and sovereign states, i.e. those institutions which propped capitalism up).

By the 1920s, outside of Russia, efforts to incite violent revolt had failed. A long-term strategy of changing hearts and minds was needed.

---

5   'Free markets and growth necessary to lift people out of poverty', *The Economist,* 1 June, 2013, https://www.economist.com/leaders/2013/06/01/towards-the-end-of-poverty (accessed 31 July 2020).

6   See James, S, *How Christianity Transformed the World,* (Christian Focus Publications, 2021).

A number of radical thinkers downplayed the need to smash capitalism by means of violent revolution. They set out, instead, to undermine the *ideas* which propped up the establishment. Any *beliefs* incompatible with revolutionary thought must be silenced. Calls for 'free speech' would be re-defined as a repressive effort to prop up the status quo.

But how do you get people to repudiate the old ideals of freedom and dignity? Get them to question the concept of truth and the meaning of language. Tell them that 'freedom' and 'dignity' are 'just words' and 'words have no universal meaning'. Persuade them that those transcendent ideals are a fraud exploited by the powerful elites (the 'hegemony') in order to sustain their own selfish interests. Prompt them to think that believing such stuff is 'false consciousness'.

Societies' deepest convictions wouldn't be changed overnight. These revolutionary thinkers knew that their ideas would be unacceptable at first, and maybe for a long time to come. They were willing to plant the seeds and await the outcome. Let's meet some of these radicals, beginning with Antonio Gramsci.

UNDERMINE 'COMMON SENSE'

In May 1922 a 30-year-old Italian, **Antonio Gramsci (1891-1937)**, travelled to Moscow as a delegate to the Communist International (a body set up to promote world revolution). When he returned to Italy he was arrested for his revolutionary activities. In 1928 he was sentenced to twenty years' imprisonment. While in prison, he compiled a series of reflections in thirty-three notebooks.

Gramsci reflected that Lenin had underestimated the power that bourgeois values had on working people. These values were passed on through the various cultural institutions that preserved the status quo. People were trapped in *false consciousness,* which made them complicit in a system which institutionalised inequality. The values formed by the 'hegemony'[7] (or establishment) were so embedded in Western

---

7   The name adopted for the overarching establishment which supposedly sustained this 'false consciousness' was hegemony, from the Greek word hēgemonía, meaning 'authority' or 'political supremacy'. Gramsci, A, *Prison*

culture that they were accepted by ordinary people as 'common sense'. Ideas which sustained this *psychological oppression* were passed on by the *family, the church, schools, universities, law, the media, businesses, literature, science and politics*.[8] It seemed impossible that this cultural mindset could be overturned. Gramsci reflected that it would be a huge task to launch:

> ...[a] cultural movement which aimed to *replace common sense* and old conceptions of the world in general.[9]

But, sitting in prison, he believed that 'the tide of history is working for me in the long term'.[10] He reckoned that the hegemony of common sense could ultimately be toppled, not least if activists remembered:

> Never to tire of repeating arguments ... repetition is the best didactic means for working on the popular mentality.[11]

Gramsci described ideas as a 'material force', and described philosophy as a 'critico-practical activity', or 'praxis' (in other words, a revolutionary tool). *You achieve revolution if you change ideas.*[12]

USE CRITICAL THEORY TO DESTABILIZE HIERARCHIES

In 1923, (the year after Gramsci left Italy for Moscow), a Marxist study-centre was established in Frankfurt, Germany. A safe-sounding name, The Institute for Social Research was chosen. The scholars associated with this 'Frankfurt School' initiated a way of seeing reality which became known as *critical theory*. Like Gramsci, they aimed to destabilise capitalist societies by means of *ideas*, rather than *violence*.

Notebooks, 1929-1935, pp. 641-2, http://courses.justice.eku.edu/pls330_ louis/docs/gramsci-prison-notebooks-vol1.pdf (accessed 31 July, 2020).

8   Gramsci, A, *Prison Notebooks*, 1929-1935, pp. 626, 654, http://courses. justice.eku.edu/pls330_louis/docs/gramsci-prison-notebooks-vol1.pdf (accessed 31 July, 2020).

9   Ibid., p. 651.

10 Ibid., p. 646.

11 Ibid., p. 651.

12 Ibid., p. 637.

Max Horkheimer (1895-1973) became the first director of the Institute in 1930. After Hitler took power in Germany in 1933, the Institute was moved to Geneva in Switzerland, and then to New York City. It affiliated with Columbia University in 1935, was based in the United States during the 1940s, and returned to Frankfurt in 1951. **Theodor Adorno (1903-1969)** took over as Director in 1953.

Horkheimer and Adorno both believed that the influence wielded by academia, the law, the church and the press in propping up the capitalist establishment could be undermined by critical theory.[13] Their target was the whole framework of ideas upholding liberal Western societies.

Viruses are microscopic parasites, sometimes ten thousand times smaller than a grain of salt. Yet in 2020, most countries in the world were locked down by a virus.

During the twentieth century, first universities, then all the institutions of Western society, were invaded by the 'virus' of radical doubt. Critical theory hijacked certainty about *everything*. This theory was built on a lie. Horkheimer began with the false premise that there is no transcendent reality – no God. From that he concluded that the world of perception is a product of human activity. *We make our own reality.*

As Horkheimer considered the 'authoritarian structure' of capitalist society, he, and the others associated with the Institute, concluded that the problem with liberalism (free societies) was that people were free to sort themselves into the *'illusory harmonies'* which allow natural inequalities to exist (because of the distribution of various abilities).[14]

According to critical theory *all hierarchies are oppressive*. The pseudo-stability of Western capitalism disguises the rotten reality. Multitudes are psychologically oppressed by inequality. This stability can only be shaken if the ideas underpinning it are challenged. Everything must be questioned. There are no universal 'truths'. All is

---

13   Horkheimer, M, *Critical Theory: Selected Essays,* (Continuum, 1975).

14   Ibid., p. 247.

relative. 'Natural privileges' must be forcibly eliminated in order to iron out inequality.

Horkheimer and Adorno co-authored *The Dialectic of Enlightenment (1947)*, which argued that Western culture (films, music, radio and magazines) seduced people into accepting the establishment. Hollywood perpetrated the myth of happiness, freedom, and the possibility of success in life. This bourgeois fraud had to be unmasked.

In 1950 Adorno published *The Authoritarian Personality*. The traditional family was painted as a repressive institution which brainwashed people into giving up individual liberty, and conditioned them into accepting 'father figures'. They were then softened up to demonstrate blind patriotism and acceptance of dictatorship. Adorno presented traditional ideas about family, religion, or patriotism as pathological. Capitalising on revulsion against Hitler's atrocities, Adorno and his colleagues labelled all authority as 'fascist'.[15]

For the American audience, Adorno packaged demand for revolution in the language of democracy. If you control language, you control the debate. In order to shift popular thinking from belief in absolute morality to acceptance of relativism, he redefined the concept of 'phobia' (an irrational fear) to make it refer to moral disapproval of certain behaviours. He associated 'phobia' with 'bigotry'. People with traditional and authoritarian 'phobias' (against homosexuality for example), he suggested, needed re-education.

That tactic was spectacularly successful. By the end of the twentieth century, many clergy refused to proclaim biblical morality because they were scared of appearing 'bigoted'.[16]

THE 'HELL OF THE AFFLUENT SOCIETY'
By the time Adorno and Horkeimer published their manifestos against traditional values, Gramsci had died in prison in 1937, aged only forty-six. He had wanted all hierarchies to be overturned, but didn't

---

15 Another member of the Frankfurt School was psychologist Erich Fromm, author of *Escape from Freedom* (1941).

16 See chapter 6.

see his vision fulfilled. His prison notebooks would not be published until the 1950s.[17] But his ideas then inspired the revolutionary activism that erupted among students in the Western world during the late 1960s. In Germany, the Baader-Meinhof gang tried to bring down the capitalist establishment by means of kidnapping, murder, bombs, terrorism and intimidation. In France, the university in Paris was brought to a standstill. Beautiful old buildings were defaced with obscene anti-Christian graffiti and calls for revolution.

Graffiti in Paris During the 1968 Student Uprising[18]

Theme of Graffiti in Paris Student Uprising May 1968	French Graffiti	English Translation
Smash the old	*Et si on brûlait la Sorbonne?*	What if we burned the Sorbonne?
	Ici, bientôt, de charmantes ruines!	Coming soon - charming ruins!
	Fin de l'Université!	Terminate the university!
	Violez votre Alma Mater!	Rape your Alma Mater!
	Pas de replâtrage, la structure est pourrie	No replastering, the structure is rotten
	Cours, camarade, le vieux monde est derrière toi !	Run, comrade, the old world is behind you!
	La passion de la destruction est une joie créatrice	The passion of destruction is creative joy!
	Examens = servilité, promotion sociale, société hiérarchisée	Exams = servility, social promotion, hierarchical society
	Le conservatisme est synonyme de pourriture et de laideur	Conservatism is a synonym for rottenness and ugliness

---

17 They were not translated into English until 1974. Scottish poet and socialist Hamish Henderson translated the Prison Notebooks into English; they were published in serial form in 1974 in the New Edinburgh Review, and as a book in 1988.

18 'May 1968, Graffiti', http://www.bopsecrets.org/French/graffiti.htm (accessed 13 October, 2020).

Overthrow society	*À bas l'État!* *Ne travaillez jamais!* *Abolition de la société de classes!* *L'anarchie, c'est je!*	Down with the state! Never work! Abolish class society! Anarchy is me!
Use violence (and dehumanise the 'enemy')	*Révolution, je t'aime!* *La plus belle sculpture, c'est le pavé qu'on jette sur la gueule des flics!* *Je t'aime! Oh! dites-le avec des pavés!* *Les frontières on s'en fout!* *Soyons cruels!* *L'humanité ne sera heureuse que le jour où le dernier capitaliste aura été pendu avec les tripes du dernier bureaucrate!* *Si tu veux être heureux pends ton propriétaire!* *Cache-toi, objet!*	Revolution, I love you! The most beautiful sculpture is a paving stone thrown at a cop's head! I love you! Oh, say it with paving stones! To hell with boundaries! Be cruel! Humanity won't be happy till the last capitalist is hung with the guts of the last bureaucrat! Happiness is hanging your landlord! Hide yourself – Object!
Destroy Christianity	*La religion est l'escroquerie suprême!* *Ni dieu ni maître!* *Même si Dieu existait il faudrait le supprimer.* *Savez-vous qu'il existait encore des chrétiens?* *À bas le crapaud de Nazareth!* *Comment penser librement à l'ombre d'une chapelle?*	Religion is the ultimate con! Neither God nor master! If God existed it would be necessary to abolish Him! Can you believe that some people are still Christians? Down with the toad of Nazareth! How can you think freely in the shadow of a chapel?

Theme of Graffiti in Paris Student Uprising May 1968	French Graffiti	English Translation
Material comfort not enough (cry for meaning)	*Vous finirez tous par crever du confort* *À bas la société de consommation* *Nous ne voulons pas d'un monde où la certitude de ne pas mourir de faim s'échange contre le risque de mourir d'ennui* *L'alcool tue. Prenez du LSD!*	You will end up dying of comfort Down with consumer society! We don't want a world where the guarantee of not dying of starvation brings the risk of dying of boredom Alcohol kills. Take LSD!
Claim to victimhood	*Debout les damnés de l'Université!*	Arise, you wretched of the university!

GRIEVANCE POLITICS

Another slogan often daubed on campus walls was: 'Marx, Mao, Marcuse!' **Herbert Marcuse (1898-1979)** was associated with the Frankfurt school, and he too viewed the ideals of Western civilisation as a fraud. Old ideals sedated people into acceptance of their inauthentic place. They were merely cogs in the machine of oppressive capitalism. Such capitalism had achieved:

> ... overpowering productivity. Its supreme promise is an ever-more-comfortable life for an ever-growing number of people ... whose life is *the hell of the Affluent Society* ...[19]

This 'hell', the 'Affluent Society' had to be overthrown. Marcuse was realistic enough to know that those who achieved comfort by earning a living would not welcome revolution.

The working classes had no desire to 'throw off their chains'. They had too much to lose.

---

19 Marcuse, *One-Dimensional Man,* Routledge, 1964, second edition, 1991, https://libcom.org/files/Marcuse,%20H%20-%20One-Dimensional%20Man,%202nd%20edn.%20(Routledge,%202002).pdf (accessed 11 September, 2020), p. 26, emphasis mine.

Marcuse argued that it was more realistic to incite non-earners to revolt against the system:

> However, underneath the conservative popular base is the substratum of the outcasts and outsiders, the exploited and persecuted of other races and other colours, the *unemployed and the unemployable ...* [20]

We should acknowledge the partial truth recognised by Marcuse and his colleagues. Material wealth alone cannot satisfy the human soul. But Marcuse didn't point people to the One who alone can satisfy. He promoted the politics of envy and grievance. During the 1960s Marcuse welcomed the growing activism among students, and became something of a guru for the hippy counterculture.

THROW OUT RESTRAINT!

In *Eros and Civilization* (1955), Marcuse drew together the ideas of Marx and Freud in order to demand a non-repressive society, liberated from traditional moral norms.[21] Throw out restraint. Traditional morality must be left behind. Some of the rebellious students of the 1960s found this idea irresistible. Graffiti appeared around the university in Paris in 1968 which could have been lifted straight from *Eros and Civilization.*

These students wanted to end the 'hell' of the affluent society, *and* the inequalities of free societies, *and* the moral restraints of traditional family structures.

---

20   Ibid., p. 260, emphasis mine.

21   Freud had described (what he regarded as) the 'sexual desires' of infants as undifferentiated, focused on any part of the body, and likely to be bi-sexual or incestuous (he called this 'polymorphous perversity'). The idea that infants have sexual desires was utterly perverted. Freud suggested that the child's raw desire would later be constrained by education into social norms. Marcuse advocated unravelling those norms to achieve complete enjoyment of 'polymorphous perversity'.

Graffiti in Paris, 1968: Sexual Liberation[22]

French Graffiti	English Translation
Déboutonnez votre cerveau aussi souvent que votre braguette!	Unbutton your mind as often as your fly!
Je prends mes désirs pour la réalité car je crois en la réalité de mes désirs!	I take my desires for reality because I believe in the reality of my desires!
Plus je fais l'amour, plus j'ai envie de faire la révolution! *Plus je fais la révolution, plus j'ai envie de faire l'amour!*	The more I make love, the more I want to make revolution! The more I make revolution, the more I want to make love!
Jouir sans entraves!	Enjoy Unhindered! (colloquial, total orgasm!)
Il est interdit d'interdire!	No forbidding allowed!
Camarades, l'amour se fait aussi à Sc. Po,[23] pas seulement aux champs!	Comrades, people are making love in the politics classrooms, not only in the fields!

In 1968, millions were dying in the Soviet gulags. Millions more were being brutalised during the Chinese cultural revolution. The legacy of Marx and Mao was in plain sight, and yet these privileged Western students regarded Marx, Mao and Marcuse as heroes. They wanted to topple the *inequalities* of capitalism, in order to usher in the *equality* 'enjoyed' by the oppressed populations of the 'People's Republic' of China and the 'Union of Soviet Socialist Republics'.

When more than eleven million workers joined in sympathy strikes with the students, France was brought to a standstill. President de Gaulle fled the country at one point, but ultimately regained control.

---

22 'May 1968, Graffiti', http://www.bopsecrets.org/French/graffiti.htm (accessed 13 October, 2020).

23 Sc. Po. is an abbreviation of The Paris Institute of Political Studies.

At the same time, campuses in America were seeing widespread student violence.

Robert H Bork (1927-2012) was teaching law at Yale during the 1960s. When he caught sight of bonfires of textbooks on his way to lectures, he realised that this was just one symbol of what was spreading across university campuses: 'violence, destruction of property, mindless hatred of law, authority and tradition.'[24] In 1968, radicals in Berkeley, California, also began demonstrating in support of the Paris students:

> What ensued was a full-fledged riot, in which police battled demonstrators for the first time and in which they were physically assaulted for the first time by radicals using steel bars, chunks of concrete and Molotov cocktails. 'We set barricades on fire,' one of the rioters later wrote euphorically, 'and someone even had the xx to set a cop on fire.'[25]

But revolution didn't bring down governments anywhere in the West. Amid the burning, rioting and looting of the late 1960s, the establishment stubbornly survived.

THE LONG MARCH

Forty-four years after the founding of the Institute for Social Research in Frankfurt, a German newspaper published an article entitled 'Der lange Marsch'. The author was **Rudi Dutschke (1940-1979)**, a German student leader.[26] If violent activism didn't overthrow the establishment, Dutschke (like Gramsci and the Frankfurt School) called for a long-term ideological struggle. In 1967 he came up with

---

24 Bork, R H, *Slouching Towards Gomorrah: Modern Liberalism and American Decline,* (Regan Books, 1996), p. 1.

25 Horowitz, D, Collier, P, *Destructive Generation – Second Thoughts about the Sixties,* (1989, second edition, Encounter Books, 2006), p. 228.

26 'Rudi Dutschke and the struggle of the 1968 student movement', *DW Akademie,* 5 December, 2012, https://www.dw.com/en/rudi-dutschke-and-the-struggle-of-the-1968-student-movement/a-16429124 (accessed 31 July, 2020).

this powerful new slogan. He called for 'Der lange Marsch' or the 'Long March' through the cultural institutions of Western society.[27] In 1971 Herbert Marcuse wrote approvingly to Rudi Dutschke, telling him that the 'notion of the long march through the institutions' was the 'only effective way' to achieve revolution.[28] In 1972, Marcuse again commended Dutschke's strategy of 'the long march through the institutions: working against the established institutions while working in them.'[29]

Like Gramsci, Rudy Dutschke never saw his vision fulfilled. He died aged just thirty-nine on Christmas Eve, 1979.

THE REPUDIATION OF TOLERANCE

Five months before that, in July 1979, Herbert Marcuse had died, aged eighty-one. In his old age, Marcuse had become the idol of rebellious students, as he demanded freedom without boundaries. But what would freedom without boundaries look like? In a letter on 'Repressive Tolerance', later printed as an essay, Marcuse said that the current state of society could justify *'strongly discriminatory tolerance on political grounds'* including the *'cancellation of the liberal creed of free and equal discussion'.* Tolerance must be withdrawn from 'regressive movements'. There should be *'discriminatory tolerance in favor of progressive tendencies'.*

> Such extreme suspension of the right of free speech and free assembly is indeed justified only if the whole of society is in extreme danger. I maintain that our society is in such an emergency situation, and that it has become the normal state of affairs.[30]

---

27 He was alluding to Mao's 'Long March' through China (actually a series of marches) in 1934-5 which successfully consolidated Mao's authority in the Chinese Communist Party and ultimately in the nation.

28 Quoted in Sidwell, M, *The Long March: How the left won the culture war and what to do about it,* (The New Culture Forum, 2020), p. 47, emphasis mine.

29 Ibid., p. 47, emphasis mine.

30 Marcuse, H, 'Repressive Tolerance', Lecture at Brandeis University 1965, https://www.marcuse.org/herbert/publications/1960s/1965-repressive-

This is the pretext by which you can get rid of any who believe in absolute moral standards. This is the justification for censoring those who advocate such 'repressive ideas' as marital fidelity, or heteronormativity, or childhood innocence.

Marcuse has been described as the father of the new left, as well as the inspiration for the student protests of the 1960s. His legacy was the unravelling of any confidence in truth. He aimed to break the established universe of meaning. You just had to persuade a gullible population of students that words don't actually mean anything, they are just tools to achieve what the writer or speaker wants. This was the project of *deconstruction, aka* critical theory, *aka* the project of cultural subversion. It has been stunningly successful. That's why intelligent people can say, with a straight face, that girls can have a penis and boys can have a vagina.

DEATH OF THE AUTHOR

The Frankfurt School was a seedbed of radical theories. The seeds took root in progressive university departments through the Western world. The movement calling for 'deconstruction' continued. This claimed that human language (spoken or written), doesn't necessarily relate to objective truth. It's a series of linguistic signs to be interpreted by the hearer or reader. That claim is nonsense. Words do relate to objective truth. But it gained traction. It was usually clothed in such pretentious academic language that students were intimidated into thinking they should accept it without question.

In 1967, the French author **Roland Barthes (1915-1980)** wrote an essay entitled 'La mort de l'auteur,'[31] or 'The death of the author'. In traditional literature courses, students were expected to examine the background and intent of the author as a vital way into understanding the text. But for Barthes, once the word was on the page (or out of the speaker's mouth), that was the end of the writer or speaker's control of meaning. For literature is:

tolerance-fulltext.html (accessed 31 July 2020).

31   An allusion to the famous Le Morte d'Arthur (The Death of Arthur), a fifteenth-century work by Sir Thomas Malory.

... the trap where all identity is lost, beginning with the very identity of the body that writes ... the author enters his own death.[32]

One cannot discern the original intent of what an author meant when they wrote a text. The meaning has to be created by the reader, by means of analysis of the text. The 'plain meaning' of the text can always be challenged, or subverted. Written words can convey meanings that the author did not intend. (The irony, of course, is that we must not apply Barthes' theory to Barthes' own words.)

Applying critical theory to literature, feminist literary criticism rejects traditional interpretations as 'phallocentric'. 'Gynocentric' concerns are imported into every text. It is regarded as oppressive to focus on the author's intention. Reader response is all-important.[33] It's common to hear that 'dead white males' can't have anything worthwhile to say to women, or people of other races, or gay people. You need to balance the curriculum with equal resources from every possible group identity. Get rid of the 'Western Canon' (the collection of 'great works' previously taught in schools and universities). It's patriarchal, sexist, heteronormative and racist.

'MUGGED BY REALITY'

French philosopher and author **Michel Foucault (1926-1984)** also believed that 'liberation' would only be possible if truth claims were discredited. He claimed that knowledge is a cultural construct, used to keep the privileged in positions of power. Science is 'powerknowledge' or 'biopower'. He and other leaders of the deconstruction project wanted to live as they pleased; 'transgressiveness' was celebrated. God's moral law had to be neutralised. They needed a way to frame Christian morality as dangerously repressive. Foucault proclaimed that all truth claims are disguised ways of maintaining power over

---

32 Barthes, R, 'The Death of the Author', 1967, https://web.archive.org/web/20200419132326/http://www.ubu.com/aspen/aspen5and6/threeEssays.html#barthes (accessed 4 August, 2020).

33 Hoff Sommers, C, *Who Stole Feminism? How Women Have Betrayed Women*, (Simon & Schuster, 1994), p. 60.

others. Personal liberation would be achieved by the deconstruction of truth claims. Foucault:

> ... devoted his work to unmasking the bourgeoisie, and showing that all the given ways of shaping civil society are reducible in the last analysis to forms of domination ... The unifying thread in Foucault's earlier and most influential work is the search for the secret structures of power. Behind every practice, every institution, and behind language itself lies power, and Foucault's goal is to unmask that power and thereby to liberate its victims.[34]

Famously, Foucault developed the concept of authorities exerting domination through the 'gaze', whether of the warder in the prison, or the medics in a hospital or mental asylum. He condemned such institutions as authoritarian.[35] Ironically, when he was dying of AIDS, he was cared for in *La Salpetriere,* a hospital he had condemned. He received there 'the compassion that he needed and which he had dismissed twenty years earlier as one of the masks of bourgeois power'.[36] Theory had been 'mugged by reality'.[37]

DEATH OF THE TEXT

The Algerian philosopher **Jacques Derrida (1930-2004)** pushed forward the project of deconstruction by opposing 'logocentrism': a supposed over-reliance on logic, reason and clear definition. He challenged any privileging of the written word over speech. For Derrida, truth claims were a mark of either immaturity or dangerous authoritarianism. He wanted to deconstruct the assumptions propping up Western culture. Take, for example, The American Declaration of Independence:

---

34   Scruton, R, *Fools, Frauds and Firebrands: Thinkers of the New Left,* (Bloomsbury Continuum, 2015), p. 99.

35   Ibid., p. 105.

36   Ibid., pp. 105-6.

37   Ibid., p. 113.

We hold these truths to be self-evident, that all men are created equal; that they are endowed by their Creator with certain unalienable rights; that among these are life, liberty and the pursuit of happiness.[38]

You can overturn the 'surface' meaning by arguing that the Declaration enshrined inequality. It failed to recognise the rights of women or slaves, and it represented a power grab on the part of privileged males.

The American philosopher **Richard Rorty (1931-2007)** argued that each person constructs truth for themselves. Truth is 'made' not 'found'. When you read anything, you, the reader, control the meaning of the text. This means *the death of the text* as something with a definite meaning that would apply to all readers. By implication, it means the death of the authority of Scripture: each reader can determine for themselves what it means 'for me'.

In 2013 a family in England were told that their four-bedroom home would have to be demolished. A deadly weed had spread from wasteland nearby, and penetrated the walls of their home. The only way to remove it would be to knock the house down, kill the plant, and rebuild.[39] Today, like that poisonous knotweed, the lie – that there is no ultimate truth – has penetrated every institution in the West.

Let's summarise five of the claims of critical theory, all of which undermine confidence in any authority, whether in the home, the lecture room, the workplace or in society.

Five Ways to Destabilize Society

I 'TRUTH CLAIMS ARE POWER GRABS'

The architects of critical theory wanted to subvert confidence in the structures of society, which they believed were intrinsically oppressive.

---

38 Declaration of Independence, 1776, https://www.ushistory.org/declaration/document/ (accessed 4 August 2020).

39 'Japanese knotweed: the plant that could cost you your home', *Love Money*, 26 June, 2013, https://www.lovemoney.com/news/21501/japanese-knotweed-the-plant-that-could-cost-you-your-home (accessed 31 July 2020).

They aimed to persuade people that truth claims are grabs for power. Words don't 'mean' anything, they are 'tools' to achieve what the writer or speaker wants. Critical theory (sometimes shortened to 'Theory') was influencing many university humanities programmes by the 1980s. Students were expected to assess texts, to see if the author demonstrated sexism, racism, or homophobia. Critical theory could be used to deconstruct every subject on the curriculum, as the idea of truth itself was radically undermined.

For example, it is true that no historian is totally objective. There is a measure of interpretation in the study and writing of history. But this was pushed further, to say we can never know *any* truth about the past, and to say that historians have constructed the past to suit their own (usually privileged) agenda. History has been used as a tool of oppression. But it can be deconstructed, or 'un-made' to progress the cause of liberation, as Edward Said has claimed:

> My argument is that history is made by men and women, just as it can also be unmade and unwritten.[40]

II 'Universal Explanations Are Suspect'

To bolster the claim that those who held power through the centuries used truth claims to protect their privilege, the next step was to label 'universal' human values (metanarratives) as deceptive ploys to keep powerless people from rising up. 'Metanarratives' are narratives about narratives; overarching explanations of events.

In 1979, **Jean-François Lyotard (1924-1998)** defined 'postmodernity' as 'incredulity towards metanarratives'.[41] The

---

40   Said, E, *Orientalism,* 1978, quoted by Pluckrose, H, Lawson, J, *Cynical Theories,* (Swift, 2020), p. 71.

41   Lyotard, J F, *The Postmodern Condition: A Report on Knowledge,* 1979, trans. Bennington, G, Massumip, B, (Manchester Universtiy Press, 1984), p. xxiv, https://www.investigatingtheterror.com/documents/files/Lyotard%20 The%20Postmodern%20Condition.pdf (accessed 28 July, 2020). Lyotard is said to be the first to use the term 'postmodern' with regard to philosophy; it had been used in reference to art and architecture earlier in the twentieth century.

book in which this statement appeared had been commissioned by several universities in Quebec, Canada. Lyotard later admitted he had very little knowledge of the science he was to write about, and to compensate he had invented stories and referred to books he had never read. He described this book as a parody, and his worst book.[42] But it was widely quoted, and used to argue that metanarratives are ways of legitimising institutions of power.

According to this thinking, rather than respecting tradition, history, faith or moral codes, we need to consult individual stories and especially non-privileged stories. The multiplicity of these experiences opens the prospect of multiple (contradictory) truths.

Take the statement *'heterosexuality is natural'*. This assertion is classed as a 'discourse', a power grab on behalf of the heterosexual majority in order to oppress the gay minority. Critical gender theory claims that binaries such as male/female, or fact/fiction, or reason/emotion, are used to prop up the hegemony. They must be challenged, or at least blurred.[43] To insist on fixed categories of anything is regarded as suspect.[44] The 'metanarrative' of a universal human nature is challenged. There is no way of accessing a truth that is true for everyone.

The claim is that powerful groups use metanarratives to oppress the powerless. Christianity is viewed as a metanarrative, and God's moral law is regarded as a major force of repression. Denying the validity of universal morality, we are left with my story, your story, their story. Each of us constructs our own morality, our own identity, our own meaning and our own truth. We'll look at the impact of this within the church in chapter 6. It's easy to see how it contributed to situational

---

42 https://www.newworldencyclopedia.org/entry/metanarrative (accessed 27 October, 2020).

43 Pluckrose, H, 'The Evolution of Postmodern Thought', 22 June 2020, https://newdiscourses.com/2020/06/helen-pluckrose-evolution-postmodern-thought/ (accessed 28 July, 2020).

44 Ironically, there's an exception for race. 'White' and 'Black' are regarded as fixed identities. The truth, we argue in Part Two, is that humans are all one race.

ethics: 'Don't be so dogmatic and absolutist! Do what seems right to you in your individual situation!'

III 'REASON, LOGIC AND SCIENCE ARE TOOLS OF OPPRESSION'

In 1987 protesters gathered outside Stanford University in California shouting:

> Hey hey, ho ho, Western Civ has got to go!

They demanded the abolition of the introductory humanities program known as 'Western Culture'.[45] But critical theory didn't stop at the challenge to humanities programmes. It never stops. Like the idea of evolution, it's a 'universal acid' that leaks out to affect every field it touches. Science is now said to be a metanarrative that upholds the establishment. 'Straight white cis males' from privileged Western societies are said to have invented logical methods of legitimising knowledge in order to oppress other people.[46] Asking to test truth claims by means of science or evidence is disallowed, as it's playing the game by rules set by the privileged.

'Tools' used by the privileged (science, rational argument, evidence), it is said, should be replaced with the lived experience of people in oppressed groups. Authentic knowledge is achieved *within* different communities. People *outside* those groups don't have access to that knowledge.[47] For example, if one particular cultural group uses 'traditional medicine' (including witchcraft or magic), if someone *outside* that group wants to test that medicine scientifically, that could be viewed as cultural oppression.

---

45 https://www.intellectualtakeout.org/article/hey-hey-ho-ho-western-civ-has-got-go/ (accessed September 2021).

46 Sommers, C H, *Who Stole Feminism? How Women Have Betrayed Women*, (Simon & Schuster, 1994), pp. 50-86.

47 This concept is often called 'standpoint theory'.

Take the idea that scientific innovation can be used to help deaf people to hear. Critical theory, as applied to 'Disability Studies',[48] interprets that as application of the 'bio power' of science to minimise (disrespect) the authentic *lived experience* of a deaf person.

Half a century ago 'women's studies' courses were introduced in many universities. Critical theory was applied. The 'patriarchal thinking' that permeated academia had to be replaced with a woman-centred philosophy. Western culture was viewed as having been infused with a conceptual error of vast proportion, the androcentric (man-centred) fallacy.[49] The foundation of Western culture is rational ('straight line', logical, scientific) discourse. This was denounced as 'male' thinking. The bias of male thinking, the 'rape of our minds', must be eliminated.[50] All human thought, it was claimed, had been communicated from the male viewpoint, and was distorted. All areas of study had to be restructured from scratch, beginning with a female perspective. Such courses were not to be based on the traditional criteria of objective reason, logic and science. Subjective (female) experience and opinion were seen as more authentic. Female experiences could be used to demand social transformation. The aim was to 'transform the world to one that will be free of all oppression.'[51]

But remember, *the universal acid of critical theory cannot be contained.* By the twenty-first century it had dissolved the category 'woman'. Women's studies had to be replaced by gender studies. Now there's fierce debate about what 'gender' means, and whether it's a valid

---

48 https://plato.stanford.edu/entries/disability-critical/ (accessed 28 July, 2020).

49 Lerner, G, *The Creation of Patriarchy,* (Oxford University Press, 1986), pp. 220, 42-3 https://radicalfeministbookclub.files.wordpress.com/2018/03/women-and-history_-v-1-gerda-lerner-the-creation-of-patriarchy-oxford-university-press-1987.pdf (accessed 6 August 2018).

50 Lerner, G, *The Creation of Patriarchy,* p. 225.

51 National Women's Studies Association Constitution, 1977, revised 1982, http://science.jrank.org/pages/11659/Women-S-Studies-PREAMBLE-CONSTITUTION-NATIONAL-WOMEN-S-STUDIES-ASSOCIATION-ADOPTED-1977-REVISED-RATIFIED-1982.html (accessed 6 August 2018).

concept at all.[52] Critical theory can be used to subvert any academic discipline.

Today some activists use the internet (built by and maintained by science) to propagate their implausible claim that logic and science are patriarchal western inventions designed to oppress and demean others. Asking for scientific proof to back up an individual's claims can be interpreted as proof of your cultural dominance, and a demonstration of your 'fragility' (unwillingness to believe the testimony of someone from a minority group). Asking for evidence to back up a claim can be silenced with: 'You're victim-shaming!'

IV 'DON'T QUESTION MY EXPERIENCE!'

The 'existential' movement denied the reality of God and made individual experience supreme. Each person is to seek their own 'authenticity'. Everyone can decide for themselves what is right for them. Individual experience is all-important, not an external moral or religious code.

Western societies in the twentieth century saw the 'old' morality based on a Christian worldview replaced with this 'new morality' of individual freedom. Leading sociologist, **Anthony Giddens (b. 1948)**, describes this as the 'democracy of the emotions'. The 'pure relationship' is based on 'confluent' love, and partners must be free to leave at any time.[53] The authentic experience of each individual must be unfettered by external rules.

In this worldview, culture and religion are matters of personal choice. It's wrong to claim that one religion or culture is superior to another. This all fed into the movement for pluralism.

But some experiences *are* given more credence than others: the experiences of those without privilege. Increasingly, propositions are assessed, not on their rational merit, but on the status (privileged or

---

52 Sophie Lewis, for example, pursues the 'cause of gender abolition'. Lewis, S, *Full Surrogacy Now: Feminism Against Family,* (Verso, 2019), p. 23.

53 Giddens, A, *The Transformation of Intimacy: Sexuality, Love and Eroticism in Modern Societies,* (Polity Press, 1992), p. 62.

not) of the person making the claim. Ultimately, only those who are victims, or self-proclaimed allies of victims, have the right to speak at all.

V 'ALL AUTHORITY STRUCTURES ARE REPRESSIVE'

In order to destabilise society, people need to view authority as oppressive. After the Second World War, horror evoked by the uncovering of Nazi atrocities was exploited in order to stigmatise all authority as 'fascist'. Trust in traditional authorities (teachers, parents, clergy, police, lawyers and politicians) was undermined. Such authorities were accused of protecting the powerful and suppressing the powerless. From the 1960s on, popular entertainment jumped on this bandwagon. Politicians, clergy, teachers, fathers, were derided as idiotic, or painted as villains. The culture of repudiation undermined those who had previously been esteemed. 'Outdated virtues' of respect and deference were derided as infantile grovelling.

The student protests of the 1960s encouraged violence against the police. They were accused of complicity in upholding capitalism, regarded as 'an army of occupation', and decried as 'pigs' who could legitimately be attacked, even killed.[54]

David Horowitz and Peter Collier took part in the radical activism of the '60s. They explain that crime was regarded as 'existential rebellion'. When one of their friends, a fellow radical, was murdered, they sought justice. By that time the police in Berkeley had been thoroughly demoralised as radical politicians had stripped them of many of their powers.[55] Lawyers had successfully defended murderers and rapists (any from minority groups were thought to be engaged in legitimate protest).[56] Peter Collier recalls going to a police lieutenant, appealing for justice, as the identity of the murderer was known. The response?

---

54   Horowitz, D, Collier, P, *Destructive Generation – Second Thoughts about the Sixties,* (1989, Encounter Books second edition, 2006), p. 151.

55   Ibid., p. 230.

56   Ibid., p. 58.

Yeah, well how can we? You guys have been cutting our xx off for the last ten years. You destroy the police, and then you expect them to solve the murders of your friends.[57]

It wasn't only the police whose authority was undermined. The authority of parents was challenged too. In the campaign to question the authority of the traditional family, even children's literature had to be censored. Traditional values had to be replaced with 'realism'. The late Roger Scruton described this as a culture of repudiation, involving 'a systematic, almost paranoid attempt to examine the charming images of that former life, and to cast them one by one into the pit'.[58] Reading books with pictures of mummy at home and daddy going to work were deemed to be so offensive that they had to be banned in schools. Books depicting every kind of unhappy, abusive and dysfunctional home situation were introduced in their place.

In the campaign to undermine the authority of employers, one strategy was to persuade people that all wealth creation is greedy and all private property is evil. The State should control all production and own all property. 'Smash Capitalism' became a common rallying cry.[59] Many of the revolutionaries also opposed sovereign nation states. Patriotism was derided as un-progressive; nationalism was vilified as racist.

THE DEPARTURE OF COMMON SENSE: 'WE'RE ALL MAD HERE!'

During the 1930s, shut up in an Italian prison, Antonio Gramsci had looked forward to the day when common sense would have been dissolved. By the 1950s the theorists of the Frankfurt School had concocted a preposterous method of criticism calculated to smash

---

57 Ibid., p. 313.

58 Scruton, R, *An Intelligent Person's Guide to Modern Culture,* (Duckworth, 1998), p. 115.

59 See chapter 8: removing wealth production from individuals, families and businesses removes freedom, and puts control in the hands of the State (ironically, a greater authority).

down the whole 'universe of meaning'. They came up with critical theory: words were characterised as tools of oppression.[60] You could claim that words can mean anything!

In 1865 and 1871 *Alice's Adventures in Wonderland* and *Through the Looking-Glass* by Lewis Carroll had been published; perhaps the greatest children's novels ever written in the 'literary nonsense' genre.

> 'But I don't want to go among mad people,' Alice remarked. 'Oh, but you can't help that,' said the Cat. 'We're all mad here. I'm mad, You're mad.' 'How do you know I'm mad?' said Alice. 'You must be', said the Cat, 'or you wouldn't have come here.'[61]

Famously, Alice asks Humpty Dumpty 'Must a name mean something?' To which he replies: 'When I use a word... it means just what I choose it to mean – neither more nor less.'[62]

Children laugh. They get the point. This is utter nonsense.

Yet this was the level of nonsense taught by pretentious academics in university lecture rooms worldwide by the mid-twentieth century. Students should have laughed out loud, but they didn't dare, for fear of being labelled as stupid or reactionary.

The universal acid of critical theory didn't stay in the lecture room. During the 1960s, many students joined violent demonstrations. In subsequent decades, relativism and doubt corrupted all the institutions of the West. Today, a common-sense assertion, such as 'a boy cannot be a girl' can be denounced as an outdated truth claim. If words no longer have universal meaning, we end up in a society where two and two can equal five, if 'that's what you believe', just as a boy can be a girl.

In 1949, *Nineteen Eighty-Four* was published, the final novel written by British author George Orwell. It offered a chillingly accurate description of life under a totalitarian regime, where the

---

60 https://www.christian.org.uk/wp-content/uploads/Identity_politics_briefing.pdf (accessed September 2021).

61 Carroll, L, *Alice's Adventures in Wonderland and Through the Looking-Glass,* (London: Regent Classics), p. 59.

62 Ibid., pp. 185, 190.

'Ministry of Truth' continually rewrites history as propaganda to prop up current Party policy:

> Every book has been rewritten. Every street has been renamed. Every date has been altered.[63]

The Party forces people to reject the evidence of their eyes and ears. That is 'their final, most essential command.' To survive, citizens have to be able to exercise 'doublethink', the power of holding two contradictory beliefs in one's mind simultaneously, and accepting both of them. The 'heresy of heresies' is common sense. Awakening to the grotesque, terrifying, inexorable power of the Party, the protagonist, Winston, realizes that:

> In the end the Party would announce that two and two made five, and you would have to believe it. It was inevitable that they should make that claim sooner or later: the logic of their position demanded it. Not merely the validity of experience, but the very existence of external reality, was tacitly denied by their philosophy. *The heresy of heresies was common sense.* And what was terrifying was not that they would kill you for thinking otherwise, but that they might be right. For, after all, how do we know that two and two make four? Or that the force of gravity works? Or that the past is unchangeable? *If both the past and the external world exist only in the mind, and if the mind itself is controllable what then?*[64]

Winston wants to hold on to reality. He 'knows' that two and two make four. But how does he know? And how do we know? What if we come to believe that the past and the external world exist only in the mind? What if the Party decides to control what's in our mind? In *Nineteen Eighty-Four* the Party decides what is truth and reality. The Party claims the power to re-programme 'false consciousness'. Winston is not allowed to speak truth, or even believe truth. And yet,

---

63 Orwell, G, *Nineteen Eighty-Four: A Novel,* (Secker & Warburg, 1949), Part 2, Section 5, http://www.telelib.com/authors/O/OrwellGeorge/prose/NineteenEightyFour/part2sec5.html (accessed 4 August, 2020).

64 Ibid., Part I Chapter 7, emphasis mine.

his crucial moment of realisation stands as an authentic witness to the reality of universal truth:

> Freedom is the freedom to say that two plus two make four. If that is granted, all else follows.[65]

In 2017, three academics wrote twenty nonsensical papers and submitted them to respected journals in various academic fields. Seven of the papers were accepted and published. The first was entitled: *Human Reactions to Rape Culture and Queer Performativity in Urban Dog Parks in Portland, Oregon.* The thesis was:

> That dog parks are rape-condoning spaces and a place of rampant canine rape culture and systemic oppression against 'the oppressed dog' through which human attitudes to both problems can be measured. This provides insight into training men out of the sexual violence and bigotry to which they are prone.[66]

This paper advocated the ethically outrageous idea of training men like dogs, and included the patently ridiculous claim that the genitals of nearly ten thousand dogs had been inspected whilst interrogating owners as to their sexuality. The paper was based on nothing more than the imagination of the author. But it was published! Two of the 'peer reviews' had concluded:

> This is a wonderful paper – incredibly innovative, rich in analysis, and extremely well-written and organized given the incredibly diverse literature sets and theoretical questions brought into conversation ... The fieldwork executed contributes immensely to the paper's contribution as an innovative and valuable piece of scholarship that will engage readers from a broad cross-section of disciplines and theoretical formations.

---

65 Ibid., Part I Chapter 7.

66 Pluckrose, P, Lindsay J A, Boghossian, P, 'Academic Grievance Studies and the Corruption of Scholarship', *Areo,* 2 October, 2018, academic-grievance-studies-and-the-corruption-of-scholarship/ (accessed 5 August, 2020).

I believe this intellectually and empirically exciting paper must be published ...[67]

In 2018, the three authors went public with what they were doing. They had proved their point. Something had gone badly wrong in some fields of academic study.

Scholarship based *less upon finding truth and more upon attending to social grievances* has become firmly established, if not fully dominant, within these fields, and their scholars increasingly *bully students, administrators, and other departments into adhering to their worldview.*[68]

Common sense should have told all those involved in the publication of those hoax papers that they were absurd. And common sense should tell us that the lies described in this chapter are preposterous too.

But remember – the pioneers of critical theory had set out to destroy common sense! They regarded it as part of the false consciousness that upheld the hegemony. The task before them had seemed formidable. But the universal acid of critical theory has now corroded all the major institutions of the West. It is promoted in the media, and pushed into the workplace (and some churches) via 'sensitivity training' or 'implicit bias training'. Common sense assumptions? Today they may be denounced as the heresy of heresies.

FURTHER RESOURCES

Baucham, V, *Cultural Marxism,* https://www.youtube.com/watch?v=GRMFBdDDTkI&t=2605s

Defining Social Justice, https://www.youtube.com/watch?v=YFNOP2IqwoY

Ethnic Gnosticism, https://www.youtube.com/watch?v=Ip3nV6S_fYU

---

67 https://areomagazine.com/2018/10/02/academic-grievance-studies-and-the-corruption-of-scholarship/ (accessed 27 October, 2020).

68 Ibid., emphasis mine.

Murray, D, *The Madness of Crowds: Gender, Race and Identity,* (Bloomsbury Continuum, 2019)

Pluckrose, H and Lawson, J, *Cynical Theories: How Activist Scholarship Made Everything about Race, Gender, and Identity: And Why This Harms Everybody,* (Pitchstone, 2020)

Summary: Without a transcendent authority, who, or what, is left to judge between competing claims to truth? Confidence that problems could be solved by human reason and science collapsed into the radical doubt of 'postmodernism'. The pioneers of critical theory wanted to bring about a society where all inequalities in outcome were removed. The 'hegemony' of established institutions had to be undermined. This could be attempted by using radical doubt (aka critical theory) to question all objective truth, including scientific truth (and much that had previously assumed as 'common sense'). Critical theory has taken root in all the major institutions of the West.

5 'No Universal Humanity': Divided We Fall

In 2020 a Nevada school teacher informed her class that they had to declare their various identities and characteristics, which were then scored according to their 'privilege' or 'oppression'. To identify as either white or Christian was defined as oppressive, malicious, unjust and wrong. William Clarke was the only student in the class who appeared white (he is of mixed-race heritage). As a Christian, he knew that something was wrong about being told to 'unlearn' Christianity. He asked to change to an alternative civics class, but was refused any accommodation, and ultimately suspended from school.[1]

What is going on? In this chapter we trace the rise of a worldview which divides and alienates us from each other, rather than uniting or reconciling us.

The students of the 1960s had grown up in a culture that said 'there is no God'. But they (rightly) sensed that people cannot live by bread alone.[2] Some of them rebelled against the 'hell of the affluent society'. Instead of turning back to God, their response was nihilistic: smash

---

1   Interview with Mrs Clarke, *Fox News,* 28 December, 2020, https://profam. us2.list-manage.com/track/click?u=71b5ff0a93830214b96a42bf6&id= b18758fb9d&e=c02fad7011 (accessed 28 December, 2020).

2   Deuteronomy 8:3; Matthew 4:4.

down what's left! Let's enjoy absolute freedom (and equality) in the middle of the ruins![3]

Half a century later, many youngsters in the West also (rightly) want something beyond immediate gratification. They (rightly) object to suffering, unfairness and injustice, and demand Social Justice.

It is true that sometimes abuse or exploitation characterises groups of people, as well as individuals. Sometimes an individual may suffer from discrimination for a number of different reasons, and these intersect to make their experience particularly painful. The sense that all this is wrong is God-given. It attests that we have been created in the image of God. The demand for Social Justice is a quest for moral certainty. It's an attempt to fill the vacuum (the 'God-shaped hole') left by the decline of authentic Christian faith.

The tragedy is that while we want injustices to be confronted, 'solutions' that are not based on the truth of God's Word make those problems worse. We will see in this chapter that the current narrative of identity politics ends up destroying the concept of our universal humanity.

FROM THEORY TO ACTIVISM

The pioneers of critical theory were brilliant at obfuscation: writing in a way that was confusing and ambiguous. Taking deconstruction to the extreme led to despair. During the 1960s and 1970s they deconstructed culture and 'left the bits all over the floor'.[4] A new generation was on the way that would translate deconstruction into activism. When you are calling people to action, cloudy academic jargon doesn't work. You need slick, powerful slogans *('My Body – My Choice!')*, and clearly defined enemies *(Men, Homophobes, Transphobes, Racists)*.

---

3   See Graffiti in Paris During the 1968 Student Uprising, chapter 4, pp. 110--12

4   Pluckrose, H, 'The Evolution of Postmodern Thought', 22 June 2020, https://newdiscourses.com/2020/06/helen-pluckrose-evolution-postmodern-thought/ (accessed 28 July, 2020).

WOMEN'S LIB

The first wave of feminists (liberal feminists) wanted equal opportunities. Second wave (radical) feminists weren't content with that. They demanded equal outcomes – something very different. From the 1960s increasing numbers of women imbibed the ideas of radical feminism (some in university classes, others in 'consciousness raising' groups in homes). Marxist theory (oppressor v. oppressed) was applied to male/female relationships. 'The Patriarchy' joined 'Capitalism' as the enemy. This overarching narrative (so much for ditching all metanarratives!) claimed that *All Men have oppressed All Women right through History!'*

There was enough truth hidden in this cartoon version of history to make it plausible. Because of the fall into sin, men *have* all too often used their superior physical strength to abuse women. But the demand for equal outcomes hit up against the brick wall of reality. Women, not men, bear and nurse children. Men and women are different! Exactly *equal outcomes* in society are a false aspiration. They can only be achieved by overriding individual choices and intrusive state intervention.[5] As I have argued elsewhere, radical feminism resulted in *more abuse* of women.[6] Claims such as 'all men hate all women', (Germaine Greer), and 'all men are potential rapists' (Susan Brownmiller) exacerbated hostility between the sexes. And as the one-sided narrative of radical feminism gained ground, all too often *new injustices* were perpetrated against men.[7]

Systemic sexism is the idea that there are embedded structures in a society that promote sexism, so those structures need to be overthrown (for example by affirmative action or positive discrimination). It's the idea that you can 'be sexist' without 'being sexist'. You, as an individual

---

5 Himmelstrand, J, 'Busting the myths of Sweden's family policy', Lecture at the Family Education Trust conference May 2013, *Family Bulletin,* Family Education Trust, June 2013.

6 James, S, *God's Design for Women in an Age of Gender Confusion,* (Evangelical Press, 2019), chapters 2, 3 and 4.

7 Jaye, C, *The Red Pill,* 2016. This film documents the concerns of the men's rights movement and fathers' rights groups.

may harbour no sexist ideas. But by virtue of being a man, i.e. part of a privileged group, you are assumed to be part of the hegemony (the privileged system) that must be overthrown. Denying that you are sexist proves that you are sexist, because you are displaying your ignorance of the power of the hegemony.[8]

Women may be the majority in a population but they are classed as a victim minority because of their experience of patriarchal oppression. In this cultural context, if a man invites a woman to go out for coffee, she may perceive that as a sexist power move, the first step in the road to rape. If he pays her a compliment, she might interpret it as a *micro-aggression* (a term referring to subtle forms of 'oppression', including indirect or unintentional words or behaviour deemed to reinforce stereotypes or discrimination).

IDENTITY POLITICS AND INTERSECTIONALITY

In 1977, a group of American feminists published 'The Combahee River Collective Statement'.[9] They have been credited with coining the term *identity politics,* which they defined as 'a politics that grew out of our objective material experiences as Black women.'

> We realize that the only people who care enough about us to work consistently for our liberation are us ... This focusing upon our own oppression is embodied in the concept of identity politics. We believe that the most profound and potentially most radical politics come directly out of our own identity, as opposed to working to end somebody else's oppression ... We realize that the liberation of all oppressed peoples necessitates the destruction of the political-economic systems of capitalism and imperialism as well as patriarchy ... We are not convinced, however, that a socialist

---

8   Sommers, C H, *Who Stole Feminism? How Women Have Betrayed Women,* (Simon & Schuster, 1994), p. 23.

9   As mentioned in chapter 2. In 1863, a daring raid which liberated over 750 slaves took place at the Combahee River in South Carolina. It was led by Harriet Tubman, herself an escaped slave.

revolution that is not also a feminist and anti-racist revolution will guarantee our liberation.[10]

These women experienced the prejudice that resulted from the intersection of racism and sexism. They didn't trust other civil rights groups to promote their interests. An academic called **Audre Lorde (1934-1992)** was a member of this group. She wrote extensively of her own experience, as it was shaped by issues of race, class, ageism, sexism, illness and disability. In an address entitled 'The Master's Tools Will Never Dismantle the Master's House', she accused most academic feminists of acting as puppets of the racist patriarchy because they relied on 'the master's tools'. What were these 'tools'? The methodology of 'racist, patriarchal' academics such as logic, reason, evidence and science! They were not adequate to fathom, still less resolve, injustice. Rather you need to draw on the *experience* of the oppressed.[11]

THE NEW PYRAMID OF POWER

The Combahee Collective came up with the concept of intersectionality. The term was then promoted by American feminist **Kimberlé Williams Crenshaw (b.1959)**, author of 'Mapping the Margins: Intersectionality, Identity Politics and Violence against Women of Color'.[12] As this concept has gained ground, it is assumed that if a person is marginalised due to multiple factors: racism, sexism, homophobia, transphobia and so on, then they can claim victim

---

10 The Combahee River Collective Statement, https://americanstudies. yale.edu/sites/default/files/files/Keyword%20Coalition_Readings.pdf (accessed 18 November, 2020).

11 Lorde, A, 'The Master's Tools Will Never Dismantle the Master's House', 1984, *Sister Outsider: Essays and Speeches,* (ed. Berkeley, CA: Crossing Press, 2007), https://collectiveliberation.org/wp-content/uploads/2013/01/ Lorde_The_Masters_Tools.pdf (accessed 6 August, 2020), emphasis mine.

12 Crenshaw, K, 'Demarginalizing the intersection of race and sex: A Black feminist critique of antidiscrimination doctrine, feminist theory, and antiracist politics', University of Chicago Legal Forum, 1989, pp. 139-167; 'Mapping the Margins: Intersectionality, Identity Politics and Violence against Women of Color,' *The Feminist Philosophy Reader,* (McGraw-Hill, 2008), pp. 279-309.

status. If they claim to have been offended, distressed or insulted, it's their *perception* that matters.

The division of society into oppressor and oppressed was applied to men (oppressor) and women (oppressed), but has been mapped onto other groups. New enemies have been named and shamed: Heteronormativity. Transphobia. Islamophobia. Racism. Nationalism. Christianity.

Remember the 'pyramid' of power criticised by the Marxists?[13] The old hierarchies were replaced. In the new pyramid of power, those at the top are privileged oppressors (such as 'white, educated, cisgender, able-bodied, males'). Those at the bottom are oppressed victims (such as 'people of colour, disabled, trans, uneducated people'). Those at the 'top', those with privilege, are assumed to be incapable of understanding the situation of those without privilege. They aren't allowed to question their claims or challenge their demands.

If you are regarded as part of the 'oppressor class', but you deny your guilt, you are told that you are selfishly defending your unearned privilege. If you are regarded as part of the 'oppressed class', but you deny your victimhood, you are told that you have 'internalized' your pathology, and are acting as a pawn of the oppressors.

QUEER THEORY

Systemic heteronormativity is the idea that there are embedded structures in a society that privilege heterosexuals. These structures (especially the man-woman married family) need to be overthrown, in order to achieve equality of dignity. If you deny being homophobic, it is thought to prove that you are repressing your own homosexuality, or that you are internalising your homophobia. In 1989, Marshall Kirk and Hunter Madsen published a handbook for gay activists entitled *After the Ball*. They deliberately constructed the concepts of 'born gay' and 'gay orientation', in order to shift attention from behaviour and choice to 'fixed identity' (over which a 'victim' had no

---

13   See chapter 2, p. 53.

control).[14] This brilliant move afforded minority status to gay people, and simultaneously shifted any questioning of homosexuality into the realm of 'persecuting a minority'.

CRITICAL RACE THEORY

Racism is an ugly reality.

American author Shelby Steele recalls that when he was young, when he arrived with his dad in any new town, the first thing they did was find someone who could give them the 'inside' story about accommodation, places to eat and other local services where they would not be turned away because of their skin colour.[15]

Until 1967, interracial marriage was still against the law in sixteen states in America.[16] The preacher and author John Piper was brought up in North Carolina at a time when the culture was permeated with racism. In 1962, his home church voted for segregated services. His mother was the only person to vote against the motion. At that time, evangelical theological schools were also committed to segregation.[17] Piper's book *Blood Lines* traces his personal journey away from that racist cultural legacy.

But we need to draw a distinction between racism, which is *always* to be opposed, and the idea of 'systemic racism', as promoted by Critical Race Theory. *Systemic* racism is the idea that there are embedded structures in a society that promote racism, so those *structures* need to be overthrown. It's the idea that you can *'be racist' without 'being racist'.* As an individual, you may harbour no racist ideas. But by virtue of being 'white', i.e. *part of a privileged group,* you are assumed to be part

---

14 Kirk, M, Madsen, H, *After the Ball: How America Will Conquer its Fear and Hatred of Gays in the 90s,* (Doubleday, 1989), p. 184.

15 Steele, S, *White Guilt: How Blacks and Whites Together Destroyed the Promise of the Civil Rights Era,* (Harper Perennial, 2006), p. 8.

16 South Carolina only removed from the state constitution the prohibition of racial intermarriage in 1998; Alabama only removed the law against intermarriage in the year 2000. Piper, J, *Blood Lines,* (Crossway, 2011), p. 204.

17 Piper, J, *Blood Lines,* p. 33.

of the hegemony (the privileged system) that must be overthrown. If you deny that you are racist, that's proof that you *are racist*. You don't understand the power of the hegemony. One generation can be held guilty for the 'sins' committed by previous generations, and called to pay reparations and make amends.[18] Richard Delgado, author of *Critical Race Theory*, writes:

> The critical race theory (CRT) movement is a collection of activists and scholars engaged in studying and transforming the relationship among race, racism, and power ... *Unlike traditional civil rights discourse, which stresses incrementalism and step-by-step progress, critical race theory questions the very foundations of the liberal order, including equality theory, legal reasoning, Enlightenment rationalism, and neutral principles of constitutional law.*[19]

But if you dismiss 'the foundations of the liberal order', and rule out legal and social reform, what is left? Brute force. 'Race' is constructed as a zero sum game of power. But the concept of 'race' itself is debatable. Ethnic and national and cultural diversity are real – but there's no biological or genetic foundation for the idea of different races.[20]

American feminist scholar **Peggy McIntosh (b. 1934)** developed the concept of 'white privilege'. Her work is a perfect example of critical theory. She doesn't attempt to use traditional research methods, properly checked surveys, quantitative analysis, and so on. Rather, she reflects on her *own experiences* of 'unearned privilege' and then extrapolates from that: 'white' people enjoy unearned privilege that they must atone for.[21]

---

18 McDermott, G R, 'Misunderstanding Race and the Bible', *Public Discourse*, 20 October, 2020, https://www.thepublicdiscourse.com/2020/10/72125/ (accessed 22 October, 2020).

19 Delgado, R, *Critical Race Theory*, 2001, third edition, (NYU Press, 2017, updated 2020), kindle edition, p. 3, emphasis mine.

20 See chapter 7 for the biblical truth that as humans we are all of one race.

21 McIntosh, P, 'White Privilege and Male Privilege: A Personal Account of Coming to See Correspondences Through Work in Women's Studies',

The politics of guilt has been carried to a new level by **Robin DiAngelo (b. 1956)**, author of *White Fragility* (2019). She believes that those who claim to see others as individuals, rather than as people of one colour or another, are 'dangerous'. 'White' people who don't own up to being racist are betraying 'white fragility'.[22] She has promoted the use of 'unconscious bias training'. This insists that if you are 'white' you are racist; if you attempt to help minorities you betray your 'interest convergence' (i.e. you are only helping because you want to reinforce your own supremacy).

CRITICAL VOICES

Critical Race Theory, albeit well-intentioned, only increases the division, suspicion, and racism it purports to oppose. Race becomes the thing to focus on, at the cost of our universal humanity. Many thoughtful commentators condemn Critical Race Theory as a new and unforgiving manifestation of racism.[23] **Professor John McWhorter (b. 1965)** has criticized *White Fragility* for 'infantilizing' and dehumanising' minority groups. He writes:

> Today's consciousness-raising on race is less about helping black people than it is about white people seeking grace ... Fifty years ago, a white person learning about the race problem came away asking 'How can I help?' Today the same person too often comes away asking, 'How can I show that I'm a moral person?'[24]

Another critic is **Dr Voddie Baucham (b. 1969)**. He was raised by a single mother in an area of South Los Angeles which was home to

---

1988, https://nationalseedproject.org/about-us/white-privilege (accessed 6 August, 2020).

22 DiAngelo, R, *White Fragility,* (Penguin, 2019).

23 Some include, Thomas Sowell, Walter Williams, Shelby Steele, John McWhorter, Tony Sewell. Trevor Phillips, Samuel Sey, and Voddie Baucham. See Further Resources.

24 McWhorter, J, 'The Great Awakening: Atonement as Activism', *The American Interest,* May, 24 2018, https://www.the-american-interest.com/2018/05/24/atonement-as-activism/ (accessed 21 December, 2020).

gangs and drug-dealers. Some of his family members were members of the Nation of Islam (a Black Power group), and both his parents were activists. He believes that Critical Race Theory fails to address the real causes of deprivation and poverty.[25] Blaming 'the system' effectively denies individual moral agency and dignity. From his own experience, Baucham argues that affirmative action is patronising and devalues achievement. He left America to study in Oxford to try to escape that.

Dr Thomas Sowell (b. 1930) criticises the 'Social Justice' vision as simplistically claiming that disparities of any kind must indicate that somebody has been wronged by someone else. Individual agency is eliminated.[26]

In October 2020 a British Equalities Minister, **Kemi Badenoch**, stated in the House of Commons:

> I want to speak about a dangerous trend in race relations that has come far too close to home in my life and it is the promotion of critical race theory – an ideology that sees my blackness as victimhood and their whiteness as oppression. I want to be absolutely clear: this Government stands unequivocally against critical race theory.[27]

A SELECTIVE NARRATIVE

Critical Race Theory focuses exclusively on 'white privilege and black victimhood'. This has led, for example, to a distorted view of slavery

---

25 Baucham, V, 'Biblical Justice', https://www.youtube.com/watch?v=VWZY woK2f7o (accessed 24 December, 2020).

26 Sowell, T, 'Discrimination, Race, and Social Justice', *The Federalist,* 13 June, 2018, https://thefederalist.com/2019/06/13/an-interview-with-thomas-sowell-on-discrimination-race-and-social-justice/ (accessed 24 December, 2020).

27 https://videos.dailymail.co.uk/preview/mol/2020/10/20/655814170 347129805/636x382_MP4_655814170347129805.mp4 (accessed 22 October, 2020). Similarly, in September 2020, the President of the United States issued an order that federal funding should not be used to promote critical race theory, which was labelled a 'divisive' and racist ideology. https://www.whitehouse.gov/presidential-actions/executive-order-combating-race-sex-stereotyping/ (accessed 5 October, 2020).

as being solely a sin of Western society. The historical reality, as Dr Thomas Sowell explains, is that in the past it has been accepted and embraced by nearly all societies:

> During the Middle Ages, Slavs were so widely used as slaves in both Europe and the Islamic world that the very word 'slave' derived from the word for Slav – not only in English, but also in other European languages, as well as in Arabic. Nor have Asians or Polynesians been exempt from either being enslaved or enslaving others. China in centuries past has been described as 'one of the largest and most comprehensive markets for the exchange of human beings in the world'. Slavery was also common in India, where it has been estimated that there were more slaves than in the entire Western hemisphere – and where the original Thugs kidnapped children for the purpose of enslavement.
>
> At least a million Europeans were enslaved by North African pirates alone from 1500 to 1800, and some European slaves were still being sold on the auction blocks in Egypt, years after the Emancipation Proclamation freed blacks in the United States.[28]

Slavery still exists in some Islamic nations. Nine out of the top ten countries where citizens enjoy the most freedom are in the West.[29] Today in some Middle Eastern countries, Westerners suffer discrimination, they are not allowed to own property or businesses or become citizens. There are still Islamic countries which enslave non-Muslims. And *Dhimmitude* is still widely accepted and practised: the belief that those not of the Islamic faith are second-rate citizens, and therefore should be denied the privileges and rights accorded to Muslims.[30]

---

28 Sowell, T, 'The Real History of Slavery', in *Black Rednecks and White Liberals,* (Encounter Books, 2005), pp. 111-169, p. 112.

29 The Human Freedom Index, 2020, *The Cato Institute,* https://www.cato.org/human-freedom-index-new (accessed 21 December, 2020).

30 Donnelly, K, 'The White Lies of Critical Race Theory', *The Conservative Woman,* 4 November, 2020, https://www.conservativewoman.co.uk/the-white-lies-of-critical-race-theory/ (accessed 21 December, 2020).

The largest number of slaves today are entrapped in the abusive networks created by global sex-slavery and sex-trafficking. The suffering is not restricted to any particular ethnic group. These evils are fuelled by prostitution and pornography.

NO FORGIVENESS

The virus of critical theory has spawned the virus of identity politics. This operates as a new religion, but one that is fiercely unforgiving. If you have privilege, you bear guilt for a sin that can never be atoned for. If you disagree with any of the claims of the less privileged, you are too *fragile* to examine your own guilt.[31] You are failing to promote Social Justice because your privilege has made you too comfortable. If you try to engage, and ask a non-privileged person to share their experience with you, you might be accused of *epistemic exploitation* (taking advantage of the experience of others to try to justify yourself).

If you are a member of a victim group, but fail to endorse the activism called for by other members of your group, you are accused of *complicity* with the oppressive system. The important thing to remember is that the focus is on *groups and structures rather than individuals*.

People are ever more afraid to speak on any contentious issues. Daily new 'trip wires'[32] or 'Kafka traps'[33] are laid, over which one might fall. We are moving towards the fearful silence experienced in all tyrannical regimes. If you are in a restaurant, you look over your shoulder and lower your voice if you are going to express views that may be judged politically incorrect. The 'wrong' words are construed as a violent attack on victim groups. *'Words are Violence'* we are told. But there's no safety in silence either. If you fail to speak out in support

---

31 DiAngelo, R, *White Fragility*.

32 The phrase often used by Douglas Murray in *The Madness of Crowds*, (Bloomsbury Continuum, 2019).

33 Burke, D, 'The intellectual Fraud of Robin DiAngelo's *White Fragility*', *New Discourses*, https://newdiscourses.com/2020/06/intellectual-fraud-robin-diangelos-white-fragility/ (accessed 25 February, 2021). You have the alternatives: 'You're Either A Fragile Racist, or A Fragile Racist'.

of victim groups you are accused of violence too. *'Silence is Violence'* as well.

But real looting and violence can sometimes be excused as part of the legitimate fight for Social Justice. Ariel Atkins, a Black Lives Matter organizer in Chicago claimed that breaking into stores and looting the goods is 'reparations':

> Anything they want to take, take it because these businesses have insurance.[34]

So violence is not real violence at all! The victims might tell a different story.

SOCIETY DIVIDED: PRIVILEGED V. VICTIMS

The promoters of critical theory insisted that societies are oppressed by a hegemony of powerful ruling interests. People can be divided between those who are complicit with the hegemony and those who resist it. Humanity is viewed as divided between powerful privileged groups and powerless victim groups (and their declared allies). *'Resource equity'* is the phrase used to demand *equal outcomes* between groups.

In terms of knowledge, only those who have lived experience of suffering oppression, can claim true knowledge of that oppression. In academic circles this is referred to as *'standpoint theory'.* Different people have access to different truths. Those deemed to have multiple layers of privilege may be stripped of any right to comment on the position of those with less privilege. They are not allowed to question their claims. They may be banned from speaking in public (*'No-platforming'* is barring someone from speaking because they do not agree with certain views). People without privilege may need to be protected from hearing any opinions which damage them (*'safe spaces'*

---

34 Banners held up in the Chicago Black Lives Matter rally said: 'Our futures have been looted from us, Loot back.' 'Reparations are about economic stability, not a looted pair of $120 Nikes', *Chicago Tribune,* 17 August 2020, https://www.google.com/search?client=firefox-b-d&q=ariel+atkins+chicago+tribune+august+17+2020 (accessed 5 October, 2020).

should be provided). The only option for those with privilege is to declare themselves to be *allies* of those without privilege (i.e. accept their accounts of 'truth').

Proponents of critical theory know that their claims can't be exposed to external critique. They have the 'hidden knowledge' of lived experience.[35] If you question them, you prove your complicity with the hegemony. If you are part of a minority group, any perceived complicity with the hegemony means that you might be excommunicated from that group. In 2016 a columnist in the LGBT newspaper *The Advocate* described openly gay PayPal founder Peter Thiel as 'not a gay man' because of his political beliefs.[36] In 2018, Kanye West was accused of not being 'truly black' because he endorsed Donald Trump.[37]

'MULTIPLE TRUTHS'

In 2017, Evergreen College in Washington State in the USA hit international headlines. The socially progressive president had been encouraging students to oppose any perceived discrimination, and he had an informal system of labelling faculty as either allies or enemies.[38]

---

35 This claim to 'hidden knowledge' is a new manifestation of an old heresy: Gnosticism. See: https://www.christian.org.uk/wp-content/uploads/gnosticism.pdf (accessed 9 October, 2020).

36 'Peter Thiel Shows Us There's a Difference Between Gay Sex and Gay', Jim Downs, *The Advocate*, 14 October 2016, https://www.advocate.com/commentary/2016/10/14/peter-thiel-shows-us-theres-difference-between-gay-sex-and-gay (accessed 25 August, 2020).

37 'I'm Not Black, I'm Kanye', Ta-Nehisi Coates, *The Atlantic*, 7 May 2018, https://www.theatlantic.com/entertainment/archive/2018/05/im-not-black-im-kanye/559763/ (accessed 25 August, l 2020).

38 Harris, U, 'How Activists Took Control of a University: The Case Study of Evergreen State', https://quillette.com/2017/12/18/activists-took-control-university-case-study-evergreen-state/ (accessed 28 July 2020). The President appointed an Equity Council who: ' ... arranged an emotionally charged meeting full of platitudes and tears, after which people were asked to step down to the stage in front of everybody and form a giant canoe in a ritualistic performance with drums beating in the background. The implication being that you were either onboard [with the Equity Plan] or

One of the teaching staff, Professor Bret Weinstein, asserted in an email:

> On a college campus, one's right to speak — or to be — must never be based on skin color.[39]

But Weinstein was told by colleagues that 'there are multiple versions of "truth" that exist at once'. And he was warned to accept the experience of minority students without question:

> If our students are telling us ... that they are experiencing a hostile environment, we must take our students at their word.[40]

On one level, there's still the belief that there's no universal truth. But some activists imply that those without privilege have access to a truth that the privileged can never enjoy. The only hope for the privileged is to sign up as allies of those without privilege.

Injustice Multiplied

A free society should ensure *equal opportunities*. All human beings made in God's image should have the opportunity to flourish. But human beings are different. There will always be a wide variety of ability, competence, energy, motivation and integrity. To *enforce equal*

---

not, with no in-between. The Strategic Equity Plan they were ostensibly affirming was never actually read.'

39 https://www.insidehighered.com/news/2018/02/22/evergreen-state-cancels-day-absence-set-series-protests-and-controversies (accessed 29 July 2020).

40 Harris, U, 'How Activists Took Control of a University: The Case Study of Evergreen State', https://quillette.com/2017/12/18/activists-took-control-university-case-study-evergreen-state/ (accessed 28 July 2020). But which students? Weinstein was subsequently accosted by students who called his email 'racist'. When two students spoke out to defend Weinstein, they were shouted down. Their 'truth' was not acceptable. The 'anti-racist' protestors went on to threaten students and staff with weapons, and even took members of the administration hostage. Lukianoff, G and Haidt, J, *The Coddling of the American Mind: How Good Intentions and Bad Ideas Are Setting Up a Generation for Failure*, (Penguin, 2018), pp. 117-118.

outcomes demands social engineering on a vast scale. It assumes state intervention in every aspect of life. It signals the end of a free society.

If you believe that society is divided into groups who enjoy unjustly accrued privilege and groups who have been unjustly deprived of privilege, your aim will be a restoration of *equity (or equal outcomes)*. Enter *critical legal theory* – the idea that law should be used as a tool to remedy past injustice. As with many worthy schemes, this idea leads to unintended consequences: even more injustices.

Critical Legal Theory: Injustice Multiplied

Critical Legal Theory: Use the Law to Right Past Wrongs	Critical Legal Theory: New Injustices Perpetrated
Ideas like 'equality before the law' and 'justice is blind' were part of the 'hegemony' of power by which the privileged kept victims oppressed.	If someone is part of a victim class, their crime may be excused if it is thought to result from their disadvantage. We are no longer equal before the law.
'Hate' legislation means that if an alleged victim (or someone else) 'perceives' that hate has motivated a crime, then the sentence can be heavier.	Justice is no longer 'blind'.
The law is a means by which to advance the 'progressive' agenda (e.g. abortion rights, same-sex marriage, or self-declaration of gender).	Judges take on too much power when they *create* laws rather than *applying* laws (judges should be fair in application of constitutionally framed laws).

THE POLITICS OF GUILT

Critical legal theory is one tool in the pursuit of equal outcomes. Another is to 'persuade' the privileged sections of society to engage in reparations and redistribution. Enter the politics of guilt, built on the narrative of systemic oppression. The privileged are not likely to voluntarily surrender their position, so they need to be *re-educated,* and then persuaded to hand over the benefits they've accrued by the accident of their birth into privilege. This is what the theorists of systemic injustice and privilege set out to do.

One aspect of re-education is to re-write history. *The New York Times* 1619 project was developed by Nikole Hannah-Jones and launched in August 2019. The project rewrote the founding of the United States, claiming that it was founded on oppression rather than freedom. Widely criticised for numerous historical inaccuracies, it was a reconstruction of the past in order to fuel present unrest. It was a significant factor in the widespread protests of 2020. Hannah-Jones explains:

> I've always said that the 1619 Project is not history. It is a work of journalism that explicitly seeks to challenge the national narrative and therefore national memory. The project has always been as much about the present as it is about the past.[41]

We can summarise the claims of those who promote the narrative of systemic injustice as follows on pages 149-152.

Systemic Injustice

Oppressor Groups: Unearned Privilege	Oppressed Groups: Undeserved Disadvantage
Their privilege is due to systemic and historic injustice.	Their oppression is due to having been robbed by the privileged class (past and present).
The group is guilty of unearned privilege (even if individuals in the group are unsuccessful and disadvantaged).	The group suffers from lack of privilege (even if individuals in the group are successful and privileged).

---

41 Furedi, F, 'Battle for America', *Spiked Online,* 28 September, 2020, https://www.spiked-online.com/2020/09/28/the-battle-for-the-soul-of-america/ (accessed 30 October, 2020).

Oppressor Groups: Unearned Privilege	Oppressed Groups: Undeserved Disadvantage
Privilege may be multiplied according to the number of privileged groups an individual belongs to.	Individuals may experience oppression at multiple levels or intersections; lack of privilege is multiplied the more levels at which it is experienced.
The group does not have 'knowledge' of suffering and lacks awareness.	The group possesses knowledge (awareness) of what it's like to suffer oppression.
Privileged groups tend to deny their unearned privilege and resources.	Suffering at various intersections leads to deeper lived experience of oppression.
Members of privileged groups must:	**Members of oppressed groups must:**
Engage in consciousness raising (equality and diversity training; 'unconscious bias training'; rewriting of the curriculum).	Affirm the reality of systemic injustice.
Check their privilege (acknowledge their part in systemic injustice and the unfairness of benefiting from historic injustice).	If they are individually successful, they must still affirm the victimhood and suffering of their group.
Work for Social Justice (take part in activism on behalf of the oppressed).	Work for Social Justice (take part in activism on behalf of their own group/s).
Accept that the guilt of unearned privilege and resources must be compensated for (forced redistribution; reparations, positive discrimination; affirmative action).	Campaign for compensation for historic and systemic injustice.

Those who developed the various liberation ideologies wanted to protect people in oppressed groups from discrimination. But each ideology has been hijacked. Each one now *aggravates* divisions between people, rather than healing them.

Humanity Divided: Divisions Exacerbated

Ideology of Liberation	Privileged Group	Privileged Group Guilty of ...	Oppressed Group	The Ideology Exacerbates Tension and Division
Feminism	Men (The Patriarchy)	Sexism/ Misogyny	Women	Affirmative action/ positive discrimination creates resentment. All men are accused of 'toxic' tendencies. Men's testimony (e.g. in rape cases) may be dismissed.
Gay/Lesbian Movement (Queer Theory)	Straight people	Homophobia/ assuming heterosexuality is normal (heteronormativity)	Gay/lesbian people	Constant promotion of gay rights leads to resentment, and sometimes backlash; disagreement is characterised as hatred (with regard to gay and trans rights).
Trans Movement (Queer Theory)	'Cis' people	Transphobia	Trans people	Erosion of protection for women leads to instances of abuse, which causes anger and resentment.
Multi-culturalism (Postcolonial Theory)	Majority culture/ Christians	(eg) Islamophobia	Minority cultures/ faiths	Failure to confront Islamic extremism creates fear and worsens community relations.
Globalism (Postcolonial Theory)	Majority culture	Nationalism/ Patriotism	Minority cultures	Failure to control immigration or control borders leads to resentment.

Ideology of Liberation	Privileged Group	Privileged Group Guilty of …	Oppressed Group	The Ideology Exacerbates Tension and Division
Anti-Racism (Postcolonial Theory/ Critical Race Theory)	Whites	Racism/ Colonialism/ Imperialism/ Slavery	Non-whites	Affirmative action/ quotas etc. leads to resentment.
Disability and Fat Studies	Able bodied/ slim people	'Othering' disabled or fat people (it is bigoted to assume it is preferable to be able-bodied, or not obese)	Disabled/fat people	Attempting treatment cure/ amelioration of condition viewed as oppressive.

FOREVER CONDEMNED

In a desperate effort to escape the guilt of privilege, some falsely claim membership of 'oppressed' groups. In September 2020, an American tenured professor, Jessica Krug, published a bizarre 'confession'. She had built her academic and activist career on a false identity. Before her lies could be exposed by others, she admitted her deception:

> To an escalating degree over my adult life, I have eschewed my lived experience as a white Jewish child in suburban Kansas City under various assumed identities within a Blackness that I had no right to claim ... doing so [was] the very epitome of violence, of thievery and appropriation ... my false identity was crafted entirely from the fabric of Black lives ... You should absolutely cancel me, and I absolutely cancel myself ... The wrath of all whom I've harmed, individually and collectively, will never erase the harm I've done ... I can't fix this ... I would never ask for nor expect forgiveness ...

There is nowhere to run. I have ended the life I had no right to live in the first place.[42]

Such is the fallout from identity politics. A woman claims a false identity to escape the guilt of privilege. She then owns up, knowing her deception is about to be exposed. But there's no hope of forgiveness. She is forever condemned.

DIVIDED WE FALL

If you want to undermine any society, you sow disunity. Western societies are experiencing dangerous levels of division. The ideal of civil rights leaders such as Martin Luther King was that in a fair society we would assess each other on the basis of character, not colour. But advocates of Identity Politics demand that we assess each other primarily on our group identity. This provokes suspicion and conflict. Community relations will only deteriorate. That was seen dramatically in the violence witnessed across many American cities and beyond during the summer of 2020 which brought terror to individuals and ruin to small businesses in cities across America:

> ... more than 10,600 incidents of what is benignly called 'unrest' were recorded between May 24 and August 22. Of these, some 570 involved violence. Of those, most have involved Black Lives Matter activists. Preliminary insurance estimates show that the damage will surpass the $1.2 billion in damages accrued during the 1992 Rodney King riots.[43]

The immediate catalyst was the protests organised after the death of George Floyd on May 25, 2020. The deeper wellspring was the ideology that has demonised American (and Western) history as being

---

42 Krug, J A, 'The Truth, and the Anti-Black Violence of My Lies', Medium, 3 September, 2020, https://medium.com/@jessakrug/the-truth-and-the-anti-black-violence-of-my-lies-9a9621401f85 (accessed 8 September, 2020).

43 Eberstadt, M, 'The Fury of the Fatherless', First Things, December 2020, https://www.firstthings.com/article/2020/12/the-fury-of-the-fatherless (accessed 30 December, 2020).

irredeemably racist and oppressive.[44] **Black Lives Matter (BLM)** was founded in 2013 by three self-described 'trained Marxists'. Before it was removed in September 2020 one section of the BLM website declared:

> We disrupt the Western-prescribed nuclear family structure requirement by supporting each other as extended families and 'villages' that collectively care for one another, especially our children, to the degree that mothers, parents, and children are comfortable.[45]

Note that fathers are missing. The vision is of a world liberated from the traditional family; and of an ideal world where 'collectivisation' replaces privately-owned business. To get to that world, you need to smash capitalism, de-fund the police, break down traditional family norms, and deconstruct the gender binary.[46]

There is no longer the common assumption that all people share the single identity of 'being human'. But history shows that when certain groups of people are regarded as 'less than human', the most heinous human rights abuses occur.

CULTURAL MARXISM?

The 2020 protests hit headlines worldwide. No one can ignore the demands made by the advocates of critical theory and identity politics. Some describe this worldview as 'Cultural Marxism'. Others dismiss any mention of Cultural Marxism as a right-wing conspiracy theory.

---

44 Furedi, F, 'Battle for America', *Spiked Online,* 28 September 2020, https://www.spiked-online.com/2020/09/28/the-battle-for-the-soul-of-america/ (accessed 5 October, 2020).

45 'What we Believe', *Black Lives Matter,* https://archive.is/oARH0 (accessed 5 October, 2020), this includes the statement: 'We disrupt the Western-prescribed nuclear family structure requirement'. https://notthebee.com/article/black-lives-matter-website-removes-controversial-what-we-believe-page (accessed 5 October, 2020).

46 During the run-up to the 2020 American Presidential election, Black Lives Matter came under pressure to remove their more controversial statements from their website, but they have not recanted their views.

But there *is* a common factor flowing from Marxism to critical theory to identity politics: the demand for equity, *aka equal outcomes*. This chart summarises these three stages in the movement:

The Demand for Equal Outcomes

	Marxism	**Critical Theory**	**Identity Politics**
Problem in Society: All are in chains	Workers are oppressed by capitalists.	Ordinary people are oppressed by the 'hegemony' (all that props up the establishment).	Oppressed groups are disadvantaged by historic and systemic injustice.
Aim	Economic equality. Bring down capitalism.	Equality of outcomes in every area of life. Undermine the traditional family, the church, the legal system. Bring down capitalism.	Equality of outcomes in every area of life, including dignity and privilege. Bring down capitalism.
Strategy	Violent revolution to overthrow the capitalist system. Divide society into 'owners of capital' v. 'workers'.	Use critical theory to undermine the establishment (the power of the 'hegemony').	Divide society into 'victim groups' v 'privileged groups'.
Demand	Owners of capital hold property by means of robbing the workers. They must repay what they have taken. They won't do this voluntarily, force will be needed.	The 'hegemony' must give up their powerful hold over the minds of ordinary people. Their hold can be weakened by denying the existence of objective truth.	Privileged groups must repay what they have taken from the oppressed (reparations etc.).

	Marxism	Critical Theory	Identity Politics
Time frame	Immediate	Long term (it would take decades for critical theory to permeate academia and then society).	Immediate direct action (looting can be viewed as taking 'reparations'). Longer term (organised programmes of reparations).
Success?	Workers in most countries in the West failed to rise up in revolution. Marxist revolution in Russia, China, and Cambodia led to mass murder and great suffering.	Critical theory has effectively permeated all the institutions in Western societies.	Some success in imposing affirmative action, positive discrimination, re-writing of educational curricula, sensitivity training, quotas. Ongoing demand for reparations. Some demand 'weighted voting' to transfer power to disadvantaged groups.

A BREAKDOWN IN THE LOGIC OF CIVILISATION

Critical theory aims to dissolve the universe of meaning by denying the existence of objective universal truth. But if we can't appeal to reason and logic there can be no reasoned debate. On what shared basis can civilisation continue? Such a society is vulnerable to tyranny. The subjective judgements of the loudest voices win. Those who resort to violence and intimidation are given a free pass. The great political philosopher Edmund Burke observed:

> Rage and frenzy will pull down more in half an hour than prudence, deliberation, and foresight can build up in a hundred years.[47]

---

47 Burke, E, *Reflections on the Revolution in France in a Letter Intended To Have Been Sent to a Gentleman in Paris,* 1790, Part VII, (3rd paragraph from end), http://www.ricorso.net/rx/library/authors/classic/Burke_E/Reflections/Reflect_07.htm (accessed 5 October, 2020).

Burke was writing in the context of the French Revolution. The dream of equality led straight to the 'reign of terror'.

Once universal truth has been denied, discrete groups claim their own 'truth' (aka experience of oppression) which others cannot comprehend. Reasoned debate is not an option. Violence is the only possible means to the end of perfect equality. That threatens the basic logic of civilisation.

However, Christians can affirm with confidence that there *is* such a thing as objective universal truth. And we *are* able to communicate with others, whatever their group identity, because *all* human beings have been given the priceless gift of reason by their Creator.

We will look at these foundational truths in Part Two. But before we get there, we need to ask: Why have so many Christians joined in the trashing of truth?

FURTHER RESOURCES

Baucham, V, Cultural Marxism, https://www.youtube.com/watch?v=GRMFBdDDTkI&t=2605s

Defining Social Justice, https://www.youtube.com/watch?v=YFNOP2IqwoY

Ethnic Gnosticism, https://www.youtube.com/watch?v=Ip3nV6S_fYU

Murray, D, *The Madness of Crowds,* (Bloomsbury Continuum, 2019)

Pluckrose, H and Lindsay, J, *Cynical Theories: How Activist Scholarship Made Everything about Race, Gender, and Identity – And Why This Harms Everybody,* (Pitchstone, 2020)

Pluckrose, H, 'The Evolution of Postmodern Thought', 22 June 2020, https://newdiscourses.com/2020/06/helen-pluckrose-evolution-postmodern-thought/ (accessed 28 July, 2020)

Scott, B, 'Black and White Are One: The Church as One New Race' *Desiring God,* 14 December, 2020, https://www.desiringgod.org/articles/black-and-white-are-one (accessed 4 January 2020)

Sidwell, M, *The Long March: How the left won the culture war and what to do about it,* (The New Culture Forum, 2020)

Tinker, M, *That Hideous Strength: A Deeper Look at How the West was Lost,* 2nd ed, (Evangelical Press, 2020)

Summary: Critical theory began in the universities, but as graduates entered all the various professions, the result at a popular level has been the rise of 'identity politics'. Many view the West as inherently evil (racist, patriarchal, capitalist). Some activists want to destroy the very structures which have created freedom and prosperity: 'Smash the patriarchy' (aka the family), 'Smash capitalism' (aka wealth creation and private property), 'Smash the police' (aka law and order), 'Smash down the statutes' (aka our collective memory and history). The essential unity of the human race, and the essential dignity of human identity, are both undermined by the current insistence on pushing people into groups defined by their diverse characteristics.

6 False Prophets: The Compromised Church

NO GUILT – NO SHAME

The beautiful and historic Southwark Cathedral in London has a Christian heritage stretching back over a thousand years. In 2019 it hosted a launch event for a new book entitled *Shameless: A Sexual Reformation*, written by Nadia Bolz-Weber, an ordained minister of the Evangelical Lutheran Church in America.

A key moment in *Shameless* is Bolz-Weber's description of a meeting with one of her parishioners. This woman tore out and burned the Bible pages referring to God's condemnation of homosexuality, and then burned all the other pages of the Bible, except the four Gospel accounts of Jesus.[1] She then felt deep peace, joy and freedom: an experience regarded by Bolz-Weber as true Christian liberty.

The message of *Shameless* is a perfect example of the 'no guilt, no shame' version of the Gospel which is so popular in our contemporary therapeutic culture. Self has replaced God as the source of 'truth' and meaning. It's often assumed that submission to external authority is unhealthy. We are expected to celebrate the release experienced by a troubled woman when she threw sections of the Bible onto a bonfire.

---

1   Bolz-Weber, N, *Shameless: A Sexual Reformation,* (Canterbury Press, 2019), pp. 71-2.

NATURALISM TO SPIRITUALISM

Many of the assumptions of the current worldview are still based on scientific naturalism: the insistence that there is no God, and nothing outside or beyond the natural world. But humans cannot live very long in a world without windows!

By the 1960s, the spiritual vacuum left by the rejection of Christianity was increasingly being filled with variations of 'New Age' thinking: astrology, crystals, occult practices, yoga, pseudo-hinduism, meditation and mindfulness (among others). Windows to the transcendent were thrown open again as some in the West experienced a 're-enchantment'. Some of the student unrest of the 1960s (described in chapter 4) had been fuelled by a (correct) sense that consumerism doesn't satisfy.

Karl Jung (1875-1961), the Swiss 'father of modern psychotherapy' was best known for introducing the concepts of extravert and introvert. Like his one-time associate Freud, Jung rejected biblical Christianity. Unlike Freud, Jung accepted the mystical and spiritual aspects of human life. From an early age he dabbled with occult activity. His psychotherapy placed self in the centre; with the understanding that self is spiritual, not just physical. Fulfilment can be found as the self is 'completed', and as the 'sub-conscious' is heeded. This all played into the sexual revolution of the 1960s: *If it feels good – do it!* and *Free Love will Save the World!*

'I'm spiritual – not religious' is heard variously from environmentalists, those adopting pagan ideas, those involved in occult activity and radical feminists who worship the 'goddess within'. That mantra channels Jung. He believed that individuals need to be 'liberated' by means of spiritual awareness, which plays well in sections of the liberal church.[2]

For many today, there is a spiritual aspect to life, but it's all about our inner self and how it relates to the 'divine' which infuses the whole earth. It is definitely *not* about the God of the Bible. Jungian ideas have contributed to the current revival of spiritualism, therapeutic psychology and popular mysticism.

---

2   Jones, P, *The Other Worldview,* (Kirkdale Press, 2015).

Biblical Worldview or Therapeutic Worldview?

Biblical Worldview	Therapeutic Worldview
GOD: the source of authority for all.	SELF: the source of authority for me.
The transcendent God defines identity, meaning, truth, morality: there is an external point of reference.	My desires and feelings are the authority for me.
God's moral law has been placed on the conscience of every human being made in God's image.	We each define our own identity and values.
God has revealed His truth in His Word, the Bible.	We don't need to submit to an external authority.

Rather than uniting to resist such challenges to biblical truth, many clergy and theologians cheered them on. Some embraced a syncretistic mix of 'Christianity' and new age type spirituality. Some have been upfront about their rejection of biblical authority, others more discreet. We should not be surprised. Throughout history the Word of God has been the target of fierce attack by the enemies of God.

GOD'S WORD ATTACKED

All Scripture is breathed out by God and profitable for teaching, for reproof, for correction, and for training in righteousness (2 Tim. 3:16, ESV).

The text of Scripture is inspired by God. It is reliable and without mistake.[3] Sometimes God's *direct* words were communicated to the human authors (there are over 400 instances of the phrase 'Thus says the Lord', eg. Exod. 4:22). At other times God providentially overruled the research of the human author (as when the doctor Luke wrote,

---

3   See the section on resources at the end of the book for more on the authority of Scripture.

'I too decided to write an orderly account for you', Luke 1:3). But it is all inspired (the phrase 'plenary' or 'full' inspiration' is often used). A mark of the true child of God is a love for God's Word.

> Oh, how I love your law! I meditate on it all day long. (Ps. 119: 97)

When one of my friends became a Christian, her enthusiasm and love for the Lord motivated her to memorise all 176 verses of Psalm 119 (an extended celebration of the Word of God). The nineteenth-century British politician, **William Wilberforce (1759-1833)**, made it his habit to recite the whole of Psalm 119 while walking home from Parliament.

Satan hates God, and makes God's Word the target of attack. Sometimes he uses atheistic regimes (such as those we looked at in chapter 2). Other times he uses the 'Christian' religious establishment to forbid access to Scripture. In October 1526 there was a great bonfire on the steps of St Paul's Cathedral, London. The clergy of the established church burned the first English New Testaments to have been printed on the newly developed printing presses of Europe. Sometimes the attack is less obvious. False teachers within the church profess to respect Scripture, but throw doubt on some of its teachings.

As long ago as the seventh century B.C., false prophets painted evil as good, and denied that there would be a judgement (Jer. 14:14-15). God's servant Jeremiah was ridiculed when he warned that 'freedom' from God's moral laws would lead down the blind alley of slavery to sin. His most violent opponents were religious leaders. They had led the race downwards into rebellion (Jer. 5:30), and denied that God would ever bring judgement:

> From the least to the greatest,
> all are greedy for gain;
> *prophets and priests alike,*
> *all practice deceit.*
> They dress the wound of my people as though it were not serious.
> 'Peace, Peace' they say,
> when there is no peace.
> Are they ashamed of their loathsome conduct?

No, they have no shame at all;
they do not even know how to blush. (Jer. 6:13-15)

Emboldened by the false assurances of the religious establishment, King Jehoiakim had the audacity to cut up and burn Jeremiah's prophecies as they were read out to him (Jer. 36).

Centuries later, Jesus warned His followers that:

... false christs and false prophets will arise and show great signs and wonders to deceive, if possible, even the elect. (Matt. 24:24, NKJV)

And the apostle Paul cautioned young believers at Corinth about:

... false apostles, deceitful workers, masquerading as apostles of Christ. And no wonder, for *Satan himself masquerades as an angel of light.* It is not surprising, then, if *his servants also masquerade as servants of righteousness.* Their end will be what their actions deserve. (2 Cor. 11:13-15)

We shouldn't, then, be surprised when the religious establishment compromises with challenges to the biblical worldview.

LIBERAL THEOLOGY: ACCOMMODATING NATURALISM

For many centuries, the doctrine of the inspiration of Scripture was not generally questioned by Christians. If you believe in an all-powerful transcendent God who created the universe by the Word of His power, you won't find it hard to believe that He has spoken in Scripture. But by the eighteenth century, some European philosophers, such as the French intellectual **Voltaire (1694-1778)**, ridiculed the idea of a transcendent God. They derided the notion that such a God would intervene in the natural world with miracles. They rejected the idea that God inspired Scripture, and scoffed at the 'primitive' ideas found in the Bible.

In the face of such challenges, the liberal project of the nineteenth century was the attempt to *reconcile* modern thinking and science with traditional religion. Many nineteenth-century theologians believed that the way to 'rescue' Christianity and make it plausible in the scientific age was to liberate it from 'primitive' and supernatural elements. The Christian faith had to be 'demythologised'.

German theologians led the charge. Rooted in the early nineteenth-century German Enlightenment (especially the writings of Immanuel Kant) such theologians elevated human reason to assess the various parts of Scripture. Belief in the inerrancy and infallibility of Scripture was abandoned. The Bible was analysed using the same 'critical' methods as would be used for any other ancient text. German theological departments became the pioneers of 'Higher Criticism'. They were regarded as the 'best' places in the world to study theology. Students from elsewhere in Europe, as well as America, went there to study, and were exposed to this way of thinking.

In parallel with the move towards a *naturalistic* worldview (as described in chapter 1), liberal theologians separated religion from the realm of historical facts. Religion was viewed as a matter of experience.[4] It became less important to insist that Jesus physically rose from the tomb – instead the 'spiritual reality' of new life was said to motivate the early disciples. Accounts such as the Virgin Birth, the historicity of the miracles, the literal return of Christ and the resurrection of the body were all questioned. Christ's authentic teaching was said to have been 'overlaid' by later theological interpretation (especially by Paul). There was an ongoing attempt to 'get back to' the 'real' Jesus.

Friedrich Schleiermacher (1768-1834), the 'father of liberal theology', wanted to 'rescue' Christianity by making it plausible in the modern age. He rejected the doctrines of divine punishment, the eternal Deity of Christ, and substitutionary atonement. In *On Religion: Speeches to Its Cultured Despisers* (1799), he set out to defend Christianity's credibility in university circles. He made *human experience* (rather than objective, divine, authoritative revelation) the foundation of Christianity. In 1810, he founded the theological

---

4   A non-doctrinal form of Pietism, led by such as Philip Wilhelm Otterbein (1727-1813), had prepared the ground for German liberalism. Schleiermacher and Kant were both brought up in the Pietist tradition where doctrine was derogated and 'experience' celebrated.

faculty at the University of Berlin. The syllabus was based on his conviction that Christian experience was the source of the New Testament writings and doctrine (rather than the other way round). *The Christian Faith,* published in 1821-2, taught that the *experience of total dependence on God* lay at the heart of true Christianity. Schleiermacher taught generations of ministers to deny the following truths (among others):

- Creation
- The existence of angels
- The existence of the devil
- The fall into sin
- God's personal involvement in the world
- The Deity of Christ
- The Resurrection and Ascension of Christ
- Divine wrath at sin
- Final judgement
- The person of the Holy Spirit

Julius Wellhausen (1844-1918), another German theologian, was one of the originators of the 'documentary hypothesis' (the idea that several authors contributed to the first five books of the Bible at different periods).[5] His *Prolegomena to the History of Israel* (1878) argued that Christianity was a set of religious views arising from human reason, rather than being based on divine revelation. The Bible was only a collection of human documents, not the Word of God. The account of Adam and Eve, for instance, was regarded as an ancient myth. Using a study of comparative religions, Wellhausen saw the Old Testament writings as the product of a long evolutionary process, constructed by numerous human authors and editors. Increasingly, scholars regarded the ideas within the Bible as evolving from 'primitive' (anything concerning wrath and judgement) to more enlightened (the doctrines of love and grace). The idea that the Bible

---

5   In 1678, a Catholic priest named Richard Simon first suggested that the Pentateuch had at least two authors, who used the names Jehovah and Elohim for God in the different sections they wrote.

is the authoritative revelation of God, speaking with a single voice (albeit via many human authors) became less and less credible.

Jean Réville (1854-1908), a self-identified Protestant Liberal, argued that liberalism was essentially non-doctrinal, belief in the Trinity was no longer needed, and the Bible was a 'source' document, but not to be regarded as authoritative.[6] All the fundamental beliefs of Christianity, including the Deity of Christ were called into doubt.

During the nineteenth century, many protestant churches abandoned belief in the Trinity, and became Unitarian. There was then a further slide into an abandonment of any belief in a transcendent Deity. By the twentieth century many Unitarians were committed humanists. More than half of the signatories of the first *Humanist Manifesto* (1933) were religious leaders, mainly Unitarian ministers. That manifesto affirmed:

> Religious humanists regard the universe as self-existing and not created. Humanism asserts that the nature of the universe depicted by modern science makes unacceptable any supernatural or cosmic guarantees of human values.[7]

The themes that remained were the universal Fatherhood of God, the brotherhood of man, and the moral example of Jesus. Belief in the afterlife was generally replaced with the idea that social justice should be achieved here on earth. The 'Social Gospel', as preached by **Walter Rauschenbusch (1861-1918)**, took centre stage.[8]

'SOME LITTLE RAG OF FAITH'

Liberal theology destroyed confidence in the Bible as the Word of God. As a case study, let's see how it affected the Free Church of

---

6   Réville, J, *Le Protestantisme libéral, ses origines, sa nature, sa mission*, 1903.

7   *The first Humanist Manifesto* (1933), Affirmations 1 and 5, https://americanhumanist.org/what-is-humanism/manifesto1/ (accessed 11 January 2021).

8   Other theological liberals included F C Baur, George W F Hegel, Albrecht Ritschl, Adolph von Harnack, Harry Emerson Fosdick and Paul Tillich.

Scotland.[9] This denomination had been formed in 1843 by around 500 ministers who separated from the Church of Scotland on account of state interference in the church. This group was:

> ... a movement born out of a revival of evangelical faith ... marked by prayerfulness, by outreach and missionary zeal, both at home and abroad. Its leaders were revered across the Protestant world. Some spoke of the denomination as the most apostolic church in the world.[10]

By the 1880s and 1890s, critical methods had been introduced into ministerial training. **Marcus Dods (1834-1909)**, for example, taught that there were inaccuracies in the Old Testament that undermined the notion of the plenary inspiration of Scripture.[11] **George Adam Smith (1856-1942)**, a professor at the Free Church College in Glasgow, taught that the early chapters of Genesis were not historical, but composed from older Babylonian accounts. They, and others, presented themselves as orthodox evangelicals motivated with a passion to reach the modern world for Christ. They emphasised the need for a personal experience of Christ and mocked the old 'narrow' brand of Christianity. Allegiance to the authority of Scripture was viewed as a 'barrier' which inhibited a living experience of Christ. Modern thinking people couldn't possibly believe in Noah's flood, or the account of Jonah being swallowed by a great fish. It was not 'plausible' to think that Moses wrote the first five books of the Bible. The problem was that Jesus Christ affirmed belief in all this. They then had to concede that not all of Christ's words could be relied on. One

---

9   It's important to note that those who retain this same name today do not represent the legacy of the liberal wing. They are faithful to Scripture.

10 Murray, I H, 'How Scotland Lost Its Hold of the Bible', address given in 2015, and published in MacArthur, J, ed, *The Inerrant Word,* (Crossway, 2016), https://banneroftruth.org/uk/resources/articles/2015/scotland-lost-hold-bible/ (accessed 18 August, 2020).

11 Scripture is 'God-breathed', in that God supernaturally guided the authors of the Bible to write what He wanted to communicate. 'Plenary' means 'complete or full'; hence all parts of the Bible are equally authoritative.

had to strip away the unreliable additions in order to get back to the 'historical' Jesus. By the end of his ministry, Dods privately admitted:

> The churches won't know themselves fifty years hence. It is to be hoped *some little rag of faith* may be left when all's done.[12]

In 1900 Professor George Adam Smith preached at the opening of a massive new church building with an auditorium for 1,000 and many adjoining rooms. Within fifty years it was deserted and closed. Liberal theology had destroyed the church from within:

> First the Word of God was lost, the light was lost, until only an empty monument remained.[13]

'THE NEW THEOLOGY CAN DO NO GOOD AT ALL'

That was one Christian denomination in one small country. But theological liberalism was pervading churches in Europe, America, and beyond. Then, as missionaries were sent out all over the world, they took unbelief with them.

Many warned of the dangers of liberal theology. One of its strongest critics was the great English Baptist preacher **Charles Haddon Spurgeon (1834-1892)**. By the age of twenty-two he was the most popular preacher of his day. Aged twenty-three he preached to more than 23,500 people at The Crystal Palace in London. By the time of his death, he had probably preached to more than ten million people. His church, the Metropolitan Tabernacle in London, was the biggest church in the world at the time. But the later part of his ministry was overshadowed by the increasing denial of evangelical belief within his own Baptist denomination. He wrote in his church magazine, *The Sword and Trowel:*

> Believers in Christ's atonement are now in declared union with those who make light of it; believers in Holy Scripture are in confederacy with those who deny plenary inspiration; those who

---

12   Murray, I H, 'How Scotland Lost Its Hold of the Bible', emphasis mine.
13   Ibid.

hold evangelical doctrine are in open alliance with those who call the fall a fable, who deny the personality of the Holy Ghost, who call justification by faith immoral, and hold that there is another probation after death ... Yes, we have before us the wretched spectacle of professedly orthodox Christians publicly avowing their union with those who deny the faith, and scarcely concealing their contempt for those who cannot be guilty of such disloyalty to Christ.[14]

Spurgeon resigned from the Baptist Union in protest at the refusal of denominational leaders to discipline those who denied fundamental truths.[15] He stood almost alone. He warned:

Assuredly the New Theology can do no good at all ... If it were preached for a thousand years by the most earnest men ... it would never renew a soul, or overcome pride in a single human heart.[16]

Spurgeon's memory was derided by the elite in the mainstream denominations for decades.

Spurgeon's son Thomas was one of those who contributed to a careful, thorough and robust defence of orthodox Christian doctrine produced between 1910 and 1915 in America. Ninety essays, written by sixty-four authors, were published. One essay, for example, was written by Benjamin B Warfield on 'The Deity of Christ'. A quarter of a million copies of *The Fundamentals* were sent, free of charge, to Protestant church leaders, missionaries and others.

As liberal theology continued to pervade Bible seminaries and theological institutions in many nations, those ministers and churches who continued to hold to the authority of Scripture increasingly became labelled 'fundamentalists' (a name taken from that series of essays). This movement tended to become associated with

---

14   Murray, I H, *The Forgotten Spurgeon,* (Banner of Truth Trust, 1966), p. 144.

15   Ibid., pp. 149-150.

16   Spurgeon, C H, *The 'Down Grade' Controversy,* (Pasadena, Texas: Pilgrim Publications, 2009), p. 2. ISBN 1561862118.

dispensational theology, legalism, and withdrawal from the public square.

ANOTHER GOSPEL

The clearest voice to be raised against theological liberalism came from the American theologian, **J. Gresham Machen (1881-1937)**. In 1923 he wrote *Christianity and Liberalism,* which has been described as 'one of the most important books of all times.'[17]

Nearly twenty years earlier Machen had travelled over to Germany to study theology under William Hermann, one of the leading theologians of the day. Initially, Machen was enthusiastic about the devotion and warmth of Hermann and other liberal teachers. Eventually he came to believe that their teachings were directly contradictory to biblical truth. If you remove the supernatural from Scripture, you destroy the central message of Christianity. In *Christianity and Liberalism,* Machen showed how liberals wrap up worldly thinking in Christian language. Liberalism is not to be regarded as one branch of Christianity. It is a false religion. God's Word is the supreme authority in Christianity, but liberals elevate human experience to be authoritative:

> It is no wonder, then, that liberalism is totally different from Christianity, for the foundation is different. Christianity is *founded upon the Bible.* It bases upon the Bible both its thinking and its life. Liberalism on the other hand is *founded upon the shifting emotions of sinful men.*[18]

Biblical Christianity and naturalism are incompatible. If you strip the supernatural out of the Christian faith, you end up with another religion:

---

17 Murray, I H, 'How Scotland Lost Its Hold of the Bible'.

18 Machen, G, *Christianity and Liberalism,* (Eerdmans, 2009), p. 67, emphasis mine.

The conception of Jesus as a supernatural Person runs all through the New Testament.[19]

At the very centre of Christianity are the words, 'Ye must be born again.' These words are despised today. They involve supernaturalism, and the modern man is opposed to supernaturalism in the experience of the individual as much as in the realm of history. A cardinal doctrine of modern liberalism is that the world's evil may be overcome by the world's good; no help is thought to be needed from outside the world.[20]

The naturalistic worldview denies the 'transcendent' (anything beyond the realm of the natural and physical). Any presentations of 'Christianity' that compromise with naturalism pull God down to the human level. They reduce God to being a 'person', greater and more glorious than us, but just a person. Machen argued that liberalism has a tendency to pantheism, which sees all of life somehow as part of God. Such liberalism denies the transcendence of God; the biblical teaching that between the creature and the Creator a great gulf is fixed.[21] Liberalism believes that people are basically good. Machen believed that at the 'root of the modern liberal movement is the loss of the consciousness of sin.'[22] He concluded:

The greatest menace to the Christian Church today comes *not from the enemies outside, but from the enemies within;* it comes from the presence within the Church of a type of faith and practice that is anti-Christian to the core.[23]

Machen was a leader in the formation of Westminster Theological Seminary in 1929. He was expelled from the American northern Presbyterian church in 1936 for resisting the invasion of liberalism,

---

19 Ibid., p. 82.

20 Ibid., p. 115.

21 Ibid., p. 54.

22 Ibid., p. 55.

23 Ibid., p. 135, emphasis mine.

and became the first Moderator of what became the Orthodox Presbyterian Church. At the time of his death in 1937, theological liberalism was still dominant in universities and seminaries around the world.

RESCUING CHRISTIANITY OR DESTROYING IT?

Every time the gospel is diluted in order to make it appealing, it loses its power.[24] When the pioneers of liberal theology set out to 'rescue' Christianity from those who despised it, they watered it down so that it could be safely ignored:

> ... the effect of the liberal project was the opposite of its intention. Far from making Christianity more acceptable to the 'educated, intelligent and cultured', it provided them with excuses to ignore its claims. Without doubting the sincerity of the liberal theologians, it is clear that their project was disastrous for the church.[25]

American theologian **Richard Niebuhr (1894-1962)** observed that once liberalism had taken hold in the church you were left with a pitiful 'gospel' in which:

> A God without wrath brought men without sin into a kingdom without judgement through the ministrations of a Christ without a cross.[26]

One church historian argues that the real reason people in England stopped going to church was the prevailing unbelief of the clergy. Why bother going to church if the people running it don't believe in

---

24 Because, as Machen argued, it is then no gospel at all. The real gospel can't have its power diluted.

25 Reeves, C, 'Bringing Home the Bacon: The interaction of Science and Scripture Today', in *Theistic Evolution: A Scientific, Philosophical, and Theological Critique,* eds Meyer, S C et al, (Crossway, 2017), p. 723.

26 Niebuhr, R H, *The Kingdom of God in America,* (Wesleyan, 1988), p. 193.

what they are doing? If the clergy don't believe in hell and judgement, there's nothing to fear after death, and no need to seek salvation.[27]

ADJUSTING TO THE THERAPEUTIC CULTURE

Christian theology all too often adjusts in order to fall into step with the surrounding culture.

Nineteenth-century theological liberalism mirrored the *naturalistic worldview* that posed such a challenge to the Christian faith at that time. The methods of 'higher criticism' set *human reason over the authority of Scripture.* Doctrines concerning the miracles, the resurrection, and the Virgin Birth were challenged because they 'seemed incredible' within a naturalistic worldview.

By the twentieth century, confidence in human reason, as promoted by the naturalistic worldview, was collapsing. The optimistic liberal expectation that humans, (using reason and science), would progress towards a better future was punctured by the First World War. Nineteenth-century theological liberalism began to fall out of fashion too.[28]

Karl Barth (1886-1968), Emil Brunner (1889–1966), and others re-emphasised the transcendence of God and the sinfulness of humankind. While this movement, (sometimes referred to as 'neo-orthodoxy'), was a necessary corrective to liberal theology, it did not return to the conviction that all Scripture is inspired, and therefore without mistake. The new emphasis on the transcendent led Barth, for example, to teach that Scripture 'becomes inspired' when the Holy Spirit applies it to the believer. That move – placing authority at least partly in the experience of the individual – played perfectly into the culture of the mid-twentieth century. The collapse of confidence in universal truth had contributed to the idea that the only thing any

---

27 Watts, M, 'Why did the English stop going to Church?' Friends of Dr Williams' Library Forty-Ninth Lecture (London: Dr Williams' Trust, 1995).

28 Much of it was also discredited academically. For example, the scholarship of J B Lightfoot (1828-1889), Bishop of Durham, undermined the claims of the Tübingen School relating to the dating of the New Testament books.

individual could do is seek their own authentic experience. There was no point in looking for external objective reality.

Once you deny that there is a God whose character and decree defines what is right, then you deny universally valid moral laws. The remaining moral absolute is to be faithful to yourself, to find your own 'authentic' identity. This 'expressive individualism' has seeped into many sections of the church. If the Bible contradicts what 'I sincerely and deeply feel', all-too-often feelings win.

Theological liberals in the past placed *human reason* above Scripture. Their descendants now place *human experience* above Scripture. In this culture of 'limitless self-regard',[29] failure to celebrate someone's lifestyle, or refusal to endorse their claims about identity, are viewed as equally hateful. Affirmations of absolute moral truth are viewed as harsh and intolerant. Calls to repentance and a holy life are seen as abusive. Evangelism is softened. Preaching hell and judgement is almost unknown. The 'Gospel' becomes a message of 'finding fulfilment', achieving freedom from anxiety, or discovering the authentic meaning of life. The significance of God is that He can bring meaning and hope to me. Self, not God takes centre stage.

Theological controversy no longer focuses so much on issues such as denying the supernatural. *Ethical issues are in the spotlight.* By the twenty-first century, significant numbers of senior clergy endorsed same-sex partnerships, celebrated same-sex marriages, affirmed gender transition, accepted abortion, and so on. The Ten Commandments were 'out'. Every individual can interpret Scripture in line with their own experience. *Human experience is placed over the authority of Scripture.* To condemn adultery or divorce or abortion or homosexual practice seems implausible and abusive within a postmodern, therapeutic worldview.[30]

---

29   Ashenden, G, 'Redefining hate: from diabolical anti-love to any criticism of the fragile self', Guest post on Archbishop Cranmer website, 14 July 2017, see http://archbishopcranmer.com/redefining-hate-diabolical-anti-love-criticism-self/ (accessed 21 September 2017).

30   Hence the moves to ban so-called 'conversion therapy'. The Christian Institute, 'Banning conversion therapy or banning the Gospel?' https://

A 'bridge' between the older liberal project and the new therapeutic liberalism was provided by **John A T Robinson (1919-1983)**. Robinson was both Divinity Lecturer at Cambridge University and Bishop of Woolwich. His book *Honest to God* was published in 1963 to international media acclaim. Robinson carried forward and developed the 'older' liberal rejection of the idea of a transcendent 'God out there'. Having reduced God to the 'God' within, Robinson called for *situational ethics*. Each individual had to decide their own morality. 'Moral absolutes' were a shackle. Universal commands (such as the Ten Commandments) seemed dangerously authoritarian in an age influenced by the new discipline of psychotherapy.

The now-retired American Episcopal bishop, **John Shelby Spong (b. 1931)** recalls his excitement at reading *Honest to God* in 1963:

> ... when I read it—I couldn't stop. I read it three times! My theology was never the same. I had to wrestle with how I could take the literalism I had picked up in Sunday school and put it into these new categories.[31]

Spong became a leading voice in the Progressive Christian movement, which champions a diversity and inclusivity that effectively means celebration of any and every lifestyle.[32]

At a popular level, each time you hear someone say:

> *'My* God would never condemn people to an eternal hell!'

or

> *'My* God would never discriminate against women/gay people!'

---

www.christian.org.uk/wp-content/uploads/Banningconversiontherapy orbanningtheGospel.pdf (accessed September 2021).

31 Interview with John Shelby Spong, Read the Spirit, June 23, 2013, https://readthespirit.com/explore/the-retired-bishop-john-shelby-spong-interview-on-one-of-the-worlds-most-loved-and-feared-books-the-bibles-gospel-of-john/ (accessed 20 August, 2020).

32 https://progressivechristianity.org/the-8-points/ (accessed 20 August, 2020).

That is an example of placing human experience in judgement over Scripture. The Bible is interpreted in such a way as to justify our own lifestyle. We each make up our own God to suit ourselves. When you see churches advertising themselves as 'inclusive', you will probably find that there is such a strong emphasis on making everyone feel welcome, that all lifestyles are accepted. If 'sin' is talked about at all, it will be limited to 'global' or structural evils such as sexism, homophobia, or racism.

What church leaders don't often realise however, is that they are being used as 'useful idiots' by activists. In chapter 5 we mentioned *After the Ball* (1989), a handbook on how to get mainstream America onboard with gay equality. Marshall Kirk and Hunter Madsen realised that church leaders could be intimidated by claims supposedly based on 'science and public opinion'. This tactic had been successfully used to frighten many churches into acceptance of abortion and divorce,[33] so they advised a strategy of 'publicizing support by moderate churches ... [and] raising serious theological objections to conservative biblical teachings.'[34] They advocated smearing of 'homohating' conservative churches with claims of the 'hatred underlying antigay doctrines'.[35] The moral authority of churches could be undermined if they were ceaselessly portrayed as 'antiquated backwaters, badly out of step with the times and with the latest findings of psychology.'[36] This proved stunningly successful! Many church leaders have been so scared at the prospect of being called 'bigoted' that they have been willing to jettison as much Scripture as it takes to win acceptance with wider society.

Other public relations advice given by Madsen and Hunter was to make gays look good by identifying heroic historical figures as closet homosexuals, but to make churches look bad by labelling them

---

33   Kirk, M, Madsen, H, *After the Ball: How America will Conquer its Fear and Hatred of Gays in the 90s,* (Doubleday, 1989), p. 179.

34   Ibid., p. 179.

35   Ibid., p. 179.

36   Ibid., p. 179.

as having been guilty of historic discrimination and hatred.[37] Once again, many church leaders jumped into buying this narrative. They obediently repeated the lies, effectively doing the work of the activists for them. Game, set and match to Kirk and Madsen and their allies!

What happened with regard to the 'gay' issue is now happening all over again with regard to Social Justice (referring, here, to the claims based on critical theory).[38] While some Christian leaders, including some evangelicals, affirm the demands put forward by those claiming to speak for victim minorities, there are non-Christians such as Douglas Murray, James Lindsay, Helen Pluckrose and Peter Boghassian who warn: 'Don't be fooled! Don't act as "useful idiots"!' Once critical theory invades any organisation, that organisation cannot stand.[39]

'THE GREAT EVANGELICAL DISASTER'

Francis Schaeffer (1912-1984) was one of the first evangelicals to engage thoughtfully with the 1960s' 'counterculture'. Originally from America, in 1955 he and his wife Edith founded 'L'Abri' ('The Shelter') in the Swiss mountain village of Huemoz. I vividly remember hearing Schaeffer preach in the beautiful mountainside chapel at L'Abri during the 1970s. L'Abri was an open house for guests to come and participate in conversations about religion, philosophy, art and culture. It was visited by many students who had imbibed the thinking of existentialist writers such as **Albert Camus (1913-1960)** and **Jean-Paul Sartre (1905-1980)**. The Schaeffers observed, with grief, the impact of such ideas in the lives of youngsters who believed that humans are

---

37 Ibid., pp. 183, 189.

38 Allen, S D, *Why Social Justice is not Biblical Justice,* (Credo, 2020); Harris, J, *Social Justice Goes to Church: The New Left in Modern American Evangelicalism,* (Ambassador International, 2020). As we noted in the Introduction, when Social Justice is capitalised, it denotes an ideology that includes concepts such as 'systemic' injustice. The biblical worldview is the foundation for true justice (chapter 7).

39 Sovereign Nations, *The Trojan Horse,* episode 3, 'Critical Race Theory', https://sovereignnations.com/2019/10/11/trojan-horse-ep3-critical-race-theory/ (accessed 5 October, 2020) and see further resources at the end of the book.

the mere product of time and chance in a materialistic world. These young people had no solid basis for distinctions between right and wrong, and no grounds for any belief in meaning or significance. Their self-destructive moral confusion and alienation from society pushed Francis Schaeffer into a deep examination of modern culture. *The God Who is There* (1968), *Escape from Reason* (1968) and *He is There and He Is Not Silent* (1972), were among his many books.

Schaeffer's last book was *The Great Evangelical Disaster* (1984). The 'evangelical disaster', Schaeffer argued, is accommodation to the 'spirit of the age', the surrender to the enjoyment of personal peace and affluence. Many Christians aren't up to the challenge of paying the price for costly discipleship.

The title was drawn from an article published in a special edition of *Time* magazine, which argued that the 'idea characterising our age' is the question for freedom in an absolute sense: *freedom from any limits and all constraints.* The article concluded that 'when people or ideas are unfettered, they are freed but not yet free'. That is because freedom without constraints leads to chaos. Where there is 'form' without a balance of freedom you get authoritarianism, even totalitarianism. But freedom without any balance of 'form' leads to anarchy. The biblical worldview provides the balance between the two:

• God's moral law provides form.
• Belief that every human is made in God's image protects freedom.

Schaeffer argued that many evangelicals had failed to defend this biblical worldview. They had capitulated to the spirit of the age.

Professor David F Wells (b. 1939) has written a succession of books which analyse the ways in which evangelicals have often been shaped by the surrounding culture.[40] He characterises much current Christianity as 'filling out my story, being propelled on my journey'.[41] Faith becomes a private, personal, individual matter. That's why some

---

40   Wells, D, *No Place for Truth* (1993), *God in the Wasteland* (1994), *Losing Our Virtue* (1998), *Above All Earthly Pow'rs* (2005), *The Courage to Be Protestant* (2008). All explored the effects of post-modernism, materialism and relativism on Christianity.

41   Wells, D, *The Courage to be Protestant,* (IVP, 2008), p. 87.

worship services consist solely of songs about how Jesus loves *me*. Our experience in the modern world inclines us to think of God solely as the 'inside' God and to lose sight of Him as the 'outside' God.[42] We are encouraged to think of God mainly as relating to me and providing for my needs, but downplay the biblical truths concerning His holiness, transcendence, justice and sovereignty. Sin is rarely presented in relation to God (how we have offended our Creator). More often, we focus on our own experience of anxiety or pain or failure. This leads to a spirituality that is: *'... deeply subjective, non-moral in its understanding, highly individualistic, completely relativistic, and insistently therapeutic.'*[43]

EMERGING CHURCH – PROGRESSIVE CHURCH

By the end of the twentieth century, a new strand of protest had arisen within evangelicalism itself, reacting against what was viewed as traditional orthodoxy with its linear thought and rigid creeds and statements of faith, as well as against megachurches, denominations and power bases of church life. One section of the movement became known as 'emerging' or 'emergent' church.[44] Embracing of diversity, the common factor was a rejection of 'dogmatism'. Formal statements of faith and authoritative preaching were replaced with assurances of 'inclusivity': a religious expression of postmodernism.

Church leader **Brian McLaren (b. 1956)** effectively rejects the law of non-contradiction, and accepts that if 'experience' dictates, we can believe two contradictory things at once. He rejects theology based on modernist thought which presents 'orthodoxy' as 'nailed down, freeze-dried, and shrink-wrapped forever.'[45] Consider the subtitle of his book *A Generous Orthodoxy* (2004). It nearly fills the front cover and reads:

---

42   Ibid., p. 120.

43   Ibid., p. 123.

44   'An Emerging Church Primer', *9 Marks,* https://www.9marks.org/article/emerging-church-primer/ (accessed 20 August, 2020).

45   McLaren, B D, *A Generous Orthodoxy,* (Zondervan, 2004), p. 286.

> Why I am a missional evangelical post/protestant liberal/
> conservative mystical/poetic biblical charismatic/contemplative
> fundamentalist/calvinist anabaptist/anglican methodist catholic
> green incarnational depressed-yet-hopeful emergent unfinished
> Christian.[46]

Liberal theologians of the nineteenth century wanted to make
Christianity more acceptable to a scientific age. Those involved in the
'emerging' (or 'emergent') church wanted to make it more acceptable to
a postmodern age. The movement has now morphed into 'progressive'
church. Today many long for authenticity, so Christ is presented in a
personal way rather than a traditional structured setting.

Some of the movement's criticisms of modern evangelicalism (for
example, disillusionment with aspects of the megachurch movement
or evangelical 'celebrity' culture) were, and are, well-founded. And
it is true that some evangelical theology has been badly infected
with 'modernist' presuppositions.[47] But whenever we place human
experience in judgement over Scripture, we place self over God. That's
a denial of authentic biblical Christianity. Dan Doriani comments:

> [today many] believe in an experience of Jesus 'not intrinsically tied
> to any specific doctrinal formulation.' They believe 'doctrine and
> morality are finally unimportant as long as believers experience
> warm feelings about Jesus and engage in ministry to the world.'
> But *if experience is the key, then revelation is found outside Scripture*
> ... [48]

Alisa Childers was a committed Bible-believing evangelical Christian,
active in her church, and a successful Christian singer. She joined a
progressive church, attracted by the way it seemed to offer authenticity

---

46 Ibid.

47 Carter, C A, *Interpreting Scripture with the Great Tradition: Recovering the
    Genius of Premodern Exegesis,* (Baker Academic, 2018).

48 Doriani, D, 'Friendly Liberalism: A Threat in every Age', *The Gospel
    Coalition,* 7 July, 2017, http://resources.thegospelcoalition.org/library/
    friendly-theological-liberalism-a-threat-in-every-age (accessed 20 August,
    2020), emphasis mine.

and relevance to real life. But the studies she attended 'challenged my beliefs, rocked my faith and shook me to the core'.[49] Her faith had been deconstructed. She went back to the foundations, and set out to study the claims of the progressives against Scripture. She came to believe that 'the gospel can only be fully known if the Bible *actually is* the inerrant and inspired Word of God'.[50] She now believes that:

> ... progressive Christianity offers me nothing of value. It gives me no hope for the afterlife and no joy in this one. It offers a hundred denials with nothing concrete to affirm.[51]

Similarly, in 2021 a twenty-six-year-old Canadian wrote to author Rod Dreher:

> ... there is a tremendous lack of meaning and purpose with most young people ... We are living in a society that promotes people to do whatever makes them happy, even if the consequences are dire.[52]

This young man tried attending many churches, but found each of them bankrupt of moral certainty or firm convictions:

> Churches are crumbling; unable to offer a vision and path for those seeking holiness. There are plenty of us, young people, who are disillusioned with the way that society is going. I truly believe it's why so many people my age are suffering from anxiety, depression and other mental health problems. Drug usage, alcohol abuse and a hookup culture are blankets of comfort for people who have no meaning or purpose in life anymore ... And churches aren't there

---

49 Childers, A, *Another Gospel? A Lifelong Christian Seeks Truth in Response to Progressive Christianity,* (Tyndale Momentum, 2020), p. xi.

50 Ibid., p. 233.

51 Ibid., p. 238.

52 Dreher, R, 'Letter From A Struggling Young Man', *The American Conservative,* 5 January, 2021, https://www.theamericanconservative.com/dreher/benedict-option-letter-from-struggling-young-man-houellebecq/ (accessed 11 January, 2021).

to pick up the slack. It's deeply distressing ... Christianity in the West has lost its moral foundation.[53]

Sadly, he found no strong confidence in biblical truth in the evangelical churches he visited, and is looking to see whether Orthodoxy will offer a more robust moral foundation.

'SOCIAL JUSTICE GOES TO CHURCH'

Many church leaders, including some evangelicals, have embraced the cause of Social Justice. Like the liberal theologians of the nineteenth century, and the 'emerging' and 'progressive' church leaders of the twentieth century, they are well-intentioned. Of course we should pray for, and work for, biblical justice. But is Social Justice biblical justice?

The Bible teaches that 'in Adam *all* die' (1 Cor. 15:22). Proponents of Social Justice would have us believe that it is those *with privilege* who are guilty. The biblical teaching is that we are all to submit to God's moral law. Jesus calls us all to repent, to be 'born again'. Today we are expected to renounce our privilege. The real Gospel deals with real sin, real repentance, and real forgiveness. It doesn't divide us into competing groups. It unites us in Christ.[54]

In reality, the Social Justice theories promoted, for example, in many schools, universities and workplaces are often *opposed to Christianity*. In chapter 5 we mentioned William Clarke, a student who was told that those who identify as Christian are 'intrinsically privileged and oppressive', which is defined as 'malicious or unjust' and 'wrong'. Any questioning of this was an expression of 'unjust privilege expressed as denial'. When William raised objections, he was suspended from school.[55]

---

53 Ibid.

54 Harris, J, *Social Justice Goes to Church: The New Left in American Evangelicalism,* (Ambassador International, 2020).

55 Interview with Mrs Clarke, December 28, 2020, https://profam.us2. list-manage.com/track/click?u=71b5ff0a93830214b96a42bf6&id=29 1cd583fe&e=c02fad7011 (accessed 30 December, 2020).

WHAT ABOUT LOVE?

Christian theologians and ministers who adjust the biblical message to suit the times sometimes begin with good intentions. They want to make Christianity accessible and acceptable to people in their own day. Today, several generations of Christians have absorbed therapeutic assumptions. They assume that it's compassionate to affirm everyone's claims about orientation or identity. Preaching the need for repentance is regarded as unloving, even abusive.[56] Christians who 'still' believe in 'outdated' concepts such as creation, judgement, man-woman marriage, and hell are denounced.

We need to remember that we can respect people as people, without having to affirm their lifestyles, or their claims about their identity. We must always oppose bullying or cruelty. But there are many testimonies of people who have converted to Christ who look back with gratitude at those who graciously pointed them to biblical truth.[57]

How should we regard Christian leaders who deny the truth of Scripture? However warm their professions of love to God, they are guilty of deceit:

> Therefore anyone who sets aside one of the least of these commands and teaches others accordingly will be called least in the kingdom of heaven, but whoever practises and teaches these commands will be called great in the kingdom of heaven. (Matt. 5:19)

THE MOST SUICIDAL ACT THAT A CHURCH CAN COMMIT

When the Free Church of Scotland began entrusting the training of their ministers to those who denied the inerrancy of Scripture, Charles

---

56   For example, Rev Melvin Tinker, was 'disinvited' to a preaching engagement at Derby Cathedral in England due to his conservative biblical convictions, https://www.christian.org.uk/news/evangelical-banned-by-derby-cathedral-receives-widespread-support/ (accessed 21 August, 2020).

57   For example, Butterfield, R, *Secret Thoughts of an Unlikely Convert,* (Crown and Covenant, 2012); and Cook, B, *A Change of Affection: A Gay Man's Incredible Story of Redemption,* (Nelson Books, 2019).

Spurgeon warned that 'This is the most suicidal act that a church can commit'.[58] History proved him right. Gresham Machen observed in 1935:

> ... many theological seminaries today are nurseries of unbelief; and because they are nurseries of unbelief the churches that they serve have become unbelieving churches too. As go the theological seminaries, so goes the church. That is certainly true in the long run. Look out upon the condition of the Church throughout the world today, and you will see that it is true.[59]

Conclusion to Part I: Living in the Waste Land

The Waste Land (1922) is one of the most famous English poems of the twentieth century.[60] It conveys the despair of a world bereft of Christian certainty. Here are some extracts:

> 'Do
> You know nothing? Do you see nothing? Do you remember
>
> Nothing?'
> ...

---

58 Spurgeon, C H, *Sword and Trowel,* 1889. Commenting on the Free Church of Scotland appointment of two professors to train their ministers, who were promoting the 'new' theology, quoted in Murray, I, https://banneroftruth. org/uk/resources/articles/2015/scotland-lost-hold-bible/#note-23 (accessed 17 August, 2020). As noted above, we need to distinguish this 1843-1900 Free Church of Scotland from the post-1900 denomination that still exists and is faithful to Scripture.

59 Machen, G, *Christianity and the Modern World,* pp. 31-2 (adobe digital edition), Talks given in 1935, published in 1965.

60 The author, Thomas Stearns Eliot (1888-1965), was born in St. Louis, Missouri. He later settled in England, converted to Anglicanism, and became a writer, publisher and Nobel prize-winner. *The Waste Land* was written before Eliot's conversion, and he denied that it was intended to communicate the disillusionment of his generation. However, its structure, language and content convey an unmistakeable loss of confidence, vision and hope.

'What shall we do tomorrow?
What shall we ever do?'

'On Margate Sands.
I can connect
Nothing with nothing.
The broken fingernails of dirty hands.
My people humble people who expect
Nothing.'

What is that sound high in the air
Murmur of maternal lamentation
Who are those hooded hordes swarming
Over endless plains, stumbling in cracked earth
Ringed by the flat horizon only
What is the city over the mountains
Cracks and reforms and bursts in the violet air
Falling towers
Jerusalem Athens Alexandria
Vienna London
Unreal

There is the empty chapel, only the wind's home.
It has no windows, and the door swings,
Dry bones can harm no one.

I sat upon the shore
Fishing, with the arid plain behind me
Shall I at least set my lands in order?
London Bridge is falling down falling down falling down
...

These fragments I have shored against my ruins ... [61]

---

61   Eliot, T S, *The Waste Land,* 1922, https://www.poetryfoundation.org/
     poems/47311/the-waste-land (accessed 24 August 2020), extracts from
     Part II, III, V.

A century after this poem was written, we seem to be living amid the ruins of a once-thriving culture. It has been poisoned by lies, some of which have been embraced in sections of the church. The most prosperous and free nations on earth, which people from many other countries aspire to move to, have adopted a self-hating narrative. A simplistic and distorted view of history paints the West as inherently evil. Some seek to destroy the structures which have created freedom and prosperity (the family, wealth creation and private property, law and order enforcement, even our collective memory and history). Douglas Murray suggests that:

> Europe [has] *lost its faith in its beliefs,* traditions and legitimacy[62] ... Europe [has] lost its *foundational story*[63] ... For centuries in Europe one of the great – if not the greatest – sources of such energy came from the *spirit of the continent's religion.* It drove the people to war, and stirred them to defiance. It also drove Europe to the greatest heights of human creativity.[64]

Just look at the landscape! Every city, town, village and even hamlet contains significant church buildings: often historic, beautiful, and empty. Some have been transformed into restaurants, offices, shops, clubs, gyms, gambling shops or bars. Those whose doors are still open to Christian worshippers may deny the foundational biblical doctrines of the Christian faith:

> ... most branches of European Christianity have lost the confidence to proselytise or even believe in their own message. For the Church of Sweden, the Church of England, the German Lutheran church and many other branches of European Christianity, the message of the religion has become a form of left-wing politics, diversity action, and social welfare projects.[65]

---

62   Murray, D, *The Strange Death of Europe,* (Bloomsbury Continuum, 2018) p. 3.

63   Ibid., p. 212, emphasis mine.

64   Ibid., p. 209, emphasis mine.

65   Ibid., p. 264.

Crumbling church buildings are the legacy of a Christianity that tried, fatally, to accommodate the two-stage landslide in Western thinking:

- There is no transcendent God
- There is no universal truth

In the Introduction we met the 'harmless professor' described in Paul Bourget's *Le Disciple*. He wasn't so harmless after all. Tragedy unfolded when his ideas were put into practice.[66] Individual freedom, unconstrained by morality, is lethal. A worldview in which the windows to the transcendent realm have been closed has created a wasteland, without hope, morality or meaning.

But, throughout the world, there *are* Christian churches and Christian believers who affirm that God is there and He is not silent. Those churches that confidently proclaim the truth of God's Word are growing – in some countries despite fierce persecution.[67] For, as we argue in Part Two, it is the truth that sets us free.

FURTHER READING

Childers, A, *Another Gospel? A Lifelong Christian Seeks Truth in Response to Progressive Christianity*, (Tyndale Momentum, 2020)

Machen, G, *Christianity and Liberalism*, (Eerdmans, 2009)

Murray, I H, 'How Scotland Lost Its Hold of the Bible', address given in 2015, and published in MacArthur, J, ed, *The Inerrant Word*, (Crossway, 2016), https://banneroftruth.org/uk/resources/articles/2015/scotland-lost-hold-bible/ (accessed 18 August, 2020)

'An Emerging Church Primer', 9 Marks, https://www.9marks.org/article/emerging-church-primer/ (accessed 20 August, 2020)

---

66 See Introduction, p 26.

67 Jenkins, P, *The Next Christendom: The Coming of Global Christianity*, (Oxford University Press, 2011).

Summary: How has the Christian church responded to the rise of a worldview that denies God and denies ultimate truth? Confusingly, some clergy seem to have cheered it on! Challenges to the authority of Scripture lie behind the rise of unbelief within the professing church. Some 'Christian' ministers paint evil as good, good as evil, and mock the idea of judgement and hell.

Part 2

The

TRUTH

We Must Hold

'The fear of the LORD is the beginning of Wisdom.'
(Prov. 9:10)

7 The Biblical Worldview: Foundation of Truth, Freedom and Dignity

To surrender the claims of truth upon humans is to surrender Earth to thugs. (Michael Novak)[1]

Viktor Popkov was brought up in communist Russia. When he read *The Stranger* by Albert Camus[2] he realised the logical outcome of atheism: meaninglessness. At that point of despair, he was drawn to church and found hope in Christ. Professing faith would mean imprisonment. But knowing God provided the meaning he had longed for. He was now willing 'to endure anything they throw at you.'[3] A worldview that says there is no God and nothing after death offers no purpose.

The truth about God and about human beings, revealed in both nature and the Bible, provides the only firm basis for meaning, morality, ethics, justice and freedom.

---

1   Novak, M, *Awakening from Nihilism: Why Truth Matters* (Address given at Westminster Abbey on the occasion of winning the Templeton Prize, 1994), (IEA London 1995), p. 19, https://www.firstthings.com/article/1994/08/awakening-from-nihilismthe-templeton-prize-address (accessed 11 January, 2021).

2   Camus, A, *L'Etranger,* 1942. Widely translated. An English translation, *The Outsider,* translated by Joseph Laredo, was published by Penguin, 1983.

3   Dreher, R, *Live Not By Lies,* (Sentinel, 2020), p. 159.

God the Creator

In the beginning God created the heavens and the earth. Now the earth was formless and empty, darkness was over the surface of the deep, and the Spirit of God was hovering over the waters. And God said, 'Let there be light,' and there was light ... [the account continues with the rest of the creation, including man and woman] ... God saw all that he had made, and it was very good ... Thus the heavens and the earth were completed in all their vast array ... (Gen. 1:1-3, 31; 2:1)

'In the beginning' God created all things. The whole universe was a demonstration of His glory, beauty, order, creativity and design. Creation was the work of the Triune God, Father, Son and Spirit, but the Lord Jesus Christ spoke the Word that summoned all into existence.

In the beginning was the Word, and the Word was with God, and the Word was God. He was with God in the beginning. Through him all things were made; without him nothing was made that has been made. (John 1:1-3)

Christ is LORD of all, Creator of all and Sustainer of all:

The Son is the image of the invisible God, the firstborn over all creation. For in him all things were created: things in heaven and on earth, visible and invisible, whether thrones or powers or rulers or authorities; all things have been created through him and for him. He is before all things, and in him all things hold together. (Col. 1:15-17)

All your works praise you, LORD! (Ps. 145:10)

God, the great King, has good designs for the created order. He provided an astonishing array of natural resources to be developed. He gave man and woman the God-like capacity to develop those resources by means of reason, creativity, intelligence, and hard work.

The 'end', or purpose, of creation was to bring glory to the Creator. The psalmist marvelled:

> O LORD, our Lord, how majestic is your name in all the earth! You have set your glory above the heavens.
> Out of the mouth of babies and infants, you have established strength because of your foes, to still the enemy and the avenger.
> When I look at your heavens, the work of your fingers, the moon and the stars, which you have set in place, what is man that you are mindful of him, and the son of man that you care for him?
> Yet you have made him a little lower than the heavenly beings and crowned him with glory and honour.
> You have given him dominion over the works of your hands; you have put all things under his feet, all sheep and oxen, and also the beasts of the field, the birds of the heavens, and the fish of the sea, whatever passes along the paths of the seas.
> O LORD, our Lord, how majestic is your name in all the earth!
> (Ps. 8:1-9, ESV)

As David gazed up at the heavens, he was overwhelmed by the glory of the stars. We know far more now than David did about the vastness of the universe. If we took off at the speed of light we would be at the sun in 8 minutes. It would take us 4 years to get to the nearest star. To get to the centre of the Milky Way galaxy would take 26,000 years (still travelling at the speed of light), and to travel across the observable universe would take 93 billion years. There are 100 billion galaxies.

Beyond the overwhelming immensity of the cosmos is the Creator, infinite in power and might (Ps. 8:1). The stars are merely the work of His fingers (Ps. 8:3). As Genesis 1 comments, almost as an aside, 'He made the stars also' (Gen. 1:16). The only fitting response is worship:

How majestic is your name in all the earth! (Ps. 8:1, 9)

The psalmist then turned from the heavens to the glorious diversity on earth: animals, birds, and sea creatures. Only a God with great intelligence could have constructed the human eye, or engineered the cheetah with its speed. Only a God of imagination and personality could have formed every creature from the electric eel to the hummingbird, and from the otter to the ostrich. Only a God with a sense of humour could have created the sloth, the meerkat, or the warthog. Or we could consider the variety of plants, trees, flowers, crops, fruits, minerals and jewels: all display the Creator's wisdom and artistry.

God continues to care for creation. He sends His sun to shine on the just and the unjust (Matt. 5:45).[4] Christ sustains all things by His powerful Word (Col. 1:17). As we look around us, we should marvel and worship:

> For since the creation of the world His invisible attributes are clearly seen, being understood by the things that are made, even His eternal power and Godhead, so that they are without excuse. (Rom. 1:20, NKJV)

Small children instinctively know that someone made the world around them.[5] They have a sense of wonder. The transcendent God delights in the joy of little ones. He is glorified by their praises and enthroned upon their songs. His enemies can only marvel at and envy such spontaneous praise – they can never attract such heartfelt worship!

> From the lips of children and infants you have ordained praise because of your enemies, to silence the foe and the avenger. (Ps. 8:2)

It is only 'clever' adults who invent theories to suggest that the universe is the product of chance, who destroy the child's belief in God. Those

---

4   This is sometimes referred to as God's 'common grace' (available to all), or His everyday grace.

5   Barrett, J L, *Born Believers: The Science of Children's Religious Belief,* (Simon & Schuster, 2012).

adults may be intellectually brilliant. Morally speaking, the Bible calls them fools:

> The fool has said in his heart there is no God. (Ps. 14:1; 53:1)

As the Lord Jesus Christ said:

> I thank You, Father, Lord of heaven and earth, that You have hidden these things from the wise and prudent and have revealed them to babes. (Matt. 11:25, NKJV)

'SIGNATURE IN THE CELL'

Evolution is 'a theory in crisis'.[6] It has been challenged by three major scientific advances: the discovery that the universe had a beginning (which the Bible taught all along); the discovery of 'fine tuning' in the universe (ditto);[7] and the discovery of the sheer amount of information contained in every single cell (the wonder of which was intuited, if not scientifically understood, by David).

> For you created my inmost being;
>   you knit me together in my mother's womb.
> I praise you because I am fearfully and wonderfully made;
>   your works are wonderful,
>   I know that full well. (Ps. 139:13-14)

The more we understand about not only the scale, but also the extraordinary complexity of the universe, the more the folly of atheism is exposed. For fifty years **Professor Anthony Flew (1923-2010)** built his academic career on the promotion of atheism. In 2004 he shocked his colleagues by changing his mind and accepting that there must be an Intelligent Creator.[8]

---

6   Denton, M, *Evolution: A Theory in Crisis,* (Adler and Adler Publishers, 1986); Meyer S C, *Signature in the Cell* (HarpurOne, 2009).

7   McDermott, G R, *Everyday Glory: The Revelation of God in All of Reality,* (Baker Academic, 2018), pp. 63-80.

8   Flew, A, Varghese, R A, *There Is a God: How the World's Most Notorious Atheist Changed His Mind,* (HarpurOne reprint, 2008).

Evolution is an observable fact only at a small scale. We observe variations over time in response to varying environmental conditions. Small-scale, reversible population variations are usually called micro-evolution or adaptive variation. Illustrations offered for evolution in action involve no increase in complexity, or appearance of new body parts, or even permanent change of any kind. Darwin wrote:

> If it could be demonstrated that any complex organ existed, which could not possibly have been formed by numerous, successive, slight modifications, my theory would absolutely break down.[9]

Over the past two decades, an increasing number of scientists have expressed doubt about the way by which Darwin extrapolated from micro-evolution to macro-evolution.[10]

During the nineteenth century, the cell was viewed as a simple glob of plasma. Today, micro-technology reveals that every cell is filled with exquisite machinery. The cell cannot exist if one component of this machinery is missing. This realm of molecular genetics provides compelling evidence of design.

> The primary flaw in the story of macroevolution is that all plants and animals are packed with information – the complicated instructions that coordinate the many processes enabling the body and brain to function. Even Richard Dawkins, the most famous living advocate of Darwin's theory, admits that every cell in a human body contains more information than all the volumes of an encyclopedia, and everyone of us has trillions of cells in his or her body, which have to work together in marvellous harmony. The

---

9   Darwin, C, *On Natural Selection,* (Penguin Books, Great Ideas, 2004), p. 92. Darwin also acknowledged that during his own life-time the fossil record was not adequate to bear the weight of the theory. He believed that in subsequent years the gaps in the fossil record would be filled in, and his theory vindicated. But the gaps haven't been filled. Scientists today have a lot more fossil evidence than he did, but it doesn't offer any more solid support for his evolutionary theories.

10 Johnson, P E, 'Evolution: Fact or Fantasy?' *Apologetics Study Bible,* (Holman Bible Publishers, 2007), p. 7.

greatest weakness of the theory of evolution is that science has not discovered a process that can create all the necessary information, which can be likened to the software that directs a computer. Without such a demonstrated creative process, evolution is merely a story, because its supposed mechanism can neither be duplicated in a laboratory nor observed in nature.[11]

One pinhead of DNA could hold enough information to fill a stack of books stretching from the earth to the moon 500 times.[12] *God has left His signature in every cell.*

Those who try to believe in both evolution *and* a Creator God (theistic evolution) have to say that Paul was wrong in assuming that Adam was an historical person from whom all humans are descended. They have to deny that the biblical account of the fall actually happened in history. The problem is that both Jesus and Paul believed in an historical Adam and Eve. When you reject this foundational teaching, you compromise the whole Gospel message.[13]

A DAZZLING THEATRE TO DISPLAY GOD'S GLORY

The created order not only reveals the Creator's wisdom (as in the complexity in every cell), and power (as in the scale of the universe), it reveals His beauty.

In 2020 Dr Thomas Fink interviewed Sir Roger Penrose, the Nobel Prize winning Physicist. The two scientists agreed on the beauty hardwired into the universe. Fink writes:

---

11 Ibid., pp. 7-8.

12 'DNA the Language of Life', *Answers in Genesis,* 1 July, 2008, https://answersingenesis.org/genetics/dna-similarities/dna-a-summary/ (accessed 30 December, 2020).

13 Mohler, R A, 'Prettifying Darwin: A timely look at a losing strategy', http://www.albertmohler.com/2010/08/27/prettifying-darwin-a-timely-look-at-a-losing-strategy/ (accessed 25 June, 2020), Grudem, W, '2 Ideas you must embrace to affirm Theistic Evolution', https://www.crossway.org/articles/12-ideas-you-must-embrace-to-affirm-theistic-evolution/ (accessed 4 November, 2020).

I put it to him that one of the great mysteries of physics is that the laws describing the universe have such inherent beauty. So much so, in fact, that this same beauty is often used as a guide to discerning which laws are true. Penrose largely agrees, but distinguishes between different types of beauty. 'There is a beauty in mathematics, which is different from the beauty in physics.'[14]

Fink asked Penrose whether such beauty points to 'something that is beyond science'. Penrose answered:

> ... it's a bit hard to know. What is science? Where are its boundaries? Is there something going on in consciousness, which is outside of science? Well, I like not to think that. It is certainly outside the science we have now.[15]

But the Bible is clear, and it's not hard to know. Painters leave a signature on their paintings. The beauty of the creation points to the beauty of its Creator. God has left His signature on His grand design, and all glory must be given to Him:

Praise him, sun and moon,
  praise him, all you shining stars,
Praise him, you highest heavens
  and you waters above the skies.

Let them praise the name of the LORD,
  for at his command they were created
and he established them for ever and ever—
  he issued a decree that will never pass away

Praise the LORD from the earth,
  you great sea creatures and all ocean depths,
lightning and hail, snow and clouds,
  stormy winds that do his bidding,

---

14 Fink, T, 'A Singular Mind', *The Spectator*, 19 December, 2020, https://www.spectator.co.uk/article/a-singular-mind-roger-penrose-on-his-nobel-prize (accessed 4 January 2021).

15 Ibid.

you mountains and all hills,
    fruit trees and all cedars,
wild animals and all cattle,
    small creatures and flying birds,
kings of the earth and all nations,
    you princes and all rulers on earth,
young men and women,
    old men and children. (Ps. 148: 3-12)

The natural world and human society are a dazzling theatre in which God displays His beauty and glory.[16] In Psalm 148 sun, moon, stars, land, seas, weather, sea creatures, animals, birds, mountains, vegetation and trees all bring God glory. Seamlessly, the psalmist continues the list: kings, all nations, princes, all rulers on earth, young people, the elderly, and children are to praise God too. John Calvin says of the Creator:

> ... there is One whom all ought to honour and adore ... he is the fountain of every good ... not only does he sustain this universe (as he once founded it) by his boundless might, regulate it by his wisdom, preserve it by his goodness, and especially rule mankind by his righteousness and judgement, bear with it in his mercy, watch over it by his protection; but also ... no drop will be found either of wisdom and light, or of righteousness or power or rectitude, or of genuine truth, which does not flow from him, and of which he is not the cause.[17]

God is the source of all truth, all beauty, and He is the One who Himself is infinitely beautiful.

Augustine of Hippo (354-430), a fourth-century North African bishop, was one of the greatest authors and theologians in church history. Before his conversion, as a young academic, Augustine was tantalised by glimpses of ultimate beauty. After his conversion, he

---

16   Calvin, J, *Institutes of the Christian Religion,* ed. McNeill, J T, (Westminster, 1960), Book 1.5.8 (p. 61); 1.14.20 (p. 180); 2.6.1 (p. 341).

17   Ibid., Book 1.2.1 (pp. 40-41).

realised that *God's* beauty had been beckoning him. It had blazed out in the order, patterns and splendour found in the external world. It had gleamed in the capacity to reason and love and care in the inner human experience:

> Your beauty speaks from all that is:
> Your likeness pleads within ...
> Your radiance touched us far from home;
> Your beauty in us burned![18]

Whenever we catch a glimpse of reason, beauty, love, order or justice, God is reaching out to us.

> The heavens declare the glory of God;
>> the skies proclaim the work of his hands,
> Day after day they pour forth speech,
>> night after night they display knowledge...
> their voice goes out into all the earth,
>> their words to the ends of the earth,
> In the heavens he has pitched a tent for the sun.
>> it is like a bridegroom coming forth from his pavilion,
>> like a champion rejoicing to run his course.
> It rises at one end of the heavens
>> and makes its circuit to the other,
>> nothing is hidden from its heat. (Ps. 19:1-2, 4-6)

> He loves righteousness and justice;
>> the earth is full of the steadfast love of the Lord. (Ps. 33:5, ESV)

THERE IS UNIVERSAL TRUTH

There is a God, and there is objective reality. God is there, and His creation reveals His power, glory and infinite wisdom. More and more is being discovered of the extraordinary complexity of the design of every part of our universe. The rational design built into the universe means that logic, mathematics and musical principles are not

---

18 Augustine, 'O Matchless Beauty of Our God', PRAISE hymn-book, no. 737.

'inventions' of humans, they are hardwired into the way things are. They are there to be discovered.[19]

> Truth is not 'merely subjective,' not something we make up, or choose, or cut to today's fashions or the morrow's pragmatism—we obey the truth. We do not 'have' the truth, truth owns us, truth possesses us. Truth is far larger and deeper than we are.[20]

Western civilisation was built on the Christian foundation: the belief that God's creation is an objective reality that can be studied. Humans created in God's image have the capacity to investigate and reason.[21] The first universities throughout Europe, and then in America, were all based on Christian foundations. Psalm 111:2 was inscribed in Latin over the archway to the old Cavendish laboratory in Cambridge, England, at the instigation of **James Clerk Maxwell (1831-1879)**, one of the greatest scientists of all time, and a humble Christian believer:

> Great are the works of the Lord,
>   studied by all who delight in them. (Ps. 111:2)

That text is now inscribed in English over the door of the Cavendish Laboratory, home to the Physics department.

We noted in chapter 1 that secular humanists insist that science and Christianity are incompatible. But modern science was pioneered by Christians.[22] **Francis Bacon (1561-1626)**, the father of the scientific method, was a Christian who believed that the source and purpose of all knowledge was the glory of the Creator. He wrote:

---

19   McDermott, G R, *Everyday Glory*, pp. 45-84.

20   Novak, M, *Awakening from Nihilism: Why Truth Matters*, p. 15.

21   Stark, R, *How the West Was Won,* (ISI books, 2015), Mangalwadi, V, *The Book That Made Your World,* (Nelson, 2012), James, S, *How Christianity Transformed The World,* (Christian Focus Publications, 2021), chapter 8.

22   Stark, R, *For the Glory of God: How Monotheism Led to Reformation, Science, Witch-Hunts and the End of Slavery,* (Princeton University Press, 2003), section 2 'God's Handiwork: The Religious Origins of Science', pp. 121-199.

... the greatest error of all the rest is the mistaking or misplacing of the last or furthest end of knowledge. For men have entered into a desire of learning and knowledge, sometimes upon a natural curiosity and inquisitive appetite; sometimes to entertain their minds with variety and delight; sometimes for ornament and reputation; and sometimes to enable them to victory of wit and contradiction; and most times for lucre and profession ... as if there were sought in knowledge a couch whereupon to rest a searching and restless spirit; or a terrace for a wandering and variable mind to walk up and down with a fair prospect; or a tower of state, for a proud mind to raise itself upon; or a fort or commanding ground, for strife and contention; or a shop, for profit or sale; and not *a rich storehouse for the glory of the Creator and the relief of man's estate.* But this is that which will indeed dignify and exalt knowledge ... [23]

The leading scientific figures in the sixteenth and seventeenth centuries were Christians 'who believed it their duty to comprehend God's handiwork'.[24] The Puritans also believed that it is a Christian's duty to study and understand God's handiwork, as that brings Him glory. Puritan intellectuals defined science as a religious calling. During the early years of the Royal Society of London, membership was dominated by Puritans.[25] Science still attracts many Christians to study at the highest levels. In the mid-twentieth century a survey of more than 60,000 university professors in America found that the majority of those involved in the 'hard sciences' professed to be religious; unbelief was far more prevalent in the social sciences.[26] Many committed Christians are deeply involved in the scientific endeavour.[27]

---

23 Bacon, F, *The Advancement of Learning,* London, 1605, Section V.11, https://www.gutenberg.org/files/5500/5500-h/5500-h.htm (accessed 11 January, 2021), emphasis mine.

24 Stark, R, *For the Glory of God,* pp. 123; 198-99.

25 Ibid., pp. 158-9.

26 Ibid., pp. 194-5.

27 The Templeton Prize is an annual reward, instituted in 1972, larger in financial terms than the Nobel Prize, for honouring those who harness

The works of the Lord, and knowledge of those works, are universally available. This is not just something for the West. There is not some truth that is only accessible to some people. There are not multiple contradictory truths. Science is a universal discipline, it can be engaged in and tested by people whatever their group identity. Logic, science, mathematics and engineering are not 'tools' of oppression (although in a sinful world they can be abused). They can be applied to liberate people from poverty and hunger; protect people from sickness and natural disaster; and provide numerous benefits of education.

Today we have seen the dangerous erosion of the concept of universal truth. When we are encouraged to think that our emotions (what we feel) are more important than objective facts, we are each able to 'construct our own truth'. At that point the distinction between truth and lies dissolves. Rather, we should insist that because God is the ground of all reality, there is such a thing as absolute truth.

God is not silent. He has spoken. He has revealed Himself in Creation and in His Word. He is righteous, and He is truthful. Morality and justice are grounded in the nature of God.

The Rock, his work is perfect,
    for all his ways are justice.
A God of faithfulness and without iniquity,
    just and upright is he. (Deut. 32:4, ESV)

Your throne, O God, will last for ever and ever;
    a sceptre of justice will be the sceptre of your kingdom;
You love righteousness and hate wickedness. (Ps. 45:6-7, ESV)

Righteousness and justice are the foundation of your throne;
    steadfast love and faithfulness go before you. (Ps. 89:14, ESV)

---

the power of the sciences to explore religious questions; at least 12 of the recipients have been physicists, some of them theologians as well. https://www.templetonprize.org/templeton-prize-winners-2/ (accessed 11 January, 2021).

He who justifies the wicked and who condemns the righteous
   are both alike an abomination to the Lord. (Prov. 17:15, ESV)

But let him who boasts boast in this, that he understands and
knows me, that I am the Lord who practices steadfast love,
justice, and righteousness in the earth. For in these things I delight,
declares the Lord. (Jer. 9:24, ESV)

The Triune Creator God is the Creator and is the source and ground
of truth, morality and justice.

Created In His Image

We turn now from the truth about God to the truth about human
beings. Are we really just random collections of cells, merely products
of time and chance?

If we fail to understand who God is, we cannot understand who
we are. We learn from Genesis 1 and 2 that we have unique dignity as
created in the image of God, with dominion over the rest of creation.
The wonder of human identity is celebrated in Psalm 8, which brings
together the paradoxical truths: as *created* beings, in comparison to
the Creator, we are very small; but as beings created in the *image of the
Creator,* we are very great.

We Are Created: We Are Very Small!

As David the psalmist contemplated the immensity of the universe
and the greatness of the Creator, by comparison he seemed utterly
insignificant:

What is man, that you are mindful of him? (Ps. 8:4)

If we compare ourselves with the vastness of the cosmos in merely
material terms, that only underlines our minuteness and seeming
unimportance. We may appear utterly insignificant when compared
to the almost infinite distances of the stars. We might think of
ourselves as just a list of chemicals. Or we could reflect that we contain
just enough iron to make a small nail, enough lime to whitewash a
chicken house, enough sulphur to rid a dog of fleas, enough sugar to

fill a jam jar, enough potassium to fire a toy cannon and enough fat to make seven bars of soap (or so). If we are simply evolved animals, why should we have more rights than chimpanzees, or dolphins (or earthworms)?

No wonder then that so many are preoccupied with the issue of personal identity. Brought up with a worldview where the windows are firmly closed, they have no external reference point. There is no recognition of the transcendent God, or any reality beyond the material. They have to work out who they are by looking within, or else by comparison with others. This may generate insecurity, envy, preoccupation with physical appearance and an obsession with image. Loss of capacity, health, or relationships may challenge self-identity. If identity is grounded in being part of a 'group', groups may splinter and self-destruct.

WE ARE CREATED IN THE IMAGE OF GOD: WE ARE VERY GREAT!

If we are to understand who we are, we need to see ourselves in relationship to our Creator: 'You made him a little lower than the heavenly beings and crowned him with glory and honour' (Ps. 8:5). Human beings are more like God Himself than anything else on earth; just a little lower than the heavenly beings, crowned with glory and honour. That is our unique dignity and status, and it confers infinite worth. We are created to relate to God, and we have been given souls that will never die.

We are small, and may seem insignificant, but we are loved and cared for by the Lord who is infinitely greater than ourselves. Our identity is defined by our relationship with our Creator. The man and woman were the crown and pinnacle of all the rest of creation. They were given the responsibility of having dominion over God's creation as His stewards or representatives: 'You made him ruler over the works of your hands; you put everything under his feet' (Ps. 8:6).

This is the paradox by which we understand human identity. In the eyes of God we are very small, because He is infinitely greater than us.

In the sphere of this world, God has made us great, because we have pre-eminence over all that He has made.

That ambiguity is captured in the expression 'son of man' (Ps. 8:4). This phrase sometimes alludes to weakness and smallness (the prophet Ezekiel was addressed as 'son of man' over ninety times). In other places it is an expression of power and authority.[28] We need to understand both human smallness *and* human greatness.

THE ONLY FIRM FOUNDATION FOR HUMAN DIGNITY

When we see a fellow human being we see someone 'crowned with glory and honour' (Ps. 8:5) who represents God Himself. When we neglect or despise a fellow human being, we insult their Maker.

> Whoever oppresses the poor shows contempt for their Maker,
>   but whoever is kind to the needy honours God. (Prov. 14:31)

> He who mocks the poor insults their Maker;
>   whoever gloats over calamity will not go unpunished. (Prov. 17:5)

> Kindness to the poor is a loan to the LORD,
>   and He will repay the lender. (Prov. 19:17, BSB)

The only certain guarantee of human freedom and dignity is the biblical truth that every human has been created by God in His image. The life of every person, whoever they are, is of infinite worth. The truth of human equality is grounded in belief in our creation by God. When that belief is lost, there is a disastrous slide towards judging 'equality' in our own human terms. Some people judge that people without independence or capacity should not be afforded equal rights.

Many believe that the real origin of the idea of 'human rights' is the concept of the person, founded on the biblical view that all persons are created in the image of God. This is what affords equal dignity to

---

28 As in Daniel 7:13-14, with reference to the Lord Jesus Christ. Also see below: 'We Can All Be Forgiven'.

every individual. Every human life, from conception to natural death, should be protected.[29]

Christians have been in the forefront of insisting that both men and women should be educated (as all should have access to the Word of God). The biblical conviction that every human being is to be treated with respect also lay behind efforts to abolish slavery.[30] The liberties and rights that we value in free societies are largely the result of Christianity's influence. They are based on the conviction that all humans, made in God's image, are equal in dignity. In 2016, Cambridge University Press published two volumes on *Christianity and Freedom*, incorporating years of research by a team of international scholars. The overall conclusion was:

> ... free institutions hardly ever developed in places that were not influenced by Jewish and Christian ideas. Outside the Judeo-Christian tradition, it has been rare for thinkers to suppose that God endowed us with a nature of our own, [and] that freedom is part of that nature ...[31]

Today in China, Christian lawyers, despite suffering discrimination and persecution for their faith, are active in fighting for freedom rights for all – not just fellow-Christians.[32] Professor Fenggang Yang wrote in 2016:

---

29 Ling, J, When does Human Life begin? The Christian Institute, 2011, 2017, https://www.christian.org.uk/wp-content/uploads/when-does-human-life-begin.pdf; Ling, J, *Bioethical Issues,* (Day One, 2014).

30 James, S, *How Christianity Transformed the World,* (Christian Focus, 2021), chapter 1.

31 Hertzke, A D and Shah, T S eds, *Christianity and Freedom: Volume I Historical Perspectives,* (Cambridge University Press, 2016), p. 29, quoting Remi Brague.

32 Yang, F, 'The Growth and Dynamism of Chinese Christianity', pp. 161-190 in Hertzke, A D and Shah, T S, eds. *Christianity and Freedom: Volume II Contemporary Perspectives,* (Cambridge University Press, 2016), pp. 179-183.

In China today, Christians are at the front lines of practising and campaigning for individual freedoms, from the freedom of belief to freedom of assembly, freedom of speech, freedom of the press, freedom for organized efforts for public welfare, and freedom for civic engagement and participation.[33]

That is because they believe that everyone is made in God's image.

While all *people* are to be afforded equal dignity, as made in God's image, we don't have to regard all *cultures* as equally valid. There is a tendency today to romanticise indigenous cultures, and decry efforts to introduce Christianity. This is historically naive. The Human Freedom Index shows that nine out of the top ten countries where citizens enjoy the most freedom are in the West.[34]

Cultures may operate more or less in keeping with God's moral law. They may have a high view of human life, or they may have an attitude that only affords value to a few. Do we have to respect the caste system as traditionally practised in India? No! It does not recognise all human beings as possessing intrinsic dignity. Although formally outlawed, the caste system still views Dalits as inferior to others. Some believe that the scale of injustice and abuse caused by this represents one of the single most serious human rights issues in history. In India today Christians are in the forefront of offering Dalits hope and dignity and the knowledge that they, along with all people, are made in the image of God.[35]

By What Standard?

God has placed awareness of His moral law in the conscience of every human being. We all know there is a difference between right and wrong:

---

33 Ibid., p. 186.

34 The Human Freedom Index, *The Cato Institute,* 2020, https://www.cato.org/human-freedom-index-new (accessed 11 January, 2021).

35 Woods, M, 'Telling a Better Story: how India's Christians are fighting for dignity for Dalits', All India Christian Council network, 4 September, 2018. For more on cultural relativism, see chapter 1.

> They [the Gentiles who don't have God's written law] show that
> the requirements of the law are written on their hearts, their
> consciences also bearing witness, and their thoughts sometimes
> accusing them and at other times even defending them. (Rom.
> 2:15)

The Ten Commandments stand apart from the rest of the laws
recorded in the early books of the Bible. God not only spoke these
words to Moses, He wrote these commands on tables of stone:

> And he gave to Moses, when he had finished speaking with him
> on Mount Sinai, the two tablets of the testimony, tablets of stone,
> *written with the finger of God.* (Exod. 31:18, ESV, emphasis mine)

The moral law, summarised in the Ten Commandments, outlines
our obligations to God our Creator as well as to our fellow human
beings. These commands are for all times and for all people, and
their principles are placed on the human conscience.[36] We are not
abandoned to make up truth and morality for ourselves. There are
moral norms which we are responsible to obey, based on the perfectly
righteous nature of God. Morality is not relative. We will be judged by
our Creator according to the law He has placed in our hearts.

THE DIGNITY OF MORAL RESPONSIBILITY

God is King, we are His subjects. When God placed our first parents
in the Garden of Eden, the man was given a command:

> And the LORD God commanded the man, 'You are free to eat
> from any tree in the garden, but you must not eat from the tree of
> the knowledge of good and evil; for when you eat from it, you will
> certainly die.' (Gen. 2:16-17)

God gave our first parents moral agency. Would they choose obedience
to their Creator? Or would they defy His authority? As created beings
they should have submitted to their Creator. Our true humanity is

---

36   Ross, P S, *From The Finger of God: The Biblical and Theological Base for the
Threefold Division of the Law,* (Christian Focus Publications, 2010).

only fulfilled when we recognise our relation of submission to our Creator.[37] We were created by God to know Him. Genuine encounter with the transcendent, all-powerful and holy God leads to humble worship. When the prophet Isaiah was given a vision of God, he fell down in awe; as his own sinfulness was unmasked:

> I saw the LORD, high and exalted, seated on a throne; and the train of his robe filled the temple. Above him were seraphim, each with six wings: With two wings they covered their faces, with two they covered their feet, and with two they were flying. And they were calling to one another:
>
> 'Holy, holy, holy is the LORD Almighty; the whole earth is full of his glory.'
>
> At the sound of their voices the door posts and thresholds shook and the temple was filled with smoke.
>
> 'Woe to me!' I cried. 'I am ruined! For I am a man of unclean lips, and I live among a people of unclean lips, and my eyes have seen the King, the LORD Almighty.' (Isa. 6:1-5)

Similarly, when Jesus Christ revealed His divine power, Peter was overwhelmed with awe:

> When Simon Peter saw this, he fell at Jesus' knees and said, 'Go away from me, Lord; I am a sinful man!' (Luke 5:8)

ACCOUNTABILITY: UNIVERSAL AND INDIVIDUAL

In a fallen world, tragically we do find sexism, racism, and other evils. Sometimes such abuses, and others, characterise whole groups or societies, even nations. But the idea of 'collective guilt' is a travesty of justice.[38] Children should not be punished for the sin of their fathers.

---

37 As clearly recognised by the great thinkers of the Christian tradition such as Augustine, John Calvin and Jonathan Edwards.

38 McDermott, G R, 'Misunderstanding Race and the Bible', *Public Discourse,* 20 October, 2020, https://www.thepublicdiscourse.com/2020/10/72125/ (accessed 22 October, 2020).

The soul who sins is the one who will die. The son will not share the guilt of the father, nor will the father share the guilt of the son. The righteousness of the righteous man will be credited to him, and the wickedness of the wicked will be charged against him. (Ezek. 18:20)

Many today view the criminal justice system as an agency to minimise harm to society, while preparing those who break the law to reintegrate into society. It is sadly true that many of those who commit crimes have themselves been horribly disadvantaged (around 50 per cent of those incarcerated in the US grew up without fathers).[39] Rehabilitation is an important aim. But personal moral responsibility is diminished by the assumption that crime is almost always only the result of deprivation and poverty. The 'progressive' refusal to admit that there is absolute right and wrong undermines the biblical truth that the guilty should be punished. Romans 13 says of rulers that 'they are God's servants, agents of wrath to bring *punishment* on the wrongdoer' (Rom. 13:4). When a sense of individual moral responsibility is lost, civic life is undermined.

The biblical truth of moral responsibility is undermined by our therapeutic culture. Instead of teaching youngsters virtues such as character and resilience, all too often adults rush to 'validate' whatever they are feeling. This creates individuals who are in continual need of therapy and support. Sociologist Frank Furedi argues that from the youngest age, some children are encouraged to think of themselves as victims:

Therapists are even showing up at our day-care centres—and they're talking to primary school children so frequently that by the time the kids turn nine, they sound as if they've been studying Freud. 'I'm stressed out.' 'I'm so depressed.' 'I need to chill out.' We

---

39   Parker, W, 'Statistics on Fatherless Children in America', May 24 2019, https://www.liveabout.com/fatherless-children-in-america-statistics-1270392 (accessed 18 September, 2020).

have socialized a generation with self-victimization, and the kids have internalized its terms.[40]

This in time inhibits enterprise and ambition, by creating a sense of dependency and entitlement. Rather, we should afford all human beings the dignity of responsibility and moral agency.[41]

THE UNITY OF THE HUMAN RACE

The Bible consistently teaches the unity of the human race.[42]

From one man he made all the nations, that they should inhabit the whole earth; and he marked out their appointed times in history and the boundaries of their lands. (Acts 17:26)

Recent discoveries in DNA are consistent with the biblical testimony that we are all more related, even in the recent past, than most imagine.[43] There are no 'absolute' identities of 'black' or 'white'. When the Bible speaks of different nations *(ta ethne)* they were 'united by culture, not skin color'.[44]

... there is a broad consensus among biologists and anthropologists that race as a clear distinction separating groups and individuals is

---

40   Macdonald, H, Furedi, F, 'The Campus Victim Cult', *City Journal,* 13 March, 2018, https://www.city-journal.org/html/campus-victim-cult-15644.html (accessed 7 October, 2020).

41   There is a legitimate place for both therapy and medication; this section is addressing broad cultural trends rather than offering any comment on specific treatments for particular illnesses. A good overview of a Christian perspective on mental illness is Alan Thomas's book, *Tackling Mental Illness Together: a biblical and practical approach,* (IVP, 2017).

42   Genesis 1:26; 6:3; 7:21;10:32; Matthew 19:4; Acts 17:26; Romans 5:12 ff; 1 Corinthians 15:21f, 45f); Bavinck, H, *Reformed Dogmatics,* Volume 2, (Baker Academic 2004), pp. 523-26.

43   Jeanson, N, https://answersingenesis.org/genetics/shocking-and-glorious-new-science-human-race-ethnicity/ (accessed 30 December, 2020).

44   McDermott, G R, 'Misunderstanding Race and the Bible', *Public Discourse,* 20 October, 2020, https://www.thepublicdiscourse.com/2020/10/72125/ (accessed 22 October, 2020).

a notion of modern origins without solid grounding in biology or genetics.[45]

Because all human beings are created in the image of God, we can communicate with each other as fellow human beings. Whatever our nationality or ethic group, we can experience friendship and love (which is why bans on interracial marriage are so wrong).

The biblical worldview opposes the claim that humanity is divided between some who have access to certain experiences, and others who don't and can't understand those experiences. Identity politics denies our capacity to engage with others. It shuts off the God-given capacity to communicate with and trust our fellow human beings. This is a wretched restriction on social interactions, but it's the logical outworking of denying God as the source of external and universally available truth. Pastor Bobby Scott writes:

> My great-great-great grandfathers were slaves ... I tell my kids the stories of their courage and character. I remind them how their ancestors' sacrifices afforded us privileges that generations before mine only dreamed about ... Although loud, radical voices on the left and right are pulling our nation apart over the issue of race, the church has the most powerful message — the gospel ... God made the human race — *one race* — in his image and likeness, for his glory, and to spread his dominion throughout the earth ... Yet Adam rebelled, and the entire human race fell with him ... God graced Israel with a special calling to bring blessing to all the families and nations of the earth ... [And now Jesus] is building a new humanity — *one new race* — the church, and through the church he is saving people from all the nations and families of the earth, reconciling them to God and to each other.[46]

---

45   Ibid.

46   Scott, B, 'Black and White Are One: The Church as One New Race', *Desiring God,* 14 December, 2020, https://www.desiringgod.org/articles/black-and-white-are-one (accessed 4 January 2020), emphasis mine.

To view people primarily according to the group to which they belong reduces the likelihood of respecting them for who they are. The *universal respect* due to all humans is lost. The *particular respect* due to individuals on account of their own character, virtue, or achievement is lost as well. The biblical truths of creation and redemption point to the essential unity of the human race, as well as the respect to be afforded to each individual.

'Affirmative action' ('positive discrimination'), although well-intentioned, can create greater injustices than those which it seeks to address. If women are promoted to make up quotas, or if members of minority groups are given jobs to fulfil targets, who knows whether that is because of their own ability, or whether they are simply there to tick the official boxes?

Clarence Thomas (b. 1948), the first person of African descent to become a member of the American Supreme Court, regards affirmative action as patronising. The idea that those from minority backgrounds need such help robs them of the rightful pride of personal achievement. He believes that if the principles of the Declaration of Independence are followed, all benefit by virtue of their dignity being recognized as individuals, created equal and endowed by their Creator with unalienable rights. Justice Thomas insists that 'the law does not properly recognize "group rights", only individual rights':

> Individuals are the proper objects of the law's solicitude ... When groups are attended to, even with the utmost in earnest care, the result is condescension, and the losers are always individuals—both those deliberately disadvantaged by policies of preference, and those putatively advantaged by them, who are robbed of their individuality, treated as though they all think alike, and balkanized by political power ... [47]

---

47 Franck, M J, 'Declaration Man: How Justice Clarence Thomas Earned His Enemies', *Public Discourse,* 18 March, 2014, https://www.thepublicdiscourse.com/2014/03/12899/ (accessed 10 September, 2020).

Acknowledging the unity of the human race does not mean that variety of ethnicity and culture cannot also be respected.[48] A theme running through the Bible is that God is glorified as the glorious diversity of peoples come together to honour Him:

> And to him was given dominion and glory and a kingdom, that all peoples, nations, and languages should serve him; his dominion is an everlasting dominion, which shall not pass away, and his kingdom one that shall not be destroyed. (Dan. 7:14, ESV)

> And they sang a new song, saying, 'Worthy are you to take the scroll and to open its seals, for you were slain, and by your blood you ransomed people for God from every tribe and language and people and nation'. (Rev. 5:9, ESV)

We Are All Sinners

When God created the world, man and woman lived in harmony with their Creator, and with one another. They enjoyed the good things of this world in abundance. That happy state did not last (Genesis 3). Our first parents rebelled against God. Judgement was pronounced. Work became difficult and burdensome. Relationships would now, all too often, be marked by abuse and resentment. Suffering and disease became commonplace. Death entered the world.

Suffering, injustice, war, greed, violence and exploitation now mean that life often seems to consist of futility and frustration. The preacher of the book of Ecclesiastes was realistic about the tragedy of human existence. The oppressed cry out, and have no one to comfort them:

> Again I looked and saw all the oppression that was taking place under the sun:
> I saw the tears of the oppressed—
>   and they have no comforter;

---

48 McDermott, G R, 'Misunderstanding Race and the Bible', *Public Discourse*, 20 October, 2020, https://www.thepublicdiscourse.com/2020/10/72125/ (accessed 22 October, 2020).

power was on the side of their oppressors—
and they have no comforter.
And I declared that the dead,
who had already died,
are happier than the living,
who are still alive.
But better than both
is the one who has never been born,
who has not seen the evil
that is done under the sun. (Eccles. 4:1-3)

As we contemplate our broken world, it is right to weep. It is right to act on behalf of the downtrodden. Do we spare a thought for the Uighur Muslims being carted off to prison camps in China, along with other minorities who are abused and oppressed, not least the Christians? Or the countless victims of human trafficking? Or the hundreds of thousands exploited by pornographers? Life often seems downright unjust:

And I saw something else under the sun:
In the place of judgment—wickedness was there,
in the place of justice—wickedness was there. (Eccles. 3:16)

In this meaningless life of mine I have seen both of these:

the righteous perishing in their righteousness,
and the wicked living long in their wickedness. (Eccles. 7:15)

There is something else meaningless that occurs on earth: the righteous who get what the wicked deserve, and the wicked who get what the righteous deserve. This too, I say, is meaningless. (Eccles. 8:14)

The Old Testament prophets consistently denounced injustice, and warned both God's people (who had the written law) and the surrounding nations (who did not) that everyone will have to answer to God in the end. The New Testament also teaches that while individuals may seem to get away with trampling over others, justice will be done:

> For we must all appear before the judgment seat of Christ, so that each one may receive what is due for what he has done in the body, whether good or evil. (2 Cor. 5:10, ESV)

None of us can consider ourselves blameless. It is not just that we do or say wrong things. We are all sinful, in that we have inherited a sinful nature. We fail to fulfil our creation purpose of worshipping and enjoying our Creator. We fail to obey His moral law as placed in our consciences. Russian author **Nadezhda Mandelstam (1899-1980)** wrote:

> ... the feeling of sinfulness is the basic 'wealth of man' because the awareness of the actual responsibility for one's destiny and that of others makes a person spiritually free and brings him back in touch with life.[49]

We Can All Be Forgiven

When we accept that we are all sinners, we have to cultivate humility. We can then relate respectfully and genuinely with those we disagree with. When we have acknowledged our own sinfulness, and experienced God's forgiveness, we are empowered to forgive others. At a time of polarisation and social division, the capacity to demonstrate humility and forgiveness is countercultural, but beautiful. We all need to pray:

> Search me, God, and know my heart;
> test me and know my anxious thoughts.
> See if there is any offensive way in me,
> and lead me in the way everlasting. (Ps. 139: 23-24)

---

49 Mandelstam, N, quoted in Aeschliman, M D, 'Solzhenitsyn and Modern Literature', *First Things,* August 1990, https://www.firstthings.com/article/1990/08/solzhenitsyn-and-modern-literature (accessed 7 October, 2020).

We all need to be convicted by the Holy Spirit. We all stand guilty before our Creator, but His offer of grace is universal:

> Look unto me, and be ye saved, all the ends of the earth:
>   for I am God, and there is none else. (Isa. 45:22, KJV)

An essential element in *true humanity* is unbroken relationship with God. That relationship was broken by rebellion. To restore that relationship, Christ, who was eternally God, became man. Unlike us, He was obedient to the Father's will. If we want to know what it is to be *truly human* we look at Christ. The New Testament author of the letter to the Hebrews wrote:

> But we see him who for a little while was made lower than the angels, namely Jesus, crowned with glory and honour because of the suffering of death, so that by the grace of God he might taste death for everyone. (Heb. 2:5-9, alluding to Ps. 8:6, ESV)

Here we see Jesus embracing smallness. The Son of God gave up the glory of heaven, and took human flesh: born in poverty, rejected by the religious and political leaders, despised by His own people. Ultimately He suffered the agonising death of the Cross.

But then He defeated death and has been exalted to the highest place.[50] Jesus also embraced greatness: not by grasping or self-promotion, but by submission to the will of God. He has been honoured with the place of supreme authority over all creation.

Jesus fulfilled God's original creation purpose for humanity, but He is not merely an example of what it means to be a perfect human being. His perfect obedience to the law of God is reckoned to those who look to Him for salvation. His sacrificial death paid the penalty of God's wrath.

If we think too highly of ourselves, we should remember that our guilt is so great that only Christ's death could bring us back to God. If we think too lowly of ourselves, we can reflect that God sent His only Son, and Christ gave His own life: such was the value God placed on restoration of relationship with us. The apostle Paul marvelled: 'The

---

50   Philippians 2:6-11.

Son of God loved me, and gave himself for me' (Gal. 2:20). Through Christ's sacrifice on the cross we can have peace with God. To know, relate to and enjoy God is what we as humans were created for. Without that, we cannot enjoy true fulfilment.

Timo Krizka was just a toddler when communism ended, in what was then Czechoslovakia. He has only known freedom and relative prosperity, but he senses a lack of purpose among his own generation. He set out to investigate what gave meaning to those who resisted communism:

> Timo ... went around his country talking to elderly people who had been in the gulag for their faith and just trying to find out what their experiences were like ... [he found that] even today [they don't have much of anything but are] so serene and so happy because their time in prison had taught them that there is nothing more important than the love of God.[51]

The identity that has eternal importance is whether or not we are united with Christ. In union with Him, we can fulfil our original creation purpose of knowing, enjoying, worshipping and serving our Creator, now and forever.

Nothing, and nobody, can remove that joy, that dignity, that significance, and that hope.

FURTHER READING

Ascol, T, 'The Right Use of God's Law' (sermon on 1 Timothy 1:8-11) https://founders.org/sermons/the-right-use-of-gods-law/

Hoekema, A A, *Created in God's Image,* (Eerdmans, 1986)

James, S, *How Christianity Transformed the World,* (Christian Focus, 2021)

---

51   Bluey, R, 'Could It Happen Here? The Parallels Between Soviet Bloc and Modern US', Interview with Rod Dreher, *The Daily Signal,* 5 October, 2020, https://www.dailysignal.com/2020/10/05/rod-dreher-discusses-parallels-between-soviet-bloc-and-modern-us/ (accessed 11 January, 2021).

Ling, J T, *When Does Human Life Begin?* The Christian Institute, https://www.christian.org.uk/wp-content/uploads/when-does-human-life-begin.pdf

Mackay, J, *The Moral Law,* The Christian Institute, https://www.christian.org.uk/wp-content/uploads/the-moral-law.pdf

McDermott, G R, *Everyday Glory: The Revelation of God in All of Reality,* (Baker Academic, 2018), chapters 3 and 4

Ross, P S, *From The Finger of God: The Biblical and Theological Base for the Threefold Division of the Law,* (Christian Focus Publications, 2010)

Stark, R, *For the Glory of God: How Monotheism Led to Reformation, Science, Witch-Hunts and the End of Slavery,* (Princeton University Press, 2003), section 2 'God's Handiwork: The Religious Origins of Science', pp. 121-99

Summary: God is the Creator, and the ground of truth, justice and morality. Our creation in the image of God is the only firm foundation for the respect of human rights. The Bible affirms both the dignity of every individual person, and the essential unity of the human race. Because of the fall into sin, oppression and suffering are endemic to human existence. Every individual is morally responsible, but forgiveness is offered to all in Christ.

8 The Biblical Worldview: Foundation of Human Flourishing

The biblical worldview is the only secure basis for respecting *individual* dignity, and also the only solid foundation of human flourishing *in society*.

God's Good Design: Family

Imagine, if you will, a divinely-designed institution perfectly tuned toward maximal human flourishing – dynamic, responsive, devoted, fecund [fruitful/fertile], nurturing. Now consider any concerted opposition to such an institution. Would it be motivated by hatred toward God? Or man?[1]

Many intellectuals during the twentieth century demonstrated unremitting hostility towards the natural family.[2] But the first two chapters of the Bible tell us that God's design for humanity starts with the family: husband, wife, and their own children. In Genesis 2:24 we read that a man 'leaves his father and mother and is united to his wife, and they become one flesh'. When God created humankind male and

---

1   Smothers, C J, 'Discovering Bavinck's The Christian Family', *EIKON*, Spring 2020, 2:1, pp. 8-15, p. 8.

2   See chapters 2-5.

female, he told them to 'be fruitful and increase in number, fill the earth ... ' (Gen. 1:28).

Our first parents, and those to follow, were to fill the earth with more human beings, made in their likeness, and in the image of God. God's good design was for children to be brought up by the two people, mother and father, whose loving union brought them into existence. When questioned about divorce, the Lord Jesus Christ referred back to this creation pattern of a life-long partnership between husband and wife:

> Some Pharisees came to Jesus to test him. They asked, 'Is it lawful for a man to divorce his wife for any and every reason?' 'Haven't you read,' he replied, 'that at the beginning the Creator made them male and female, and said, "For this reason a man will leave his father and mother and be united to his wife, and the two will become one flesh"?' (Matt. 19:3-5).

The fifth commandment reads:

> Honour your father and your mother, so that you may live long in the land the LORD your God is giving you. (Exod. 20:12)

Together with the seventh commandment, 'You shall not commit adultery', these principles are foundational for family life and society. The rest of the Bible confirms the need to uphold the family.

A stable, happy, peaceful society depends on the members of that society learning to obey authority:

> No other institution can top the family's ability to transmit what is pivotal—character formation, values, virtues, and enduring love— to each new generation. Where is dignity learned, self-restraint modelled, and caring demonstrated if not first from our mothers and fathers? Without healthy families, other institutions quickly begin to show signs of crippling stress.[3]

---

3   George, R P, Vaughan, H W, 'The Five Pillars of a Decent and Dynamic Society', *Public Discourse,* October, 2018, https://www.thepublicdiscourse. com/five-pillars/ (accessed 5 January, 2021).

THE STATE – NO SUBSTITUTE FOR FAMILY

Children born within marriage know who their parents and grand-parents are; they are given a genealogy on both sides linking them to past generations; they are assured of the care of both sides of the family. If their parents cease being able to support them, other relatives are likely to step in. Marriage has always been the way in which society has 'cemented' the bonds of parents to their children. Throughout history, and throughout the world, we find moving examples of the tenacious determination of parents to provide for their own children.

At the other end of life, the biblical injunction is for people to care for their mothers and fathers when they need support:

> Honour widows who are truly widows. But if a widow has children or grandchildren, let them first learn to show godliness to their own household and to make some return to their parents, for this is pleasing in the sight of God ... If anyone does not provide for his relatives, and especially for members of his household, he has denied the faith and is worse than an unbeliever. (1 Tim. 5:3-4, 8, ESV)

There is inbuilt welfare provision in societies which respect the family (albeit backup may be needed from the wider community). The assault on the natural married family in many Western societies has undermined the institution designed by God to provide care for children and the elderly.[4] As the ideology of sexual freedom gained ground, public policy shifted from supporting married families to ensuring state support for all lone parents and their children. To suggest that the married family was the best situation for children was viewed as stigmatising 'families of all shapes and sizes'.[5]

---

4 Morgan, P, *The War Between the State and the Family: How Government Divides and Impoverishes,* Institute of Economic Affairs, 2007, https://iea. org.uk/wp-content/uploads/2016/07/upldbook406pdf.pdf (accessed 5 January, 2021).

5 The family has been under relentless attack for more than a century; Lasch, C, *A Haven in a Heartless World,* (Basic Books, 1977). Evolutionary theory saw the family as just another phase of social development, as did Marxism – the family was 'merely the temporary product of a particular

Queer theory has further 'de-normalised' the married family: binaries and boundaries, such as male/female or heterosexual/homosexual, are condemned as power grabs which wrongly disadvantage some. The legalising of same-sex marriage and rights for transsexuals further redefined family. The advent of artificial reproductive technologies enables individuals (outside of any relationship) to claim the 'human right' to have children.[6] Increasing numbers of children are born who may never know who one or both of their natural parents are.

But knowledge of one's lineage is important to human identity.[7] One youngster testified:

> Almost five months ago now I found my bio mom on ancestrydna.com. I messaged her and immediately went from years of pain and wondering (from my strong belief that I would never know her or anything about her) to anxiety that she'd never see, read, or respond to my message. But she did and we have been in contact ever since ... She is wonderful and I'm so happy that I come from her ... I still feel a lot of anger and sadness about the circumstances of my conception, and all of the psychological hurt I endured (and still endure) but by some miracle I got what I wanted, and

---

stage of economic development' (Bosanquet, H., *The Family,* 1906). More pragmatically, others doubted that the family was 'fit for purpose' in an industrial age: city life meant the family was reduced to 'a temporary meeting place for board and lodging' (Dealey, J Q, *The Family in its Sociological Aspects,* 1912). The cultural Marxists took the critique further: families were one of the ways in which people were kept trapped in a false consciousness, see chapter 4.

6   See, for example, Kaufman, D, 'The Fight for Fertility Equality', *New York Times,* 22 July, 2020, https://www.nytimes.com/2020/07/22/style/lgbtq-fertility-surrogacy-coverage.html (accessed 8 March, 2021).

7   Marquardt, E, ed., *The Revolution in Parenthood: The Emerging Global Clash Between Adult Rights and Children's Needs,* (Institute for American Values, 2006).

I am so so grateful that my bio mom was and is open to having a relationship with me.[8]

Many today who campaign for Social Justice oppose the married family. But genuine social justice is best secured by following the Creator's design for social structures. Children at least statistical risk of abuse are those living with their own biological mother and father, who themselves are in a stable marriage. A father, as a male parent, brings unique contributions to parenting.[9] A mother, as a female, brings a complementary and different perspective to parenthood.[10] Many single parents do a magnificent job, but generally children flourish best when they have the active participation of their mother and their father. Research has indicated that in the United States the 'marriage gap' is the strongest factor behind social immobility. Children born to married parents and brought up by their own parents, do better on every measure: health, education, employment, mental stability.

No amount of state intervention, state funding or social care, can compensate for lack of parental involvement through childhood and adolescence.[11] Being raised in a married family in the USA reduces a child's probability of living in poverty by about 80 per cent.[12] The state is a poor substitute for family. The state can provide, but it cannot love. In June 2020, American author Shelby Steele said:

---

8   Anonymous, 'I found my bio mom and couldn't be happier', 17 January, 2020, https://anonymousus.org/i-found-my-bio-mom-and-couldnt-be-happier/ (accessed 14 September, 2020).

9   Pruett, K, *Father-need: Why Father Care is as Essential as Mother Care for Your Child,* (Broadway Books, 2000).

10   Hunter, B, *The Power of Mother Love: Transforming Both Mother and Child,* Waterbrook Press, 1997; Komisar, E, *Being There,* (Random House, 2017).

11   https://www.heritage.org/marriage-and-family/heritage-explains/why-the-declining-marriage-rate-affects-everyone (accessed 15 September, 2020), *The Heritage Foundation*; Hymowitz, K S, 'The Marriage Gap', *Cato Unbound,* 16 January 2008.

12   Rector, R, 'Marriage: America's Greatest Weapon Against Child Poverty', *The Heritage Foundation,* 5 September, 2012, https://www.heritage.org/poverty-and-inequality/report/marriage-americas-greatest-weapon-against-child-poverty (accessed 4 September, 2020).

Our families have fallen to pieces. 75 percent of all black children are born out of wedlock, without a father ... I don't care how many social programs you have. You're not going to overcome that. [Programs are] not going to read a story to a child that night before he goes to sleep so he's developing his mind.[13]

Over the centuries, some intellectuals have scorned the nuclear family, and idealised the 'efficiency' of collective child-rearing. But children are not simply products which roll off a production line.

It's one of the eternally paradoxical things about babies and small children that they need love as much as they need milk and warmth in order to develop properly. They need to be cuddled, spoken and sung to, played with, held close and looked at with enthusiasm – and will as good as die inside without such care. Every child needs to experience what one could term 'Primary Parental Delight,' a basic feeling that they are limitlessly wanted by those who put them on the earth and are capable of generating intense pleasure through their very being. Without this, a child might survive, but it can never thrive. Their right to walk the earth will always be somewhat in doubt, they will grow up with a sense of being superfluous, disruptive and, at core, unappealing and shameful. Such emotions feed directly into a broad range of mental illnesses – chronic anxiety, self-harm, suicidal ideation, depression – all have roots in a sense of not mattering enough to anyone over long childhood years.[14]

---

13   https://thefederalist.com/2020/06/16/how-black-lives-matters-antagonism-to-marriage-and-family-hurts-black-americans/ (accessed 25 February, 2021), emphasis mine.

14   'The Role of Love in Mental Health', *The School of Life,* 2020, https://www.theschooloflife.com/thebookoflife/the-role-of-love-in-mental-health/?utm_source=pocket-newtab-global-en-GB (accessed 23 November, 2020).

God's pattern for human life was designed for human flourishing. When public policy dis-incentivises family stability, poverty increases, and children suffer.[15]

The Bible affirms the duty of children to respect both their mothers and fathers.[16] In a sinful world, authority can be abused and there should be safeguards to protect children. But challenging the principle of parental authority introduces greater risks. Children need boundaries to protect them from abuse and exploitation. Dr Aric Sigman is a psychologist, and also a parent. He looks at the evidence from different societies and cultures (not from a Christian perspective) and concludes:

> By shying away from being in control and maintaining a clear position of authority, we have engaged in a type of parental and societal self-harm. Children today urgently need the most secure network possible, in the form of boundaries, discipline and order, to keep them from crumbling. Yet instead, the adult world at every turn – from parents and teachers, to social workers, police, the courts and politicians – has retreated from authority, and in so doing has robbed children of their basic supporting structures.[17]

The home is where we are to learn the principle of submission. Then in later life we are better prepared to live as good citizens and employees under the other authorities ordained by God. That is why there is a promise attached to this command: 'that your days may be long in the land that the LORD your God is giving you.'

FAMILY – NOT THE ULTIMATE LOYALTY

The Bible is realistic about the horrible effects of sin on family life. God has designed human government to restrain evil, so if there is

---

15 Ells, K, *The Invincible Family: Why the Global Campaign to Crush Motherhood and Fatherhood Can't Win,* (Regnery Gateway, 2020).

16 Proverbs 6:20; Ephesians 6:1-4; Colossians 3:20; note the example of the Lord Jesus, Luke 2:51.

17 Sigman, A, *The Spoilt Generation: Why Restoring Authority Will Make Our Children and Society Happier,* (Piatcus, 2009), p. 26.

violent abuse, the law must protect the victims. The family does not have ultimate authority over individuals. If human families forbid family members to follow Christ, the principle that 'Jesus is Lord' takes precedence over family loyalty.

And, in a fallen world, we may find ourselves in broken, messy, painful family situations. We may have hurt others and damaged ourselves by the decisions we've taken. Whoever we are, whatever our situation, the Gospel offers forgiveness and a new start and hope for the future.

Human beings have been created in the image of God for relationships. That doesn't mean that we all have to be married. The New Testament teaches that to be single is a high calling. Whether we are married or single, God has provided moral boundaries within which relationships will best flourish. When we defy those moral boundaries, we damage both individuals and community.

God's Good Design: Work

THE CREATION COMMAND

Adam and Eve were placed in a garden which was cultivated, but the rest of the earth was, as yet, untamed. They were commanded not only to 'fill' the earth, but to 'subdue' it:

> Be fruitful and increase in number, fill the earth and subdue it. Rule over the fish of the sea and the birds of the air and over every living creature that moves along the ground. (Gen. 1:28).

Our first parents were given stewardship over the inanimate creation (such as minerals, plants, forests), and dominion over animate creation (such as animals, fish, birds).

Once the fall into sin had occurred, that would involve 'subduing' the thorns and thistles that would continually hinder productivity. Nature would only reach its potential by means of human cultivation. Adam was given responsibility to 'tend and care for' the garden (Gen. 2:15). He was to work with the woman, who would bring her complementary skills, and with the offspring who would join them in fulfilling the creation mandate. So humans are to:

> ... explore the resources of the earth, to cultivate its land, to mine its buried treasures ... [They are] called by God to develop all the potentialities found in nature and humankind as a whole. [They are] to develop not only agriculture, horticulture and animal husbandry, but also science, technology, and art. In other words, we have here what is often called the cultural mandate: the command to develop a God-glorifying culture.[18]

Good stewardship means due care of the environment; regard for the preservation of the earth for future generations. Equally, the resources of the earth, including other living creatures, have been given to humans for our benefit and blessing. God as the Creator permits humans to use other living creatures for food:

> Then God said, 'I give you every seed-bearing plant on the face of the whole earth and every tree that has fruit with seed in it. They will be yours for food.' (Gen. 1:29)

> Everything that lives and moves about will be food for you. Just as I gave you the green plants, I now give you everything. (Gen. 9:3)[19]

God expects us to treat other living things with care and consideration, which is why eighteenth-century Evangelicals initiated the first society for the prevention of cruelty to animals.[20]

> You shall not muzzle an ox when it is treading out the grain. (Deut. 25:4, ESV)

> Whoever is righteous has regard for the life of his beast. (Prov. 12:10, ESV)

---

18 Hoekema, A, *Created in God's Image,* (Eerdmans, 1986), p. 79.

19 See also Romans 14:2-3.

20 Bready, J W, *England Before and After Wesley,* (Hodder and Stoughton, 1939), pp. 150-5; 407-8.

God has filled the earth and the seas with rich resources. We are to use those responsibly for the benefit of our fellow humans. Wayne Grudem and Barry Asmus write:

> ... it is right to use the energy resources that are found in the earth for our benefit and to do so with thanksgiving to God. We are convinced that God has given us an immensely abundant earth, filled with rich storehouses of energy supplies of different types, and these energy resources, many of which can substitute for each other, are unlikely ever to be exhausted.[21]

WORK AND REST

The fourth commandment reflects and expands on the creation mandate.

> Remember the Sabbath day by keeping it holy. Six days you shall labour and do all your work, but the seventh day is a sabbath to the LORD your God. On it you shall not do any work, neither you, nor your son or daughter, nor your male or female servant, nor your animals, nor any foreigner residing in your towns. For in six days the LORD made the heavens and the earth, the sea, and all that is in them, but he rested on the seventh day. Therefore the LORD blessed the Sabbath day and made it holy. (Exod. 20: 8-11).

The sabbath principle goes back to creation, when God set a cycle of six days of labour and one day of rest. This pattern is for all people, everywhere. Like marriage, this is a creation ordinance. We set aside time in the week to acknowledge and give thanks to the Creator. All can sense from nature that there is a God to whom thanks should be given (Rom. 1:21).

The command to rest from work for one day in seven is a protection from exploitation and overwork. Matthew Sleeth was working as a doctor when he realised that many of his patients were suffering life-threatening conditions because they refused to stop working. Their

---

21 Grudem, W, Asmus, B, *The Poverty of Nations: A Sustainable Solution,* (Crossway, 2015), p. 283.

driven lifestyle was killing them. He came to see the wisdom and humanity of the sabbath principle.[22]

Alongside the command to rest is the command to work. God stamped us with His image and gave us the privilege of managing His creation on His behalf. He has equipped humans with an astonishing array of different gifts and abilities, not just for 'paid work', but for all forms of creativity: economics, art, music, literature, science, cooking, agriculture, architecture and engineering. People created in the image of God were created to create. Work and creativity reflects the Triune God, because God is the original worker:

> The heavens declare the glory of God. The skies proclaim the work of his hands. (Ps. 19:1)

When we see a glorious sunset, a beautiful mountain, or an exquisite flower, we are to praise the Maker. When we see an amazing piece of art, or architecture, or engineering, or listen to a wonderful piece of music, we instinctively think of the human creator. But we should also thank God for making them in His image with the capacity, energy, and desire to create. That's why we see works of art in every culture and civilisation, not just 'Christian' ones. We live in an amazing and gloriously diverse social system.

WORK TO BLESS OTHERS

God created a beautiful world for His glory and pleasure, and for our enjoyment. God made us to reflect Him: if we create something of beauty or usefulness, it's not just about self-fulfilment. We take joy in giving pleasure to others, serving them, and providing for their needs. That is a reminder of the image of God in every human being.

We are made in God's image, and are most *truly fulfilled* when we glorify our Creator and serve our fellow human beings. We are to work hard, and use what we earn to support our own family and do good to others.

---

22 Sleeth, M, *24/6: A Prescription for a Happier Healthier Life,* (Tyndale House Publishers, 2012).

Anyone who has been stealing must steal no longer, but must work, doing something useful with their own hands, that they may have something to share with those in need. (Eph. 4:28)

In all things I have shown you that by working hard in this way we must help the weak and remember the words of the Lord Jesus, how he himself said, 'It is more blessed to give than to receive.' (Acts 20:35, ESV)

Whoever is generous to the poor lends to the Lord, and he will repay him for his deed. (Prov. 19:17, ESV)

They are to do good, to be rich in good works, to be generous and ready to share, thus storing up treasure for themselves as a good foundation for the future, so that they may take hold of that which is truly life. (1 Tim. 6:18-19, ESV)

One of the reasons for the rapid spread of Christianity in the early centuries was the way that unbelievers saw how willing the Christians were to care for the needy.[23]

WORK AFTER THE FALL

In a fallen world, sin impacts every area of human activity, including work. It is often difficult, frustrating, and seemingly unrewarding. Throughout history, the norm has been for people to have to work to survive. Often that work has been agonisingly hard. Those in agrarian economies seem to be at the mercy of the elements; those in industrial and technological economies seem to be at the mercy of market forces. Unpaid work, including looking after a family and home can be boring, repetitive, and frustrating. The workplace can be a place of injustice, harassment, petty infighting, backbiting, and ethical dilemmas. But in all these areas of work, paid or unpaid, we are to seek to glorify God, to be salt and light, and to bless others.

---

23 Stark, R, *The Rise of Christianity: A Sociologist Reconsiders History*, (Princeton University Press, 1996), p. 155.

Whatever you do, work at it with all your heart, as working for the Lord, not for human masters. (Col. 3:23)

History is filled with those who abuse and oppress. We see the horrible effects of sin wherever there is exploitation of other people, or of the environment, as well as in the excesses of big business or consumerism. In all these cases, there has been a failure to humbly acknowledge that we are accountable to the Creator. When we have access to resources and opportunities in this world, we are to use them to bless others and glorify God. Love God. Love neighbour. Paul warns the rich:

Command those who are rich in this present world not to be arrogant nor to put their hope in wealth, which is so uncertain, but to put their hope in God, who richly provides us with everything for our enjoyment. (1 Tim. 6:17)

Prosperity in Place of Poverty

God endowed humans with almost limitless potential in terms of creativity and achievement. Human capital, and freedom for people to innovate and create, is the single most important asset for any nation.

If we truly love our neighbour we should be deeply exercised by the terrible poverty suffered by great numbers of people in so many nations. It is a tragedy that some of the *poorest* nations on earth are among the *richest* in terms of natural resources, but all incentive or capacity to manage those resources well is crippled by tyrannical regimes. When individuals are unable to secure documented property ownership, it is impossible to escape from poverty.[24] The strong then prey on the weak, and the weak can get no justice. Achieving the wealth creation necessary to enable human flourishing demands not only skill and energy, but also freedom to initiate businesses and other enterprises,[25] the rule of law, and respect for property rights.

---

24 Grudem, W, Asmus, B, *The Poverty of Nations*, pp. 149-53.

25 Jraissati, J, 'A Tale of Two Countries: How Norway Embraces Markets While Venezuela Does Not', *Public Discourse,* September 9, 2020, https://

Myanmar (Burma), for example, is abundantly blessed with forests, precious gems, plentiful minerals, fertile soil for agriculture and off-shore oil and gas deposits. Most of the population live at subsistence level, and the majority of children are malnourished. This is a shocking failure to fulfil the creation mandate given to human beings by God the Creator, the ultimate owner of the whole earth:

> The earth is the Lord's, and everything in it, the world and all who live in it (Ps. 24:1; 1 Cor. 10:26).

God as the Great King appointed humans to manage the earth on His behalf. This can only be achieved where the exercise of initiative is allowed. That means respecting private property. In the Bible, property is seen as belonging not to the government or to society as a whole but to individuals. The sixth commandment, 'You shall not steal', implies the legitimacy of owning property (Exod. 20:15). In ancient Israel, during the Jubilee year, each person was to return to their family property (Lev. 25:10). It was a crime to 'move your neighbour's boundary stone' (Deut. 19:14). God was angry when King Ahab took family property away from Naboth, even though he offered to pay full compensation (1 Kings 21).

The medieval theologian Thomas Aquinas wisely pointed out:

> Every man is more careful to procure what is for himself alone than that which is common to many or to all: since each one will shirk the labor and leave to another that which concerns the community.[26]

When property is held in common, incentive is removed, and work is often badly done. Collective farms in the Soviet Union were a disaster. During the 1980s the Soviets had to buy grain from America, even

---

www.thepublicdiscourse.com/2020/09/70415/ (accessed 16 September, 2020).

26 Quoted by Spencer, A, 'Five Reasons Why Aquinas Supported Private Property', *Institute for Faith, Work and Economics,* 13 April, 2018, https://tifwe.org/reasons-aquinas-private-property/ (accessed 23 November, 2020).

though the USSR had just as much arable land dedicated to grain production as the United States.[27]

Until around 1800, across the globe average life expectancy was under thirty years. It doubled by 2001 because of the innovations brought in by the agricultural and industrial revolutions.[28] Some romanticise the idea of subsistence farming, but the lived reality is brutal. The creation mandate indicates that God's design for humanity is not just for us to survive, but to flourish on earth.[29]

SMASH CAPITALISM?

Well-intentioned Christians often join with 'progressive' demands to 'smash capitalism'. But capitalism is simply the free exchange of privately held goods and services. Free exchange allows for personal incentive. If a business is to succeed it has to meet the buyer's needs.

Adam Smith was a moral philosopher, and his classic book *The Wealth of Nations*, as well as *The Theory of Moral Sentiments* showed that *morality* was the key to capitalism. He explained that self-interested behaviour motivated economic activity. 'Self-interest' is not 'selfishness'. It means that in serving the needs of others, we also receive financial reward:

> It is not from the benevolence of the butcher, the brewer or the baker that we expect our dinner, but from their regard to their own interest.[30]

If nations are to escape poverty, they need to be free to increase the production of goods and services. People must be able to create businesses in order both to make profits and serve the needs of others.

> After [Smith's] book, 'Wealth of Nations', was published and its principles took hold, wages quadrupled in the next 50 years, and

---

27 Ibid.

28 Grudem, W, Asmus, B, *The Poverty of Nations*, p. 110.

29 Ibid., p. 111.

30 Smith, A, *An Inquiry into the Nature and Causes of the Wealth of Nations*, 1776, Soares, S M, ed, 2007, p. 16.

then quadrupled again over the next 50. Every society that has leaned into free enterprise has prospered and benefited the poor and needy. Profits are good. They are not a four letter word. They are the incentive for work.[31]

In a sinful world, we are all corrupted, and the Bible warns against greed and exploitation. But temptation to greed doesn't mean that we should all stop eating; nor should it shut down free markets.[32] We should guard against selfish consumerism, but also defend the human freedom to work, and to profit from that work.[33]

> People in our [free] societies own things, their labour included, and can trade those things freely with others. They can buy, sell, accumulate, save, share, and give. They can enjoy all that their freely exercised labour can secure for them and even, if they choose, do nothing and still survive. You can take away the freedom to buy and sell; you can compel people to work on terms that they would not freely accept; you can confiscate property or forbid this or that form of it. But if those are the alternatives to 'capitalism' there is, now, no real alternative save slavery.[34]

In a sinful world no economic or political system will function perfectly. But capitalism has been better for the poor than either socialism or traditional pre-industrial economies. Just observe the direction in which the poor of the world migrate. They:

---

31 Hovind, C, author of *Godonomics,* (Multnomah, 2013), author interview, https://www.christianbook.com/godonomics-protect-through-biblical-principles-finance/chad-hovind/9781601424785/pd/37086EB#CBD-PD-Description (accessed 7 October, 2020); Kilcoyne, M, 'Why Edinburgh's Adam Smith statue should stay', *The Spectator,* 7 March 2021, https://www.spectator.co.uk/article/adam-smith (accessed 8 March, 2021).

32 Leach, G, 'Thoughts on a biblical economic worldview: or Godonomics', https://theceme.org/wp-content/uploads/2020/04/Part-2.pdf (accessed 7 October, 2020).

33 Scruton, R, *Fools, Frauds and Firebrands: Thinkers of the New Left,* (Bloomsbury Continuum, 2015/2019), pp. 213-4.

34 Ibid., p. 276.

... know better than the intellectuals. They seek opportunity and liberty. They seek systems that allow them to be economically creative, as God made them to be.[35]

A Sea of Blood

A just society should provide equal opportunities, including education. Individuals vary in capacity, competence, and determination to take advantage of those opportunities. God has gifted people made in His image with moral responsibility, creativity, and the capacity to work. The biblical worldview respects individual responsibility, choices, family and property. It is the only certain bulwark against totalitarian tyranny.

Today, those calling for Social Justice want advantages and resources to be re-distributed (forcibly if necessary) to iron out the inequalities between different groups of people. They demand the smashing down of institutions regarded as 'oppressive' and the redistribution of resources to ensure 'equity', or equal outcomes. The twentieth century is replete with examples of the injustice and suffering that follows such efforts. Templeton Prize winner Michael Novak observed in 1994:

No system that devalues the initiative and creativity of every woman and every man, made in the image of their Creator, is fit for human habitation. On the first day that the flag of Russia snapped against the blue sky over the city hall of St. Petersburg, where for seven decades the Red flag had flown, a Russian artist told me: 'The next time you want to try an experiment like socialism, try it out on animals first—men it hurts too much.' Indeed, once the Iron Curtain was joyfully torn down, and the Great Lie thoroughly unmasked, it became clear that in the heartland of 'real existing socialism' the poor were living in Third World conditions; that a

---

35 Novak, M, *Awakening from Nihilism: Why Truth Matters,* (Address given at Westminster Abbey on the occasion of winning the Templeton Prize, 1994), (IEA London 1995), p. 18, https://www.firstthings.com/article/1994/08/awakening-from-nihilismthe-templeton-prize-address (accessed 11 January, 2021).

large majority of the population was in misery; that both the will to work and economic creativity had been suffocated ...[36]

British author Peter Hitchens abandoned his revolutionary socialist ideals when he saw, first hand, the outworking of that ideology.[37] He marvels that with so much evidence of failure, people still pursue the false Utopia of equal outcomes. Reflecting on communist Russia he writes:

> The sunlit modern cities turned out to be concrete slums. The promised prosperity ended in meat queues, corruption, and squalor. The equality of man was mocked by a secretive and corrupt privileged class living sequestered lives behind high, green fences. The armies that broke Hitler and smashed down the gates of the death camps went on to crush human liberty in Berlin, Budapest, and Prague. And yet in millions of minds the fantasy still persists that we can begin the world over again, and that after all the broken eggs there will in fact be an omelette rather than a useless mess ... I sense that they are taking bookings to Utopia yet again. *Nobody will mention that the route takes you across a sea of blood, and you never get there.*[38]

When we destroy all disparities, a grim kind of equity is achieved: equality amid the rubble. The ideology of Social Justice is not biblical justice.[39]

---

36 Ibid., p. 17.

37 See chapter 2.

38 Hitchens, P, 'Bookings to Utopia', *First Things,* October 2020, https://www.firstthings.com/article/2020/10/bookings-to-utopia (accessed 7 October, 2020), emphasis mine.

39 Allen, S D, *Why Social Justice Is Not Biblical Justice,* (Credo House Publishers, 2020); Brunton, J, 'The Theological Problem With Tim Keller's So-Called Social Justice', https://christianintellectual.com/the-theological-problem-with-tim-kellers-so-called-social-justice/ (accessed 25 February, 2021).

God's Good Design: Communities

Our Triune God is relational, characterised by love, self-giving and serving. We are created in His image with the capacity to love others. We are designed to live in communities, in which we are to work and care. In every neighbourhood there are people with a whole range of needs.

CHRISTIANITY: A TRACK RECORD OF CARE

Our Triune God is a God of mercy and compassion.

> The LORD is gracious and compassionate,
>   slow to anger and rich in love.
> The LORD is good to all;
>   he has compassion on all he has made. (Ps. 145:8-9)

God insists that anyone who wants to honour Him will have mercy on the needy:

> Whoever oppresses the poor shows contempt for their Maker,
>   but whoever is kind to the needy honours God (Prov. 14:31).

Compassion characterised the ministry of Christ:

> When Jesus landed and saw a large crowd, he had compassion on them and healed their sick. (Matt. 14:14)

When Jesus was asked specifically how Christian love (agape) was to be shown, and to whom, He answered with the story of the Good Samaritan, and said, 'go and do likewise' (Luke 10:25-37).[40] Such self-giving love was a revolutionary concept. The account of the Good Samaritan has been described as the parable that changed the world.

---

40 Flemming, H, 'Post-Hippocratic Medicine: The Problem and the Solution: How the Christian Ethic Has Influenced Health Care', *Kuyper Foundation*, 2010, https://www.kuyper.org/s/TextPost-HippocraticMedicine.pdf (accessed 17 April, 2020), p. 22.

Over the centuries, the followers of Christ have been at the forefront of efforts to relieve suffering and need.[41] The West has a tradition of philanthropy and a culture of giving and sharing that is unmatched in any other civilisation in history. Indian author Vishal Mangalwadi observes the contrast between the biblical ethic, and the Hindu concept of a hierarchical society where Brahmins are at the top and 'untouchables' at the bottom.[42]

In pagan culture, compassion to the needy was often regarded as foolish. The Greeks praised strength, courage and self-control, but viewed compassion as weakness. Plato, and other philosophers, thought that the poor should be left to die if they could no longer work. By contrast, Christians were widely noted for their compassion, and willingness to give without expecting reward. In A.D. 40, there were probably no more than a few thousand Christians. By A.D. 350 there were possibly over thirty-three million Christians in the Roman Empire out of a total population of sixty million.[43] Rodney Stark describes how their ethic impacted the misery and brutality of life in the urban Greco-Roman world:

> To cities filled with the homeless and impoverished, Christianity offered charity as well as hope. To cities filled with newcomers and strangers, Christianity offered an immediate basis for attachments. To cities filled with orphans and widows, Christianity provided a new and expanded sense of family. To cities torn by violent ethnic strife, Christianity offered a new basis for social solidarity. And to cities faced with epidemics, fires and earthquakes, Christianity offered effective nursing services.[44]

Christian response to poverty was grounded in beliefs about human dignity. No pagan cult insisted that caring for the sick, the

---

41 Some of this section taken from James, S, *How Christianity Transformed the World,* chapter 6.

42 Mangalwadi, V, *The Book That Made Your World,* (Thomas Nelson, 2011), p. 300.

43 Stark, R, *The Rise of Christianity,* (HarperCollins, 1997), p. 7.

44 Ibid., p.155.

poor, widows, and orphans was an essential religious duty.[45] Once Constantine became emperor the church became the first organised institution of public welfare in Western history.[46]

Whenever God has moved to revive the church, there has been an outpouring of mercy and compassion. During the evangelical awakenings of the eighteenth and nineteenth centuries, despite opposition, many were born again, their lives were transformed, and this inspired a nationwide moral reformation and outpouring of mercy ministries. The awakenings in Britain and America created a culture where 'benevolence', 'sympathy', 'compassion' and 'fellow-feeling' became a social ethos which found expression in numerous reform movements and philanthropic enterprises.

In France, a more aggressively secular enlightenment resulted in Revolution, but the French enlightenment didn't produce the community of philanthropists or the multitude of private societies that were so prominent in Britain.[47] The poor were worse off at the end of the French Revolution than at the beginning.

A second Great Awakening at the end of the eighteenth century, and continuing through the nineteenth century, led to tens of thousands more people on both sides of the Atlantic converting to living Christianity. Evangelical Christians were responsible for a remarkable range of social reforms: prison reform, care of the mentally ill, factory reform, rescuing women and children from sexual abuse, provision of education, and of course, the abolition of the slave trade. Probably three-quarters of the total number of voluntary charitable organisations in Britain during the second half of the nineteenth century were evangelical.[48] Large numbers of lay men and women gave time, energy and money to help an extraordinary variety of

---

45 Bentley Hart, D, *Atheist Delusions: The Christian Revolution and Its Fashionable Enemies,* (Yale University Press, 2009), p. 164.

46 Ibid., pp. 163-4.

47 Himmelfarb, G, *The Roads to Modernity: The British, French and American Enlightenments,* (Vintage, 2008), p. 181.

48 Heasman, K, *Evangelicals in Action,* (Geoffrey Bles, 1962), p. 14.

organisations reaching out to help street children, prostitutes, orphans, prisoners, the sick and disabled, and other needy people.

By contrast, Russian communists despised philanthropy as a 'betrayal of all mankind', as it delayed necessary revolution. During the terrible famine of 1891-1892, Tolstoy and Chekhov initiated food distribution to those who were suffering, but Lenin said it would be better to hoard food to speed up the demands for revolution: in his view the worse social conditions were the better.[49]

What about today? *Half the Sky: How to Change the World* (2010) was written by liberal feminists who document female oppression worldwide. They found that Christians are at the forefront of working against discrimination in the hardest places on earth, and that they significantly out-give political liberals (who decry social injustice, but tend to lobby governments to give aid, rather than digging deep themselves).[50]

In 2006 a survey of the UK found that Christians give seven and a half times as much as others of their salary to charities, churches and good causes.[51] In the United States, a large proportion of the volunteers who mentor prisoners and their families are Christians. Shutting down a city congregation will often damage a neighbourhood's viability and socio-economic health, whereas active churches, religious schools, and church-based ministries have a positive impact on local communities.[52]

---

49 Morson, G S, 'Suicide of the Liberals', *First Things,* October 2020, https://www.firstthings.com/article/2020/10/suicide-of-the-liberals (accessed 12 January 2021).

50 Kristof, N D, WuDunn, S, *Half the Sky,* (Virago, 2010), pp. 157-60; see James, S, *God's Design for Women in an Age of Gender Confusion,* (Evangelical Press, 2019), chapter 1.

51 Quoted in Rose, L, ed, *What Are They Teaching the Children?,* (VFJ/Wilberforce Publications, 2016), p. 263. A contrast between Christian and secular generosity is found in Coppenger, M, *Moral Apologetics for Contemporary Christians,* (B&H Publishers, 2011).

52 Zinsmeister, K, 'Less God, Less Giving?' *Philanthropy Roundtable,* Winter 2019, https://www.philanthropyroundtable.org/philanthropy-magazine/less-god-less-giving (accessed 27 March, 2020).

GOD'S MORAL LAW PROMOTES THE COMMON GOOD

Many today imagine that freedom means that each individual can do as they wish, choose their own morality, and live free from the external constraints of God's law. Absolute morality is equated with 'authoritarian control'. But between moral relativism on the one hand, and authoritarian control on the other, is the situation where individuals exercise self-restraint because they are following the moral law, as laid upon the human conscience by God.

If you were given the choice of living in a community where the majority obeyed the Ten Commandments, or one where they were consistently broken, which would be the safer and happier community? There cannot be a flourishing and free society where the majority of citizens routinely steal, cheat, lie, fail to keep agreements or pay debts, or behave violently to others.

> If a people composed of 100 million citizens is guarded by 100 million inner policemen—that is, by 100 million self-governing consciences—then the number of policemen on its streets may be few. For a society without inner policemen, on the other hand, there aren't enough policemen in the world to make society civil. Self-control is not authoritarianism but rather the alternative to it.[53]

The creation mandate and God's moral law both uphold the principles of family and work. Compassion and care should be provided for all in genuine need. But well-intended welfare provision which has the *unintended* consequence of *discouraging* stable family formation, or the work ethic (or both), does more harm than good. Individual responsibility and agency should not be denied or suppressed. The 'wisdom literature' of the Bible instructs people to cultivate diligence and prudence. Cultures influenced by a biblical Christian worldview recognise the importance of taking responsibility. They encourage qualities such as hard work, perseverance, generosity and courage.

---

53 Novak, M, *Awakening from Nihilism: Why Truth Matters,* p. 21, https://www.firstthings.com/article/1994/08/awakening-from-nihilismthe-templeton-prize-address (accessed 11 January, 2021).

The practical impact of revival was obvious in Wales during the early twentieth century. Dr Martyn Lloyd-Jones, one of the greatest preachers of the twentieth century, took up his first pastorate in a poor area in his native Wales. Many of those who heard his preaching were converted to living Christianity. One little boy told his school teacher: 'We had a dinner today, Miss! We had gravy, potatoes, meat, and cabbage, and rice pudding ... My father has been converted!'[54] Up until then, the father's pay packet had gone on drink. The family rarely had a proper meal. Home life was now transformed.

The poor suffer most when moral restraints are derided and cast aside. Christianity has spread rapidly in Latin America, Asia, and Africa during the twentieth century. A major factor in that growth has been the fact that evangelical churches have a high view of the family, and emphasise responsibility and fidelity.[55] Women and children benefit when men are discouraged from squandering family resources on drinking, gambling or prostitutes.

LEARNING FROM THE WISDOM OF OTHERS

One generation commends your works to another;
  they tell of your mighty acts. (Ps. 145:4)

Many today claim that we all need to discover our own values.[56] But human society is a covenant between present, past, and future generations. Each generation is not meant to start from scratch, and discover all the branches of learning by themselves. We are to learn from the wisdom of others, and build on that. We are to learn from God's works ('general revelation' including nature and history) and from God's Word.

The Czech reformer **Jan Comenius (1592-1670)** has been described as 'the father of modern education'. He believed that *God's*

---

54 Murray, I, D. *Martyn-Lloyd Jones, The First Forty Years, 1899-1939*, (Banner of Truth Trust, 1982), pp. 220-1.

55 Jenkins, P, *The Next Christendom: The Coming of Global Christianity*, (Oxford University Press, 2011), pp. 96-7.

56 See chapter 1.

world is the greatest textbook of all: we learn of God through learning about His world. He wanted classrooms to be 'happy workshops of humanity'; each one should be 'an imitation of heaven'.[57] He was passionate about providing excellent education to every single child, as each is made in God's image.

One of the great educational pioneers of the twentieth century was **Dr Rochunga Pudaite (1927-2015)**. When he was born in a remote area of India, among a tribe who were widely feared for their violence, the nearest school was 96 miles away. At the age of ten, he was sent by his father on foot through dense jungle to learn to read and write, with a view to one day translating the Bible into their native Hmar language. Ultimately Rochunga created a romanized script for the Hmar, and translated the New Testament into the Hmar language from the original Greek. He founded an organisation which opened 85 schools, a college and hospital for the Hmar people. By 2011, the literacy rate was 85 per cent (compared with an average 60 per cent rate in India). He helped several other people groups translate the Bible into their own languages. His motto was 'Transforming A Nation Through Education'. He worked tirelessly against the caste system, and for the equality of all people. His friend Vishal Mangalwadi writes:

> The Bible set his imagination free to dream what his tribe ought to be – educated; free to interact with neighbours and enemies; able to overcome hunger, hate and disease; and ready to contribute to the world ... Ro became a linguist because he believed that language links our minds together to make us the only culture-creating creatures on this planet. It enables us to store and transmit ideas and to improve upon existing ideas.[58]

Wherever Christian missionaries have gone, literacy for all, boys and girls, has been one of the first priorities.[59]

---

57 Mangalwadi, V, *The Book That Made Your World*, pp. 213-4.

58 Ibid., p. 368.

59 Woodbury, R D, 'Protestant Missionaries and the Centrality of Conversion Attempts', in Hertzke, A D, Shah, T S, eds, *Christianity and Freedom:*

Amid the fragmentation of individual experiences, amid the diversity of group identities, we share a common human history, and we live in a shared world, created by one God. The great literature of all ages describes our mutual humanity. In 2001 Dr Theodore Dalrymple visited North Korea. He describes a memorable encounter in the main square in Pyongyang:

> A young Korean slid surreptitiously up to me and asked, 'Do you speak English?' An electric moment: for in North Korea, unsupervised contact between a Korean and a foreigner is utterly unthinkable ... 'Yes,' I replied. [The young Korean whispered] 'I am a student at the Foreign Languages Institute. Reading Dickens and Shakespeare is the greatest, the only, pleasure of my life.' It was the most searing communication I have ever received in my life. We parted immediately afterwards and of course will never meet again. For him, Dickens and Shakespeare (which the regime permitted him to read with quite other ends in view) guaranteed the possibility not just of freedom but of truly human life itself.[60]

God's Good Design: Nations

After the fall into sin God provided that evil should be restrained: communities were to enforce law and order.

> And for your lifeblood I will surely demand an accounting. I will demand an accounting from each animal. And from each man, too, I will demand an accounting for the life of his fellow man.
>
> Whoever sheds the blood of man,
> By man shall his blood be shed;
> For in the image of God
> Has God made man. (Gen. 9: 5-6)

Volume I Historical Perspectives, (Cambridge University Press, 2016), pp. 367-90, p. 373.

60 Dalrymple T, *Our Culture: What's Left of It: The Mandarins and the Masses*, (Ivan R Dee, 2005), p. 114.

Rulers, including non-Christians, are appointed by the Creator to restrain wrongdoing (Rom. 13:1-7). God expects that they should administer justice. Scripture is filled with teaching about how God hates injustice. God watches over all the affairs of all the nations. He is angry when rulers acquit the guilty and accuse the innocent; when they accept bribes; and when they govern in their own self-interest.

> He who justifies the wicked and he who condemns the righteous are both alike an abomination to the Lord. (Prov. 17:15, ESV)

The Bible shows unbelieving rulers being used by God to further His own purposes, as in the example of Cyrus of Persia:

> Thus says the LORD to his anointed, to Cyrus, whose right hand I have grasped, to subdue nations before him and to loose the belts of kings, to open doors before him, that gates may not be closed. 'I will go before you ... I call you by your name, I name you, though you do not know me. I am the LORD, and there is no other, besides me there is no God; I equip you, though you do not know me.' (Isa. 45:1-5, ESV)

In the New Testament, believers were commanded to respect their rulers:

> Let every person be subject to the governing authorities. For there is no authority except from God, and those that exist have been ordained by God. Therefore whoever resists the authorities resists what God has appointed, and those who resist will incur judgement. For rulers are not a terror to good conduct but to bad. Would you have no fear of the one who is in authority? Then do what is good, and you will receive his approval, for he is God's servant for your good. But if you do wrong, be afraid, for he does not bear the sword in vain. For he is the servant (deacon) of God, an avenger who carries out God's wrath on the wrongdoer. Therefore one must be in subjection, not only to avoid God's wrath, but also for the sake of conscience. (Rom. 13:1-5, a parallel passage is found in 1 Pet. 2:13-17, ESV).

In many ways, the Roman Empire was wicked and dissolute. But a state exercising law and order is still a great benefit to citizens, compared to a state of anarchy or civil war.

Governments should protect citizens from crime, foreign invasion, bribery, corruption, and (where possible) from the spread of epidemics of disease. They should protect natural resources from unnecessary destruction.[61] Good governments promote universal education and laws that protect stable family structures. They should ensure the freedom of citizens to own property, buy and sell, and to relocate and live anywhere within a nation. They should promote freedoms for all.[62] All human beings equally are under law; all equally should have access to justice. God expects rulers to dispense justice fairly:

> Do not pervert justice; do not show partiality to the poor or favouritism to the great, but judge your neighbour fairly. (Lev. 19:15)

That biblical principle of equality before the law is undermined when critical legal theory is applied in a way that means that justice is no longer 'blind'.[63]

In a sinful world, civil authority can veer into oppression. But life in a society without any law enforcement is even worse. During the 1980s there was no functioning government in Somalia. Evil was not restrained. Destitution and terror reigned.

A research project of many years' duration documented that where there has been the most impact of Bible-believing mission in the world, there are governments which are most respectful of human rights and the rule of law, and least prone to tyranny.[64]

61　Grudem, W, Asmus, B, *The Poverty of Nations: A Sustainable Solution,* (Crossway, 2013) chapter 7.

62　Ibid., chapter 7.

63　See chapter 5.

64　Woodberry, R D, 'Protestant Missionaries and the Centrality of Conversion Attempts for the Spread of Education, Printing, Colonial Reform, and Political Democracy', in *Christianity and Freedom, Volume 1,* pp. 367-90.

Rulers Are Accountable

Obedience to God includes submission to the human authorities He has ordained.

But the fact that human leaders have to answer to God also limits their power. Leadership is to be exercised for the benefit of those being led. The truth that all have to answer to God limits the extent of necessary submission. It protects against totalitarian tyranny.

By contrast, in atheistic regimes where no God is acknowledged, the State can 'become God' with horrific consequences. The twentieth century was the century of terrifying dictatorships. Between 1900 and 1987 *170 million* people were killed by their own governments, more than *four times* the total number killed in all the wars of that period.[65] But the State is not God. If agents of the State, or any other authorities, command us to do anything that God forbids, we respond 'We must obey God rather than men' (Acts 5:29).

Martin Niemöller (1892-1984), a Lutheran pastor in Germany, was imprisoned between 1938 and 1945 for his opposition to the Nazi regime. On one occasion, when interrogated by Hitler himself, Niemöller responded:

> You can imprison me and you can torture me and you can kill me, but, one day you will give an account to one who is the King of kings and the Lord of lords.[66]

Individual human dignity, founded on our relationship to God our Creator, is the foundation of individual liberty of conscience.

Protection from Global Tyranny

In a fallen world, nationalism can be a force for evil. States can tyrannise their own citizens, or they can attack and subdue other states. Some think that humanities' problems can only be solved by global government. The humanist aim, as set out in the Second Humanist Manifesto, was to eliminate national sovereignty, in order to achieve

---

65 Rummel, R J, *Death by Government,* (Transaction Publishers, 1997).

66 Dockery, D S, George, T, *The Great Tradition of Christian Thinking: A Student's Guide,* (Crossway, 2012), Kindle Edition, 1123-6.

a new world order: 'based upon transnational federal government'.[67] The framework policy for UNESCO[68] published in 1946 said that to secure world peace there would need to be 'some form of world political unity, whether through a single world government or otherwise'.[69]

But in a fallen world, global government could form the ultimate totalitarian regime. In Genesis 11, after the building of the Tower of Babel, humanity was divided into different nations. That was God's provision to *protect* them from global tyranny.[70]

Diversity between nations is not intrinsically negative. The vast variety of cultures and social systems reflects the diversity found throughout the created order. Roman Catholic scholar Charles Chaput writes:

> We do need to be wary of excessive national pride. It has caused great harm in the modern era. A nation can become so corrupt and Babylon-like that it's not worth defending ... We also need to remember that the nation-state, however happily we conceive it, is distinct from, and finally less important than, the purpose of our life in this world. Man's purpose is to know and love God ... Our true and lasting commonwealth is in heaven, and therein lies our real citizenship (Phil 3:20) ... [But] we need a healthy patriotism. We need to entertain the possibility that love for our country might lead us to sacrifice greatly, even radically, in order to preserve the best that remains in it. That love is not an evil. It's a source of liberation. It breaks the bonds of our addiction to lesser things. It leads us to stand as brothers, sisters, and friends with others. Fidelity to the good in our nation is not our final end. It

67   Kurtz, P, Wilson, E H, *Humanist Manifesto II,* 1973, https://www.google.com/search?client=firefox-b-d&q=Second+Humanist+Manifesto (accessed 16 September, 2020).

68   The United Nations Educational, Scientific and Cultural Organization.

69   Huxley, J, *UNESCO: Its Purpose and its Philosophy,* (UNESCO, 1946), p. 13, https://unesdoc.unesco.org/ark:/48223/pf0000068197 (accessed 16 September, 2020).

70   Mangalwadi, V, *The Book That Made Your World,* pp. 170-7.

doesn't deliver us from sin and death. It doesn't have an absolute claim on our souls. It doesn't replace our hunger for heaven. But it is a natural grace; a partial but real deliverance from the prison cell of a world without loyalties, and the confines of self-love.[71]

Rather than utopian schemes for world government, the biblical teaching is that all rulers should recognise that they are answerable to God. They should govern justly for the good of those they rule.

THE LORD IS KING!

God is Creator and Lord of all. The Father has exalted His Son, Jesus Christ, to have authority over all other rulers (Psalms 2, 110). All will answer to Him at the Last Day. No earthly authority (whether in family, workplace or state) has ultimate authority. We are all under God. Abusive parents, unfair teachers, harsh employers, brutal law enforcement officers, and tyrannical rulers will all have to give account to Him. God has ordained structures of law and order which should *protect* children from violence or abuse, employees from unreasonable working conditions, and citizens from injustice whether at the hands of the police or the law.

In a sinful world, such authorities do sometimes abuse their trust. Some then demand the abolition of all authority – but the resulting anarchy is most damaging for the weak, the vulnerable and the poor.

The Bible is realistic about human sin, and the need for authority structures; but because it is realistic about sin, no authority is absolute. Those societies that have been impacted by the biblical worldview have promoted 'liberal values' such as:

- Limits on the power of government (by means of political democracy)
- Equal access to law
- Freedom of religion, speech, expression and conscience
- Respect for reason and evidence

---

71   Chaput, C J, 'Dulce et Decorum Est: In Defense of Healthy Patriotism', *Public Discourse*, 7 March, 2021, https://www.thepublicdiscourse. com/2021/03/74524/ (accessed 8 March, 2021).

- Measures to ensure safe living and working conditions for all

Increasing numbers of people, even if they don't profess to be Christian, accept that these 'liberal values' have been founded on the biblical insistence that all human beings equally are created in God's image, and that all will be held accountable to God.[72]

FURTHER RESOURCES

Grudem, G, *Business for the Glory of God,* (Crossway, 2007)

Leach, G, 'Thoughts on a biblical economic worldview: or Godonomics', https://theceme.org/wp-content/uploads/2020/04/Part-2.pdf

London Institute of Contemporary Christianity (LICC): *Fruitfulness on the Front line* (DVD series and study guide) https://www.licc.org.uk/resources/discover-fruitfulness-on-the-frontline/

Mackay, J L, *The Dignity of Work,* (The Christian Institute, 2011), www.christian.org.uk/wp-content/uploads/dignityofwork.pdf

Mangalwadi, V, *The Book That Made Your World: How the Bible Created the Soul of Western Civilisation,* (Thomas Nelson, 2011)

Morgan, P, *The War Between the State and the Family: How Government Divides and Impoverishes,* (Institute of Economic Affairs, 2007), https://iea.org.uk/wp-content/uploads/2016/07/upldbook406pdf.pdf

Needham, N R, *Common Grace,* (The Christian Institute, 2017), http://www.christian.org.uk/wp-content/uploads/common-grace.pdf

Traeger, S, Gilbert, G, *The Gospel at Work: How working for King Jesus gives purpose and meaning to our jobs,* (Zondervan 2013), http://www.thegospelatwork.com/

---

72 Authors such as Tom Holland, Douglas Murray and Rodney Stark. See also Further Resources.

Summary: The biblical worldview is the foundation of human flourishing in society. God designed family and work. The married family should not be undermined. Property should be protected, work should be rewarded. We need to learn from the past and allow for innovation in the present. Civil authorities should be supported. All human institutions are answerable to God, which provides a bulwark against oppression. The division of the world into nation states offers protection from the threat of global tyranny.

9 The Biblical Worldview: Christ Is King – Hope for the Future

Without God: Without Hope

Without God, hope is eclipsed.[1] Many anticipate ever greater environmental damage, civil unrest, escalating terrorism, correspondingly authoritarian governments, and deadlier pandemics. Some resolve never to bring children into this world. There is a ready market for dark dystopian novels and films.[2] A world where each person believes they are at the centre of the universe is bleak. If the only purpose of life is to fulfil ourselves, when life does not deliver our desires, what hope is there?

By April 2020 fear of a new virus, Covid-19, had led to half the world's population being instructed to stay at home.[3] Covid is a serious disease, but other diseases have killed, and are killing, many more people. The deeper contagion sweeping the globe in 2021 is fear. When a godless worldview dominates, death is the end, and so fear of

---

1   Ephesians 2:12. Paul writes that, prior to their conversion, the Ephesian Christians had been 'without hope and without God in the world'.

2   A 'dystopia' is an 'imaginary place where everything is as bad as possible'. Concise Oxford Dictionary.

3   'Coronavirus: Half of humanity now on lockdown as 90 countries call for confinement', *euronews,* 3 April, 2020, https://www.euronews.com/2020/04/02/coronavirus-in-europe-spain-s-death-toll-hits-10-000-after-record-950-new-deaths-in-24-hours (accessed 18 August, 2020).

death becomes a 'lifelong slavery' (Heb. 2:15). Extending life becomes the all-consuming concern, even at the cost of other aspects of human flourishing. Nations are locked down, economies are crashed, governments intrude into family and church life. In some countries care homes closed the doors to visitors. The elderly have been unable to see their own children, or even their spouses. Relatives have been banned from entering each other's homes. Churches have been closed. Ministers have been barred from visiting the sick and dying.

But fear isn't the exclusive preserve of unbelievers. The devil wants to discourage Christians because a demoralised army will never gain ground. Many evangelicals in the West seem to be traumatised by the strength of opposition. They display little confidence that Christ's cause will prevail. Ambition appears to be limited to survival rather than advance. 'Let's just hang on until the return of Christ!'

CHRIST IS KING

It's right to look forward to the return of Christ when His Kingship will be universally acknowledged.[4] But it's wrong to be paralysed by pessimism in the here and now. The defeat of the devil and all his works has been guaranteed by Christ's finished work of salvation.

> The reason the Son of God appeared was to destroy the works of the devil. (1 John 3:8 ESV)

> He too (Jesus Christ) shared in their humanity so that by his death he might break the power of him who holds the power of death—that is, the devil— and free those who all their lives were held in slavery by their fear of death. (Heb. 2:14-15)

Christ's final command to His disciples was that they should go to all nations. It was accompanied by the promise of His continued presence and universal authority:

> Then Jesus came to them and said, '*All authority* in heaven and on earth has been given to me. Therefore go and make disciples of all

---

4   Philippians 2:10-11.

nations,[5] baptizing them in the name of the Father and of the Son and of the Holy Spirit, and teaching them to obey everything I have commanded you. And surely *I am with you always, to the very end of the age.*' (Matt. 28: 18-20)

Writing to persecuted believers in the great Roman city of Corinth, Paul assured them: 'For he *must reign* until he has put all enemies under his feet' (1 Cor. 15:25).

The Son is reigning at the Father's right hand. His victory over Satan at the Cross is being worked out in the present age as His enemies are brought into submission. Rulers may defy God, but their defiance is futile. Christ will be seen to triumph. One by one they will submit to His Lordship. This is vividly described in Psalms 2 and 110, both often alluded to by the New Testament writers.[6]

> The kings of the earth rise up
> and the rulers band together
> against the LORD and against his anointed, saying,
> 'Let us break their chains
> and throw off their shackles.'
> The One enthroned in heaven laughs;
> the Lord scoffs at them.
> He rebukes them in his anger
> and terrifies them in his wrath, saying,
> 'I have installed my king
> on Zion, my holy mountain.'
> I will proclaim the LORD's decree:
> He said to me, 'You are my son;
> today I have become your father.
> Ask me, and I will make the nations your inheritance,
> the ends of the earth your possession.

---

5   The Greek word used could be literally translated as 'people groups'.

6   Among other references, Psalm 2 is alluded to in Acts 2:36; 13:33; Hebrews 1:15; Revelation 2:26-7; 6:15-17; 19:15; 19:16,20,21; Psalm 110 is alluded to in Acts 2:33-5; 1 Corinthians 15:25-7; Hebrews 7:15-17; 20-21; 10:11-13.

You will break them with a rod of iron;
  you will dash them to pieces like pottery.' (Ps. 2:2-9)

The LORD says to my lord:
'Sit at my right hand
  until I make your enemies
  a footstool for your feet.'
The LORD will extend your mighty sceptre from Zion, saying,
  'Rule in the midst of your enemies!' (Ps. 110:1-2)

In this present age we are to pray for, work for and expect Christ's kingdom to be acknowledged among every people group on earth.[7] That is not to be achieved by force, but as people voluntarily and willingly submit to Him. By nature we all resist the command to submit to God, but the Holy Spirit works to bring new life (John 1:12-13). We are to long for the earth to be filled with the knowledge of the glory of the Lord:

For the earth will be filled with the knowledge of the glory of the LORD, as the waters cover the sea. (Hab. 2:14)

It is right to lament as people suffer, and creation itself suffers as a result of evil. But gloominess about the prospects of God's Kingdom betrays a failure of faith. With God's people in every age we are to live by faith and not by sight.[8]

GOD'S CAUSE WILL TRIUMPH

Promises of universal blessing in the Old Testament are best understood in the framework of the 'prophetic perspective'. When you are high in

---

7   Some Christians argue that it's wrong to have any firm confidence in gospel progress as they suggest it's incompatible with the New Testament teaching about the imminent return of Christ. But none of us knows the time of His return (Matt. 24:36). We are to live holy lives, as if it may take place today. We are to pray and work faithfully as if it may not take place for many centuries or millennia. Murray, I, *The Puritan Hope*, (Banner of Truth, 1971).

8   2 Corinthians 5:7; and see Hebrews 11.

the Alps, looking out at the next mountain range, peak after peak may *appear* to be close together; in reality they may be many miles apart.

As the prophets looked forward, various events in the future often seemed to blend into one great 'mountain range': the restoration of the Jews from the Babylonian captivity, the first coming of the Messiah, the pouring out of the Spirit at Pentecost, the extension of the Kingdom through subsequent millennia, and the second coming of the Messiah. Many of the prophecies had 'layers' of meaning, and can be applied to one, more, or all of those events in salvation history. They reach their *fullest and final* fulfilment in the establishment of the new heavens and the new earth after the second coming of Christ. They *also* point to the blessings of the present gospel age.

For example, God's heart for justice is seen in the prophet Isaiah's depiction of the coming Messiah:

> Here is my servant, whom I uphold,
>   my chosen one in whom I delight;
> I will put my Spirit on him,
>   and *he will bring justice to the nations.*
> ...
>   he will not falter or be discouraged
> till he establishes justice on earth.
>   In his teaching the islands will put their hope. (Isa. 42: 1, 4)

This vision would find *one* level of fulfilment with the coming of Christ to earth. There would be *further* realization as the gospel was taken to all nations during the whole gospel age (the period between Christ's first and second coming). The *final* fulfilment will be when Christ returns in glory to usher in the new heavens and new earth.

JESUS IS LORD OF HISTORY

As we look over human history, it's not a straight steady line of kingdom progress. There are advances and retreats; periods of gospel blessing, and times of terrible opposition. The book of Revelation shows that as history progresses we expect to see the spread of the gospel and the hostility of Satan advancing *together*. The devil 'makes war' on God's people (Rev. 12:17). As they increase in number, his opposition intensifies. But the Lord Jesus is Lord of history. As He 'opens the seals' history unfolds. He is King of kings and Lord of lords (Rev. 19:16; 1:5).

The sixteenth-century French reformer John Calvin was sure that we should expect the kingdom of God to advance on earth. Although exiled from France for his faith, he wrote confidently:

> ... whatever resistance we see today offered by almost all the world to the progress of the truth, we must not doubt that our Lord will come at last to break through all the undertakings of men and make a passage for his word. Let us hope boldly, then, more than we can understand; he will still surpass our opinion and our hope.[9]

During the Puritan era of the seventeenth century, many ministers encouraged their congregations to pray for the conversion of all peoples (including the Jews). They expected that widespread gospel advance would take place by means of powerful outpourings of the Holy Spirit. Had they adopted a short-term view:

> ... the problems of the Church in their day might justifiably have seemed hopeless, but they faced them with an unflinching sense of duty towards posterity. Succeeding centuries would reap the advantage of an uncompromised witness to the Word of God. Their work could not be in vain for *the testimony of Christ's Church was yet to encircle the earth.*[10]

This 'Puritan Hope' was passed on through their writing, and motivated many of the early missionary pioneers. In 1793 the 'father of modern missions', **William Carey**, sailed from England, never to return. His desire to take the gospel to India seemed ridiculous and foolhardy. But he was confident that 'I have God, and His Word is true ... God's cause will triumph.'[11]

---

9   Murray, I, *The Puritan Hope*, p. xii.

10   Ibid., p. 97, emphasis mine.

11   Ibid., p. 140.

In 1812, **Henry Martyn** died in Asia Minor aged just thirty-one. By then he had accomplished significant work as a pioneer Bible translator in both India and Persia (now Iran). When a Muslim leader asked him why Christianity was so weak in the world, Martyn responded confidently that God's purposes had not yet been fulfilled. The helpers in his translation work, he said, were making provision for *future* Persian Christian believers. Prayers would be answered and the work honoured in God's time.[12] Two centuries later, there is remarkable gospel advance in Iran, despite fierce opposition.[13]

Also in 1812, **Adoniram and Ann Judson** left America to take the gospel to Asia. They endured extreme privations and discouragements. When asked how they could persevere, Adoniram Judson replied that future prospects for the gospel are 'As bright as the promises of God', and 'Nothing is difficult for omnipotence.' Near the end of his life he explained the basis of their perseverance:

> The world is yet in its infancy; the gracious designs of God are yet hardly developed. Glorious things are spoken of Zion, the city of our God. She is yet to triumph, and become the joy and glory of the whole earth. Blessed be God that we live in these latter times – the latter times of the reign of darkness and imposture. Great is our privilege, precious our opportunity, to cooperate with the Saviour in the blessed work of enlarging and establishing his kingdom throughout the world.[14]

As the gospel advances, we should expect that this will lead to human flourishing. It is tragic to see nations, rich in natural resources, torn apart by conflicts, mismanagement, corruption and unjust rule. Biblical promises of future blessing give us grounds to pray for people to be liberated spiritually, but *also* physically and materially.

---

12 Ibid., p. 154.

13 Elam, 'Church Growth in Iran', https://www.elam.com/page/rapid-church-growth-how-it-happening (accessed 25 February, 2021).

14 Quoted in James, S, *Ann Judson: A Missionary Life for Burma,* (Evangelical Press, 2015), pp. 274-5.

It is *confidence* in Christ's victory that has inspired and motivated Christians who have fought most energetically against abuses in society. During the nineteenth century, **Josephine Butler (1828-1906)** campaigned fearlessly against sexual exploitation of women and children.[15] Despite opposition from vested interests, she secured the protection for girls of the raising of the age of consent to the age of sixteen. Often facing intimidation, danger, opposition and slander, she was confident that:

> There is no evil in the world so great that God cannot raise up to meet it a corresponding glory that will blaze it out of countenance.[16]

'Why does God allow unbelief and evil to prevail for so long, in so much of the world?' **Charles Haddon Spurgeon** addressed that question in 1865, when speaking at a missionary meeting:

> When I have read some masterly tragic poem, and verse after verse has dwelt upon the horrible portion of the tale, did I wish it shortened? Would I have had the author leave out one of those dark verses? Not I! It is true when the poem ended with a shout of victory, and with the tramp of martial men through the city, when they returned in triumph, our heart leaped; we rejoiced when we came to that last stanza, but we didn't want the poem shortened ... God is writing a great poem of human history, the subject is the victory of truth, the destruction of Anti-Christ. Let the history be long. Who wants it shortened? Who wants a brief story on so exceedingly interesting a subject as this, from so great an author? No! Let it drag on what some may call its weary length, we are sure that when we come to read it, as God will write it, we shall wish

---

15 *Josephine Butler: The Age of Consent, a Warning from History,* The Christian Institute, https://www.christian.org.uk/wp-content/uploads/aoc_warning.pdf (accessed September 2021)

16 Josephine Butler, when replying to the Royal Commission on the Contagious Diseases Acts, March 1871, in answer to the question 'How could a lady of her social standing bear to contemplate such degradation in members of her own sex?' Quoted in Petrie, G, *A Singular Iniquity,* (London, 1971), p. 115.

the story longer. We will not complain of its extent, for the result is we shall see more of God, and learn more of his mind.[17]

Come the end, we won't want God's story shortened. He will be exalted in the earth (Ps. 46:10). We need to keep praying, keep working, and keep telling the truth. God will glorify His Son among all nations. His purpose cannot be thwarted.

RETURN OF THE KING

When God's purposes are completed, when He has gathered all His people into the kingdom, then Christ will return. That is our final, greatest hope:

> He who testifies to these things says, 'Yes, I am coming soon.' Amen. Come, Lord Jesus. (Rev. 22:20)

> For the Lord himself will come down from heaven, with a loud command, with the voice of the archangel and with the trumpet call of God, and the dead in Christ will rise first. After that, we who are still alive and are left will be caught up together with them in the clouds to meet the Lord in the air. And so we will be with the Lord for ever. Therefore *encourage each other* with these words. (1 Thess. 4:16-18)

We are to encourage each other as we look forward to the resurrection of the dead, the final judgement, and the new earth and heavens.

'IN MY FLESH I WILL SEE GOD'

When Jesus Christ was raised from the dead, He was raised in a physical body. We too will be raised physically. Many hundreds of years before the coming of Christ, Job testified in the darkest time:

> And after my skin has been destroyed, yet in my flesh I will see God. (Job 19:26)

---

17 Spurgeon, C H, 'Jericho Captured', Sermon 629 preached at the Metropolitan Tabernacle, Newington, 1865.

Centuries later, writing from a prison cell at the heart of the Roman Empire when the whole world seemed to be covered in ignorance of God, the apostle Paul wrote:

> But our citizenship is in heaven. And we eagerly await a Saviour from there, the Lord Jesus Christ, who, by the power that enables him to bring everything under his control, will transform our lowly bodies so that they will be like his glorious body. (Phil. 3:20-21)

The certainty of physical resurrection underlines the respect with which we should regard our bodies. It offers comfort to believers who are suffering pain, illness, and the advances of age. It gives courage and joy in the face of death.

TRUE JUSTICE

As we look out at evil and injustice, we long for wrongs to be put right. We are called to pray for and work for justice. Perfect justice won't be achieved this side of the Judgement. But whatever the terrible wrongs we may suffer, or see others suffer, we know that in the end God will not leave evil unpunished.[18] The final judgement is the time when God's just reign will be fully brought in. That's why there is a sense of longing in many of the prophetic writings.

> Oh, that you would rend the heavens and come down,
>   that the mountains would tremble before you!
> As when fire sets twigs ablaze
>   and causes water to boil,
> come down to make your name known to your enemies
>   and cause the nations to quake before you! (Isa. 64:1-2)

The coming of the judgement day will be the *ultimate* answer to all such prayers. Throughout the book of Revelation, God's people are seen *rejoicing* in the just judgements of God:

> We give thanks to you, Lord God Almighty,
>   the One who is and who was,

---

18 See, for example, Psalms 37 and 73.

because you have taken your great power
and have begun to reign.
The nations were angry;
and your wrath has come.
The time has come for judging the dead,
and for rewarding your servants the prophets,
and your saints and those who reverence your name,
both small and great –
and for destroying those who destroy the earth ... (Rev. 11:17-18)

Many sections of the professing church are embarrassed by the biblical teaching about judgement and hell.[19] But, as human beings made in the image of God, we're outraged when we see unfairness, cruelty and abuse. At the last day, the Creator and Judge of all the earth will do right, and will be seen to do right.[20] None of us will argue with Him then.

A RENEWED COSMOS

As we look around us, we rightly grieve when we see suffering, pain, injustice and need. Human beings all too often exercise dominion over the world in a greedy way:

We know that the whole creation has been groaning as in the pains of childbirth right up to the present time. (Rom. 8:22)

We all face the reality of illness, age and death: 'Dust you are, and to dust you will return'. (Gen. 3:19). But, following the return of Christ, we will be raised, and the earth itself will be renewed and restored:

But do not forget this one thing, dear friends: With the Lord a day is like a thousand years, and a thousand years are like a day. The Lord is not slow in keeping his promise, as some understand slowness. Instead he is patient with you, not wanting anyone to perish, but everyone to come to repentance. But the day of the

---

19   See chapter 6.
20   See Genesis 18:25.

Lord will come like a thief. The heavens will disappear with a roar; the elements will be destroyed by fire, and the earth and everything done in it will be laid bare. Since everything will be destroyed in this way, what kind of people ought you to be? You ought to live holy and godly lives as you look forward to the day of God and speed its coming. That day will bring about the destruction of the heavens by fire, and the elements will melt in the heat. But in keeping with his promise we are looking forward to a new heaven and a new earth, where righteousness dwells. (2 Pet. 3:8-13)

The words 'laid bare' translate a Greek work meaning 'exposed'. The image is one of purification. God's people will enjoy and serve Him forever in this purified and renewed new heavens and new earth. The scope of redemption is *cosmic,* because when Christ was raised from death, He achieved *total* victory over Satan.

> He comes to make His blessings flow
>> Far as the curse is found.[21]

Christ's victory set in train the unravelling of *all* the damage wreaked by Satan. Sin has spoiled the created order: family, education, communities, societies and nations. This results in misery for people, suffering for animals, pollution of our oceans, over-use of soil and mismanagement of forests. The work of redemption achieves the unravelling of the curse in *every* respect. It achieves the reconciliation of 'all things' to God (Col. 1:20). That does not mean that every single human being will be saved (the Bible teaches that some people are saved and some are not). It does mean that all the elements of the created order will be restored and brought back to their intended purpose. As Paul wrote:

> And he made known to us the mystery of his will according to his good pleasure, which he purposed in Christ, to be put into effect when the times reach their fulfillment—to bring unity to *all things* in heaven and on earth under Christ. (Eph. 1:9-10, emphasis mine)

---

21   Watts, I, 'Joy to the World: the Saviour comes'.

For God was pleased to have all his fullness dwell in him, and through him to reconcile to himself *all things*, whether things on earth or things in heaven, by making peace through his blood, shed on the cross. (Col. 1:19-20, emphasis mine)

All that is good in creation (possibly including the best accomplishments of human cultures) will be built upon in the new heavens and the new earth. God's good creation design will go on being developed, explored and managed for all eternity. The new creation will be no less exciting, varied and beautiful than the creation we experience now:

In this new world we will be given remarkable new tasks. Thrilling avenues of service will open before us, calling for the use of all our gifts and talents, many unsuspected or undeveloped in our present existence. 'The reason, the intellectual curiosity, the imagination, the aesthetic instincts, the holy affections, the social affinities, the inexhaustible resources of strength and power native to the human soul, must all find in heaven exercise and satisfaction.' Throughout eternity we will live full, truly human lives, exploring and managing God's creation to his glory. Fascinating vistas will unfold before us as we learn to serve God in a renewed universe. 'Every legitimate activity of (new) creaturely life will be included within the life of worship of God's people.' It is challenging to reflect that the greater our faithfulness now, the more extensive and fulfilling our heavenly responsibilities will be. 'Well done, good and faithful servant; you have been faithful over a few things, I will make you ruler over many things' (Matt. 25:23). Christ rewards us for work well done by entrusting more responsibility to us.[22]

Most wonderful of all will be unhindered friendship with our Creator God. That's what we were originally created to enjoy.

---

22   Donnelly, E, *Biblical Teachings on the Doctrines of Heaven and Hell*, (Banner of Truth, 2002), pp. 123-4; quotations from A A Hodge and C P Venema. I quote more theologians on this subject in James, S, *The Dawn of Heaven Breaks*, (Evangelical Press, 2007), 2016.

GOD WITH US

In the new earth and heavens we will realise the extent of God's love for us. Our experience of that love will be unbroken, as we will be free from all sin.

> Then I saw a new heaven and a new earth, for the first heaven and the first earth had passed away, and there was no longer any sea. I saw the Holy City, the new Jerusalem, coming down out of heaven from God, prepared as a bride beautifully dressed for her husband. And I heard a loud voice from the throne saying, 'Now the dwelling of God is with men, and he will live with them. They will be his people, and God himself will be with them and be their God. He will wipe every tear from their eyes. There will be no more death or mourning or crying or pain, for the old order of things has passed away.' (Rev. 21:1-4)

People without God have no hope in the face of death. But Christians have everything to look forward to. No wonder Adoniram Judson said near the end of his life:

> When Christ calls me home, I shall go with the gladness of a boy bounding away from his school.[23]

FURTHER READING

Hoekema, A A, *The Bible and the Future,* (Eerdmans, 1996)

Murray, I, *The Puritan Hope: Revival and the Interpretation of Prophecy,* (Banner of Truth Trust, 1971/2014)

> Summary: Christ is King. The biblical worldview is the foundation of future hope. God has good purposes for this world. He will bring about complete justice, and restoration of the whole creation, when Christ returns.

---

23   Quoted in Anderson, C, *To the Golden Shore: The Life of Adoniram Judson,* (Judson Press, 1987), p. 499.

10 What Should I Do Now?

BE PREPARED

We are living in a culture which has been poisoned with lies. We must be ready to speak truth with confidence.

During the first century, persecution meant that believers were scattered through the Roman Empire (1 Pet. 1:2; 4:12). Neighbours vilified and abused them when they turned to Christ and rejected their old lifestyle (1 Pet. 4:4). But the apostle Peter encouraged them:

> Do not repay evil with evil or insult with insult. On the contrary, repay evil with blessing... even if you should suffer for what is right, you are blessed. 'Do not fear what they fear; do not be shaken.' In your hearts revere Christ as Lord. Always be prepared to give an answer to everyone who asks you to give the reason for the hope that you have. But do this with gentleness and respect, keeping a clear conscience, so that those who speak maliciously against your good behaviour in Christ may be ashamed of their slander. (1 Pet. 3:9, 14-16)

As believers got ready to give an answer to those who opposed them, their priority was to prepare their hearts. 'In your hearts revere Christ as Lord' (v. 15). When they answered their opponents, they were to 'keep a clear conscience', and speak with respect and courtesy. 'Do not repay evil with evil or insult with insult. On the contrary, repay evil with blessing' (v. 9).

As we get ready to speak to others, we too are to prepare our hearts. Most importantly, we are to fear the Lord. Then we won't fear anyone or anything else. But we are also to love others. There's no point winning an argument if in the process we needlessly alienate the person we are speaking to. Those who persecute believers sometimes (later) admit that the gracious demeanour of the one they were tormenting remained with them, and was a factor leading to their own conversion.

Even children have been empowered to stand for Christ in the face of opposition. Nikolai Malai was born in northern Moldova in 1946. That was the year of a great famine, when many died of starvation. Nikolai survived. He and his seven siblings grew up in severe poverty. They also experienced harsh persecution because their family were bible-believing Christians. Nikolai was bullied at school, especially by a young Communist teacher, Olga Sergevna. She despised Christians, often mocked Nikolai, and punished him unfairly. But he was taught at home to follow Christ and respect his teacher. Decades later, Nikolai's daughter Evelina met an elderly woman who asked about her father. It was Olga. She had become a Christian, and told Evelina:

> I was his teacher many years ago. I remember your father. I treated him very badly when he was in my class ... Please give him my greetings and ask him to forgive me for my treatment of him.[1]

We are to love those who oppose us, and pray for those who persecute us. We want their good. We want them to be saved.

Paul's letter to Titus outlined how believers were to live in a culture infused with dishonesty, laziness and greed. They were to demonstrate contentment, hard work, generosity, self-control, and integrity:

> ... so that those who oppose you will be ashamed because they have nothing bad to say about us. (Titus 2:8)

---

1   Birnie, J, *God's Man in Moldova*, (Slavic Gospel Association, 2011), p. 79.

We live in a consumer culture; but it's not enough to denounce greed. We are to model trust in God, which liberates us to work hard and to be contented and generous:

> Keep your lives free from the love of money and be content with what you have, because God has said, 'Never will I leave you; never will I forsake you.' (Heb. 13:5)

Having prepared our hearts, we also need to prepare our minds. If we are to 'be ready to give answers to others' we need to be aware of the presuppositions that scare people away from the biblical worldview. In Part one we examined some of these, and we also looked at the disastrous results when they are put into practice. In Part two we argued, by contrast, that the biblical worldview offers the only firm foundation for human dignity and freedom. Living according to God's moral law leads to human flourishing. Here is a summary of how the biblical worldview contrasts with the lies commonly told today:

There Is No God?

Naturalistic Worldview v. Biblical Truth

Naturalistic Worldview	Implications of Naturalistic Worldview	Biblical Truth
1 No Creator God, we just evolved	No unique dignity afforded to human life. No purpose in history. Nothing after death. No ultimate meaning to life.	God created human beings in His image with unique dignity. History has meaning and purpose. There is life beyond the grave. Every human has significance.

Naturalistic Worldview	Implications of Naturalistic Worldview	Biblical Truth
2 No Creator God, no judgement	No absolute morality Freedom means no boundaries. The elevation of absolute individual 'freedom' has led to family breakdown and communal weakening.	All human beings will answer to our Creator at the Day of Judgement. God's moral law, written on the human heart (the conscience) is the basis for ethics and morality. It will be the basis for God's just judgement.
3 'True Truth' has to do with physical reality alone	We are left with 'my truth' and 'your truth'. No universal religious truth. Christians must keep their faith private.	God has designed this universe in a rational and ordered way. He created humans in His image able to reason and discern moral truth. God's truth is accessible to all by means of 'general revelation' (creation) and the conscience.

THERE IS NO UNIVERSAL TRUTH?

Critical Theory v. Biblical Truth

Critical Theory	Biblical Truth
1 Truth claims are power grabs	They would be if they were based only on individual experience. But universal truth is grounded in the fact that the cosmos is made by God, who has hardwired truth into creation and into human nature by means of the conscience.

2 Universal explanations are suspect	They would be if they had simply been devised by humans. But God has revealed Himself and His truth in both creation (general revelation) and His Word (special revelation). The biblical truth that humans are made in God's image is the basis for freedom and dignity.
3 Reason, logic and science are tools of oppression	God has created all human beings with the capacity to reason, explore and discover. Reason, logic and science can be used to harm others, but they can be used to heal the sick, lift from poverty, and bring benefits to many.
4 Individual experience cannot be challenged	Individual people must be respected, but we do not have to respect everyone's views and demands. We are all individually accountable, because God has placed His moral law on every human heart. The fact that a person is in a 'victim' group does not mean their claims or experiences can be placed above question.
5 All authority structures are repressive	God ordained authority structures for our good. In a fallen world authorities may abuse power. But abolishing them leads to disorder and anarchy, where it is the weak who suffer most.
6 Society is divided between privileged and victims (victims alone have access to 'their truth')	All human beings are made in God's image, we are all 'one race', there is more that unites us than divides us, we all have access to truth.
7 There is no forgiveness for collective guilt	Forgiveness is offered to all. Societies can be guilty of collective injustice, but every individual is morally accountable to God. Every person should be afforded respect. Individuals should not be silenced, whatever group they belong to.

The biblical worldview explains both the evil in the world *and* the good in the world. Every individual human being is both infinitely valuable (made in the image of God) *and* utterly sinful (naturally in rebellion against God).

We are to prepare our hearts and our minds to engage with the lies and speak for truth. That demands a robust understanding of biblical truth. It also demands humility. We are not to place our own experience in judgement over the Word of God. We are to submit to the authority of Scripture. Where God's Word challenges us, we are to repent.

If we love God, we will love His Word. That means studying it, memorising it, meditating on it, and obeying it:

Oh, how I love your law! I meditate on it all day long.
(Ps. 119:97)

If you love me, you will keep my commandments. (John 14:15, ESV)

LOVE AND PRAISE GOD

When we understand who God is, the only possible response is joyful praise:

Sing to the LORD, praise his name;
    proclaim his salvation day after day.
Declare his glory among the nations,
    his marvellous deeds among all peoples. (Ps. 96: 2-3)

Throughout church history when God's people have been persecuted, they have praised God. They have even gone to their deaths singing. Enemies of the gospel have gagged Christians, sometimes cut their tongues out, in desperate attempts to curb those praises.

In sixteenth-century France there was a remarkable spiritual awakening. A few beleaguered groups of believers in the early 1550s grew to around two million adherents in over a thousand congregations in 1562. Their enemies were baffled by their irrepressible urge to sing praise to God. They especially loved singing Psalms:

> They sang them in their secret meetings, they sang them at home, they sang them even when they were being tortured, they sang them when they were manacled to oars in the galleys. The Psalter was so popular that it went through 62 editions in 3 years. It sold like wildfire and many were saved through it.[2]

Today, living in a culture that overwhelmingly rejects God, we must not be intimidated. There is power in praise! As we sing, our confidence is renewed, and God is honoured.

Don't Be Afraid!

As a young teenager, I was taken to see the Tower of Constance, built into the walls of a French town called Aigues Mortes. During the later seventeenth and early eighteenth centuries, Huguenot girls and women were imprisoned there in horrible conditions, scarcely able to enjoy air or sun. At any time if they recanted their faith they would be set free. Many remained for decades rather than deny Christ. Marie Durand was imprisoned at the age of fifteen, and stayed firm in her faith for thirty-eight years until she was finally released under a new regime. You can still see the word she scratched on the wall of the prison: Resister ('Resist').[3]

'Fear not!' is the most common command found in Scripture. When Moses was summoned before the leader of the super-power of the ancient world he was not intimidated because he 'saw Him who is invisible' (Heb. 11:27). Moses trusted the God who had created

---

2   'The Huguenots', lecture by Geraint Lloyd at the Heath Evangelical Church, Cardiff, http://www.heath-church.org/missionary-outreach/french-connections/the-huguenots/ (accessed 26 October, 2020); see also MacCulloch, D, *Reformation: Europe's House Divided,* (Penguin, 2003), pp. 307-8.

3   Mentzer, R A and Spicer, A, eds, *Society and Culture in the Huguenot World 1559-1685,* (Cambridge University Press, 2002), p. 230.

Pharaoh; the One to whom the proud king would ultimately have to give account.

We are freed from fear when we understand that above and beyond all else is the God who is all-powerful, all-wise and all-good. *When we fear God, we don't fear anyone or anything else!*

In the West, the prevailing worldview has been poisoned by lies. We *can* stand against these lies because we have the truth of God's Word and the power of God's Spirit. In union with Christ and His people we can move forward, gain ground, and rescue those imprisoned by deceit:

> Put on the full armour of God, so that you can take your stand against the devil's schemes. For our struggle is not against flesh and blood, but against the rulers, against the authorities, against the powers of this dark world and against the spiritual forces of evil in the heavenly realms. Therefore put on the full armour of God, so that when the day of evil comes, you may be able to stand your ground, and after you have done everything, to stand. (Eph. 6:11-13)

Previous generations of Christians loved to read books such as the *Book of Martyrs* by John Foxe, and John Bunyan's *Pilgrim's Progress* and *The Holy War*. These taught that true Christians will suffer for their faith. By contrast today, many Christian 'self-help' books imply that God wants to make life as comfortable as possible for us. In reality, God's purpose is to make us like Christ:

> Endure hardship as discipline [or training]. God is treating you as sons. For what son is not disciplined by his father? If you are not disciplined, and everyone undergoes discipline, then you are illegitimate children and not true sons. (Heb. 12:7-9)

In the West we are not (yet) being forced to deny Christ by force. 'Soft totalitarianism' is when we are intimidated by the threat of losing social status, employment, or academic credibility. If we think that life is all about security in the here and now, we will fall at the first hurdle.

We should remember that the joy of knowing God's smile is greater joy than anything else.

In 1951, Silvester Kremery, a young Christian doctor, was arrested by the communist authorities in what was then Czechoslovakia. He was brutally tortured but refused to recant his faith. He later explained why: 'There could not be anything more beautiful than to lay down my life for God.'[4]

WORK FOR THE EXTENSION OF GOD'S KINGDOM

If we believe the devil's lie that this life is mainly about us, our security, and our comfort, we will be tempted to lie low, keep our faith private, and bunker down in our Christian communities.

If, however, we understand that our chief 'end' is to bring praise to God, we then long that He should be honoured by everyone on earth. Jesus taught His followers to pray:

> Hallowed be your name, your kingdom come, your will be done on earth as it is in heaven (Matt. 6:9-10)

If we *pray* for God's will to be done on earth, we are to *work* for that as well. To love God means loving our neighbour by doing good and campaigning against evil. To retreat and wait for Christ's coming is the equivalent of burying our talent in the ground (Matt. 25:14-30).

As I write in 2021, tens of thousands of people made in God's image are held in concentration camps in China and North Korea; Christians are being massacred in Central Nigeria; worldwide the abortion industry is destroying unborn life on an industrial scale; millions are held in sex slavery; and many others are victims of human trafficking.

Ultimately Christ will triumph over all these evils, and justice will be done. In the here and now He works through His people to confront injustice. We may variously be involved in action, advocacy, giving or prayer; but we are all called to love our God and love our

---

4   Dreher, R, *Live Not by Lies: A Manual for Christian Dissidents,* (Sentinel, 2020), p. 152.

neighbour. We are all called to extend the universal and free offer of the gospel:

> Come, everyone who thirsts,
>> come to the waters;
> and he who has no money,
>> come, buy and eat!
> Come, buy wine and milk without money and without price ...
>
> Seek the LORD while he may be found;
>> call upon him while he is near;
> let the wicked forsake his way,
>> and the unrighteous man his thoughts;
> let him return to the LORD, that he may have compassion on him,
>> and to our God, for he will abundantly pardon. (Isa. 55:1, 6-7, ESV)

FURTHER READING

Bunyan, J, *The Pilgrim's Progress* (many editions available)

Bunyan, J, *The Holy War,* modern language edition by Thelma Jenkins, (Evangelical Press, 2015)

Foxe, J, *Book of Martyrs* (original title Acts and Monuments, many editions available)

Hefley, J and M, *By Their Blood: Christian Martyrs of the Twentieth Century: A Continuation of Foxe's Book of Martyrs,* (Baker, 1979)

MacKenzie, C, *A Voice in the Dark: Richard Wurmbrand,* (Christian Focus, 1997) (for young people)

Voice of the Martyrs, *Jesus Freaks: Stories of Those Who Stood for Jesus,* (Eagle Publishing, 2000)

Summary: Christians are not just to know the truth, but to live it. We are created to live for God's glory. Worship should be the pulse of our existence. When we love and fear God, we won't fear anyone or anything else. Loving God and loving our neighbour includes sharing the good news of salvation and working for our neighbour's good.

Further Resources

Books

Allen, S D, *Why Social Justice Is Not Biblical Justice*, (Credo House Publishers, 2020)

Anderson, C, Edwards, B H, *Is It True? Evidence for the Bible*, (Day One, 2016)

Anderson, C, Edwards, B H, *Evidence for the Bible*, (Day One, 2013)

Baucham, V T, *Fault Lines: The Social Justice Movement and Evangelicalism's Looming Catastrophe*, (Salem Books, 2021)

Bentley Hart, D, *Atheist Delusions: The Christian Revolution and Its Fashionable Enemies*, (Yale University Press, 2009)

Blanchard, J, *Does God Believe in Atheists?* (Evangelical Press, 2000)

Bork, R H, *Slouching Towards Gomorrah: Modern Liberalism and American Decline*, (Regan Books, 1996)

Breese, D, *Seven Men Who Rule the World from the Grave*, available in digital format (Moody, 1990), https://www.logos.com/product/7705/seven-men-who-rule-the-world-from-the-grave

Brown, M L, *A Queer Thing Happened to America, and What a Long, Strange Trip it's been*, (Equal Time Books, 2011)

Bunyan, J, *The Pilgrim's Progress,* various editions

Bunyan, J, *The Holy War,* modern language edition by Thelma Jenkins, (Evangelical Press, 2015)

Butterfield, R, *Secret Thoughts of an Unlikely Convert,* (Crown and Covenant, 2012)

Carter, C A, *Interpreting Scripture with the Great Tradition: Recovering the Genius of Premodern Exegesis,* (Baker Academic, 2018)

Carter, J D, *Western Humanism: A Christian Perspective: A Guide for Understanding Moral Decline in Western Culture,* (Point of Grace, 2005)

Chang, J, Halliday, J, *Mao: The Unknown Story,* (Vintage Books, 2006)

Childers, A, *Another Gospel? A Lifelong Christian Seeks Truth in Response to Progressive Christianity,* (Tyndale Momentum, 2020)

Collier, P, Horowitz, D, *Destructive Generation: Second Thoughts about the Sixties,* (Encounter Books, 1989)

Cook, B, *A Change of Affection: A Gay Man's Incredible Story of Redemption,* (Nelson Books, 2019)

Cormack, D, *Killing Fields Living Fields: An Unfinished Portrait of the Cambodian Church,* (2001, rep. Christian Focus, 2014)

Dalrymple, T, *Life at the Bottom: The Worldview that Makes the Underclass,* (Ivan R Dee, 2001)

Dalrymple T, *Our Culture: What's Left of It: The Mandarins and the Masses,* (Ivan R Dee, 2005)

Darling, D, *The Dignity Revolution: Reclaiming God's Rich Vision for Humanity,* (The Good Book Company, 2018)

Dennett, D C, *Darwin's Dangerous Idea: Evolution and the Meanings of Life,* (Simon and Schuster, 1995)

Denton, M, *Evolution: Still a Theory in Crisis,* (Discovery Institute, 2016)

Dreher, R, *Live Not by Lies,* (Sentinel, 2020)

Eberstadt, M, *Primal Screams: How the Sexual Revolution Created Identity Politics,* (Templeton Press, 2019)

Edgar, W, *Created and Creating: A Biblical Theology of Culture*, (Apollos, 2017)

Edwards, B H, *All You Need to Know About the Bible*, (Day One, 2016) (six books)

Edwards, J, *History of Redemption,* (Banner of Truth, 2003)
Edwards, J, *Christ Exalted*, www.biblebb.com/files/edwards/exalted.htm

Ells, K, *The Invincible Family: Why the Global Campaign to Crush Motherhood and Fatherhood Can't Win,* (Regnery Gateway, 2020)

Emerson, L, *Deception: The Craft of Satan, the Folly of Man, the Wisdom of God,* (Vide Press, 2021)

Foxe, J, *Book of Martyrs (Acts and Monuments),* various editions

Gilson, R, *Born Again This Way: Coming Out, Coming to Faith, and What Comes Next,* (The Good Book Company, 2020)

Grant, G, *Killer Angel: A Biography of Planned Parenthood's Founder, Margaret Sanger,* (Ars Vitae, 1995)
Grant, G, *Grand Illusions, The Legacy of Planned Parenthood,* (Adoit Press,1988, 1992)

Grudem, W, Currid J, et al, *A Biblical Case Against Theistic Evolution: Is It Compatible with the Bible?* (Crossway, 2022)
Grudem, W, *Business for the Glory of God,* (Crossway, 2003)
Grudem, W, Asmus, B, *The Poverty of Nations: A Sustainable Solution,* (Crossway, 2013)

Hardyman, J, *Maximum Life: All for the Glory of God,* (IVP,2009)

Harris, J, *Social Justice Goes to Church: The New Left in Modern American Evangelicalism,* (Ambassador International, 2020)

Haugen, G, *The Locust Effect: Why the End of Poverty Requires the End of Violence,* (Oxford University Press, 2015)

Hertzke, A D and Shah, T S, eds. *Christianity and Freedom:* Volume I *Historical Perspectives;* Volume II *Contemporary Perspectives,* (Cambridge University Press, 2016)

Himmelfarb, G, *From Clapham to Bloomsbury: A Genealogy of Morals,* 1985, https://www.commentarymagazine.com/articles/gertrude-himmel farb/from-clapham-to-bloomsbury-a-genealogy-of-morals/
Himmelfarb, G, *The Demoralization of Society: From Victorian Virtues to Modern Values,* (IEA, 1995)

Hitchens, P, *Short Breaks in Mordor: Dawns and Departures of a Scribbler's Life,* (privately published, 2018)

Hoekema, A A, *Created in God's Image,* (Eerdmans, 1986)
Hoekema, A A, *The Bible and the Future,* (Eerdmans, 1996)

Hoff Sommers, C, *Who Stole Feminism? How Women Have Betrayed Women,* (Simon & Schuster, 1994)

Holland, T, *Dominion: The Making of the Western Mind,* (Little, Brown, 2019)

Honeysett, Marcus, *Meltdown: Making Sense of a Culture in Crisis,* (IVP, 2002)

James, S, *God's Design for Women in an Age of Gender Confusion,* (Evangelical Press, 2019)
James, S, *Gender Ideology: What do Christians need to know?* (Christian Focus, 2019)
James, S, *How Christianity Transformed the World,* (Christian Focus, 2021)

Jenkins, P, *The Next Christendom: The Coming of Global Christianity,* (Oxford University Press, 2011)

Johnson, P, *A History of the Modern World from 1917 to the 1980s,* (Weidenfeld and Nicolson, 1983)
Johnson, P, *Intellectuals: A Fascinating Examination of Whether Intellectuals are Morally Fit to Give Advice to Humanity,* (Weidenfeld & Nicolson, 1988/2013)

Jones, P, *The Other Worldview,* (Kirkdale Press, 2015)

Kuby, G, *The Global Sexual Revolution,* (LifeSite, 2015)
http://www.christendom-awake.org/pages/book-promotions/global-sexual-revolution/978-1-62138-154-9_int-2.pdf

Ling, J, *Bioethical Issues*, (Day One, 2014)

Lukianoff, G and Haidt, J, *The Coddling of the American Mind: How Good Intentions and Bad Ideas are Setting Up a Generation for Failure*, (Penguin, 2018)

Machen, G, *Christianity and Liberalism*, (Eerdmans, 2009)

Mangalwadi, V, *The Book that Made Your World: How the Bible Created the Soul of Western Civilisation*, (Thomas Nelson, 2011)

Mangalwadi, V, *The Legacy of William Carey: A Model for the Transformation of Culture*, (Wcl 3rd party,1999)

Marquardt, E, ed., *The Revolution in Parenthood: The Emerging Global Clash Between Adult Rights and Children's Needs*, (Institute for American Values, 2006)

McDermott, G R, *Everyday Glory: The Revelation of God in All of Reality*, (Baker, 2018)

Meyer, S C et al (eds), *Theistic Evolution: A Scientific, Philosophical, and Theological Critique*, (Crossway, 2017)

Meyer, S C, *Return of the God Hypothesis: Three Scientific Discoveries That Reveal the Mind Behind the Universe*, (Harpur One, 2021)

Miłosz, C, *The Captive Mind*, translated by Zielonko, J, (Penguin, 1953)

Mohler, A R, *Atheism Remix: A Christian Confronts the New Atheists*, (Crossway, 2008)

Mohler, A R, *We Cannot Be Silent: Speaking Truth to a Culture Redefining Sex, Marriage, and the Very Meaning of Right and Wrong*, (Nelson Books, 2015)

Mohler, A R, *The Gathering Storm: Secularism, Culture and the Church*, (Nelson Books, 2020)

Morgan, P, *The War Between the State and the Family: How Government Divides and Impoverishes*, Institute of Economic Affairs, 2007, https://iea.org.uk/wp-content/uploads/2016/07/upldbook406pdf.pdf

Murray, D, *The Strange Death of Europe: Immigration, Identity, Islam*, (Bloomsbury Continuum, 2018)

Murray, D, *The Madness of Crowds: Gender, Race and Identity*,

(Bloomsbury Continuum, 2019)

Murray, I, *The Puritan Hope*, (Banner of Truth, 1972)

Nichols, S, *A Time for Confidence: Trusting God in a Post-Christian Society,* (Reformation Trust, 2016)

Orwell, G, *Nineteen Eighty-Four: A Novel,* (Secker & Warburg, 1949)

Pearcey, N, *Total Truth: Liberating Christianity from Its Cultural Captivity,* (Crossway, 2004)

Pearcey, N, *Love Thy Body: Answering Hard Questions about Life and Sexuality,* (Baker Books, 2016)

Piper, J, *Blood Lines,* (Crossway, 2011)

Pluckrose, H, Lindsay, J, *Cynical Theories: How Universities Made Everything about Race, Gender and Identity – and Why This Harms Everybody,* (Swift, 2020)

Roberts, A, *Churchill: Walking with Destiny,* (Penguin Books, 2019)

Ross, P S, *From the Finger of God: The Biblical and Theological Base for the Threefold Division of the Law,* (Christian Focus Publications, 2010)

Rueger, M, *Sexual Morality in a Christless World,* (Concordia, 2016)

Rummel, R J, *Death by Government,* (Transaction Publishers, 1997)

Ryken, P G, *Christian Worldview: A Student's Guide,* (Crossway, 2013) (and other books in that series)

Schaeffer, F, Koop, E C, *Whatever Happened to the Human Race?* (Marshall Morgan and Scott, 1980)

Schmidt, A J, *How Christianity Changed the World,* (Zondervan, 2004)

Scruton, R, *Fools, Frauds and Firebrands: Thinkers of the New Left,* (Bloomsbury Continuum, 2015)

Sidwell, M, *The Long March: How the Left Won the Culture War and What to Do About It,* (The New Culture Forum, 2020)

Sire, J, *The Universe Next Door: A Basic Worldview Catalog,* 1973, 4th edition, (IVP Academic, 2004, 6th edition IVP Academic, 2020)

Smart, S, ed, *The Spectator's Guide to Worldviews*, (Blue Bottle, 2007)

Smiles, S, *Self-Help: With Illustrations of Character and Conduct,* http://files.libertyfund.org/files/297/Smiles_0379.pdf

Smith, C et al, *Lost in Transition: the Dark Side of Emerging Adulthood,* (OUP US, 2011)

Solzhenitsyn, A, *The Gulag Archipelago,* (Abridged edition), (Penguin, 2018)

Sowell, T, *Black Rednecks and White Liberals,* (Encounter Books, 2005)

Stark, R, *For the Glory of God: How Monotheism Led to Reformation, Science, Witch-Hunts and the End of Slavery,* (Princeton University Press, 2003)

Stark R, *The Victory of Reason,* (Random House, 2006)

Stark, R, *The Triumph of Christianity,* (Bravo, 2012)

Stark, R, *How the West Was Won,* (ISI books, 2015)

Stark, R, *Bearing False Witness: Debunking Centuries of Anti-Catholic History,* (Templeton Press, 2016)

Steele, S, *White Guilt: How Blacks and Whites Together Destroyed the Promise of the Civil Rights Era,* (Harper Perennial, 2006)

Strachen, O (author), MacArthur J (foreword), *Christianity and Wokeness: How the Social Justice Movement Is Hijacking the Gospel – and the Way to Stop It,* (Salem Books, 2021)

Tinker, M, *That Hideous Strength, How the West was Lost: The Cancer of Cultural Marxism in the Church, the World and the Gospel of Change,* (Evangelical Press, 2018/2020)

Traeger, S, Gilbert, G, *The Gospel at Work: How working for King Jesus gives purpose and meaning to our jobs,* (Zondervan 2013)

Trueman, C, *The Rise and Triumph of the Modern Self: Cultural Amnesia, Expressive Individualism, and the Road to Sexual Revolution,* (Crossway, 2020)

Vazsonyi, B, *America's Thirty Year War: Who is Winning?* (Regnery Publishing, 1998)

Wells, D, *No Place for Truth*, (Eerdmans, 1993)

Wells, D, *God in the Wasteland*, (Eerdmans, 1994)

Whelchel, H, *How Then SHOULD We Work? Rediscovering the Biblical Doctrine of Work*, (Westbow Press, 2012)

Williams, P J, *Can We Trust the Gospels?* (Crossway, 2018)

Wilson, A N, *God's Funeral*, (John Murray, 1999)

BRIEFINGS/BOOKLETS

Grudem, W, Asmus, B, *What Is at Risk for Business if We Lose a Christian Worldview?* 2010, http://www.waynegrudem.com/wp-content/uploads/2012/03/What-Is-At-Risk-For-Buisness-If-We-Lose-A-Christian-Worldview.pdf

Leach, G, 'Thoughts on a biblical economic worldview: or Godonomics', https://theceme.org/wp-content/uploads/2020/04/Part-2.pdf

Ling, J, *When Does Life Begin?* www.christian.org.uk/resource/when-does-human-life-begin/

London Institute of Contemporary Christianity (LICC): *Fruitfulness on the Front line* (DVD series and study guide) https://www.licc.org.uk/resources/discover-fruitfulness-on-the-frontline/

Mackay, J, *The Dignity of Work* www.christian.org.uk/resource/dignity-of-work/

Mackay, J, *God's Moral Law* http://www.christian.org.uk/wp-content/downloads/the-moral-law.pdf

Needham, N R, *Common Grace* www.christian.org.uk/resource/common-grace-publication/

Novak, M, *Awakening from Nihilism: Why Truth Matters*, (Address given at Westminster Abbey on the occasion of winning the Templeton Prize, 1994), IEA London 1995, https://www.firstthings.com/article/1994/08/awakening-from-nihilismthe-templeton-prize-address

The Christian Institute, *Gnosticism*, https://www.christian.org.uk/wp-content/uploads/gnosticism.pdf

The Christian Institute, *Identity Politics*, https://www.christian.org.uk/wp-content/uploads/Identity_politics_briefing.pdf

The Christian Institute, *Christianity and Liberalism*, https://www.christian.org.uk/wp-content/uploads/christianity-and-liberalism.pdf

The Christian Institute, 'Banning conversion therapy or banning the Gospel?' https://www.christian.org.uk/wp-content/uploads/BanningconversiontherapyorbanningtheGospel.pdf

9 Marks, *'An Emerging Church Primer'*, https://www.9marks.org/article/emerging-church-primer/

Articles/Chapters

Ashenden, G, 'Redefining hate: from diabolical anti-love to any criticism of the fragile self', *Archbishop Cranmer website*, 14 July 2017, http://archbishopcranmer.com/redefining-hate-diabolical-anti-love-criticism-self/

Astier, H, 'The incestuous sins of the soixante-huitards', *The Critic*, July 2021, https://thecritic.co.uk/issues/july-2021/the-incestuous-sins-of-the-soixante-huitards/

Bartholomew, J, 'Life in a Gulag', *The Spectator*, 20 May, 2017, https://www.spectator.co.uk/article/life-in-a-gulag

Bluey, R, 'Could It Happen Here? The Parallels Between Soviet Bloc and Modern US', Interview with Rod Dreher, *The Daily Signal*, 5 October, 2020, https://www.dailysignal.com/2020/10/05/rod-dreher-discusses-parallels-between-soviet-bloc-and-modern-us/

Brunton, J, 'The Theological Problem With Tim Keller's So-Called Social Justice', https://christianintellectual.com/the-theological-problem-with-tim-kellers-so-called-social-justice/

Dalrymple, T, 'Ibsen and his discontents', *City Journal*, Summer 2005, http://www.city-journal.org/html/15_3_urbanities-isben.html

DeYoung, K, 'Thinking Theologically About Racial Tensions: The Image of God', *The Gospel Coalition*, 15 July, 2020, https://www.

thegospelcoalition.org/blogs/kevin-deyoung/thinking-theologically-about-racial-tensions-sin-and-guilt/

Donnelly, K, 'The White Lies of Critical Race Theory', The Conservative Woman, 4 November, 2020, https://www.conservativewoman.co.uk/the-white-lies-of-critical-race-theory/

Doriani, D, 'Friendly Liberalism: A Threat in Every Age', The Gospel Coalition, 7 July, 2017, http://resources.thegospelcoalition.org/library/friendly-theological-liberalism-a-threat-in-every-age

Eberstadt, M, 'The Fury of the Fatherless', First Things, December 2020, https://www.firstthings.com/article/2020/12/the-fury-of-the-fatherless

Franck, M J, 'Declaration Man: How Justice Clarence Thomas Earned His Enemies', Public Discourse, 18 March, 2014, https://www.thepublicdiscourse.com/2014/03/12899/

Furedi, F, 'The Diseasing of Judgment', First Things, January 2021, https://www.firstthings.com/article/2021/01/the-diseasing-of-judgment

George, R, 'The Five Pillars of a Decent Society', Public Discourse, https://www.thepublicdiscourse.com/five-pillars/

Harris, U, 'How Activists Took Control of a University: The Case Study of Evergreen State', Quillette, 18 December, 2017, https://quillette.com/2017/12/18/activists-took-control-university-case-study-evergreen-state/

Hitchens, P, 'Bookings to Utopia', First Things, October 2020, https://www.firstthings.com/article/2020/10/bookings-to-utopia

Huxley, A, Brave New World, written 1931, published 1932, Grafton Books, 1985

Jeanson, N, 'The Shocking and Glorious New Science of Human "Race" & "Ethnicity"', Answers in Genesis, 16 June, 2020, https://answersingenesis.org/genetics/shocking-and-glorious-new-science-human-race-ethnicity/

Leach, G, 'Thoughts on a biblical economic worldview: or Godonomics', https://theceme.org/wp-content/uploads/2020/04/Part-2.pdf

McDermott, G R, 'Misunderstanding Race and the Bible', *Public Discourse,* 20 October, 2020, https://www.thepublicdiscourse.com/2020/10/72125/

McWhorter, J, 'The Great Awokening: Atonement as Activism', *The American Interest*, May, 24 2018, https://www.the-american-interest.com/2018/05/24/atonement-as-activism/

Mitchell, J, 'Maduro's Madness: How Venezuela's Great Socialist Experiment has Brought a Country to Its Knees', *The Spectator*, 25 August, 2018, https://www.spectator.co.uk/article/maduro-s-madness

Morson, G S, 'Suicide of the Liberals', *First Things*, October 2020, https://www.firstthings.com/article/2020/10/suicide-of-the-liberals

Murray, I H, 'How Scotland Lost Its Hold of the Bible', address given in 2015, and published in MacArthur, J, ed, *The Inerrant Word*, (Crossway, 2016), https://banneroftruth.org/uk/resources/articles/2015/scotland-lost-hold-bible/

Paul, D E, 'Under the Rainbow Banner', *First Things,* June 2020, https://www.firstthings.com/article/2020/06/under-the-rainbow-banner

Pluckrose, H, 'The Evolution of Postmodern Thought', *New Discourses,* 22 June 2020, https://newdiscourses.com/2020/06/helen-pluckrose-evolution-postmodern-thought/

Pluckrose, H, Lindsay, J A, Boghossian, P, 'Academic Grievance Studies and the Corruption of Scholarship', Areo, 10 February, 2018,https://areomagazine.com/2018/10/02/academic-grievance-studies-and-the-corruption-of-scholarship/

Reeves, C, 'Bringing Home the Bacon: The Interaction of Science and Scripture Today', in *Theistic Evolution: A Scientific, Philosophical, and Theological Critique*, eds Meyer, S C et al, (Crossway, 2017)

Roberts, A, https://www.telegraph.co.uk/news/2020/12/28/death-george-blake-reveals-little-now-respect-western-values/ (helpful article on moral relativism).

Salzman, P C, 'If you Love Anti-American Riots, Thank Our Universities', *Minding the Campus*, 2 July, 2020, https://www.mindingthecampus.org/2020/07/02/if-you-love-anti-american-riots-thank-our-universities/

Scott, B, 'Black and White Are One: The Church as One New Race', *Desiring God*, 14 December, 2020, https://www.desiringgod.org/articles/black-and-white-are-one

Scruton, R, 'An Unhappy Birthday to Sigmund the Fraud', *The Spectator*, 29 April 2006, https://www.spectator.co.uk/article/an-unhappy-birthday-to-sigmund-the-fraud

Sey, S, 'How to be a Racist, Slow To Write', 19 December, 2020, https://slowtowrite.com/how-to-be-a-racist/
Sey, S, 'Do not Grow Weary Rejecting Critical Race Theory, Slow To Write', 19 December, 2020, https://slowtowrite.com/do-not-grow-weary-rejecting-critical-race-theory/

Sowell, T, 'Discrimination, Race, and Social Justice', *The Federalist*, 13 June, 2018, https://thefederalist.com/2019/06/13/an-interview-with-thomas-sowell-on-discrimination-race-and-social-justice/

TALKS/SERMONS/FILMS

Ascol, T, *The Right Use of God's Law (sermon on 1 Timothy 1:8-11)* https://founders.org/sermons/the-right-use-of-gods-law/

Baucham, V, *Cultural Marxism*
https://www.youtube.com/watch?=GRMFBdDDTkI&t=2605s
Baucham, V, *Defining Social Justice*
https://www.youtube.com/watch?v=YFNOP2IqwoY
Baucham, V, *Ethnic Gnosticism*
https://www.youtube.com/watch?v=Ip3nV6S_fYU

Copan, P, 'Can truth be "your truth?"' https://www.youtube.com/watch?v=pMzhzqoQh8c

Illustra Media and Focus on the Family, *Unlocking the Mystery of Life*, 2003, http://www.unlockingthemysteryoflife.com/

Sovereign Nations, The Trojan Horse, episode 3, 'Critical Race Theory', https://sovereignnations.com/2019/10/11/trojan-horse-ep3-critical-race-theory/

The Christian Institute, *Living Christianity,* https://livingchristianity.org.uk/en_GB 5 studies for groups and individuals who want to be equipped to engage our contemporary world (videos/studyguide).

Websites

The Christian Institute: www.christian.org

Living Christianity: https://livingchristianity.org.uk

UCCF Be Thinking: www.bethinking.org/

Christian Medical Fellowship: www.cmf.org.uk/

Discovery Institute: www.discovery.org/

Answers in Genesis: https://answersingenesis.org/

The Equiano Project: https://www.theequianoproject.com/

Persons Index

Subject Index